D1478996

It's Not
What You Sign,
It's How
You Sign It

It's Not What You Sign, It's How You Sign It

Politeness in American Sign Language

Jack Hoza

Gallaudet University Press
WASHINGTON, D.C.

Gallaudet University Press
Washington, DC 20002
http://gupress.gallaudet.edu

16 15 14 13 12 11 10 09 08   10 9 8 7 6 5 4 3 2

Library of Congress Cataloging-in-Publication Data

Hoza, Jack.
  It's not what you sign, it's how you sign it : politeness in American
Sign Language / Jack Hoza
      p. c.m.
  Includes bibliographical references and index.
  ISBN-13 978-1-56368-352-7 (alk. paper)
    1. American Sign Language. 2. Politeness (Linguistics) I. Title.
  HV2474.H69 2007
  419'.7—dc22

                                                    2007009631

To Paul, Ben, and Ian

CONTENTS

Acknowledgments — ix

1 Politeness—It's *How* You Say It — 1

2 Exploring Linguistic Strategies — 32

3 Requests In ASL And English — 63

4 Rejections In ASL And English — 106

5 Two Nonmanual Modifiers That Mitigate Smaller Threats To Face — 126

6 Three Nonmanual Modifiers That Mitigate More Severe Threats To Face — 149

7 Language Fluency And Politeness — 188

8 Why It Matters How You Say It — 202

Appendix I: Transcription Conventions — 215

Appendix II: Discourse Completion Test — 218

Appendix III: Brown and Levinson's (1987) Politeness Strategies Arranged by the Categories Used in This Book — 221

References — 225

Index — 231

ACKNOWLEDGMENTS

I am pleased to acknowledge the support and guidance of the many people who have made this research and the publication of this book possible. Numerous people have been instrumental in my work and have helped shape my understanding of cross-cultural communication and linguistic inquiry.

I am thankful for my bilingual (ASL/English) family who initiated my journey into the world of language study. I want to thank my Deaf parents, Raymond and Dorothy Hoza, and my two Deaf siblings, Larry and Mike, for their gift of ASL and the Deaf world. Also, I wish to thank my hearing siblings, Peggy, Linda, Don, Pat, and Tim, for sharing this bilingual/bicultural ride with me and for deepening my awareness and appreciation of life as a bilingual/bicultural person.

My professional thinking has been shaped by too many people to list here. However, I do want to acknowledge the contributions and help from the many Deaf people, interpreters, and linguists whom it has been my pleasure to know over the years. In particular, I am indebted to Dr. Cathy O'Connor at Boston University for her years of support and guidance, and for sharing her expertise in the field of sociolinguistics. She largely informed my understanding of linguistic politeness, and her mentorship and guidance were crucial to finetuning the research design and the implementation of the study. I am also grateful for the collegiality, support, and academic direction I received during my stint with the Boston University ASL Linguistics Project—especially Dr. Carol Neidle and Dr. Ben Bahan—for what they taught me about strict adherence to linguistic inquiry.

I would also like to thank Daniel Roush for sharing his master's thesis with me. In particular, his discovery of the association between nonmanual modifiers and politeness allowed me to recognize and focus on this aspect of ASL.

The participants in the study gave willingly of their time, and although they will remain anonymous, their contributions are much appreciated and I whole-heartedly thank them for their participation in the study. There have been hundreds of Deaf and hearing people with whom I have discussed this work, and I am indebted to their discussions and critiques of this work.

I want to thank Carol Zurek for allowing me to take pictures of her producing the nonmanual modifiers and signs for the photographs that appear in the book. I also want to thank the wonderful staff at Gallaudet University Press who worked diligently on editing the manuscript and preparing it for publication.

The book is dedicated to my immediate family for their loving support and encouragement. Their inquisitiveness and interest helped me stay motivated to see this book through publication.

IT'S NOT
WHAT YOU SIGN,
IT'S HOW
YOU SIGN IT

1

POLITENESS—
IT'S *HOW* YOU SAY IT

People may not always remember the specifics of a conversation, but they do remember their overall impressions of the other person, as well as how well they felt the conversation proceeded. For example, they may recall whether or not they felt the other person was cooperative, and whether or not the other person was friendly, polite, knowledgeable, standoffish, or rude. These conclusions are usually reached without much thought, and the standards used to make these judgments are largely determined unconsciously based on social factors, which lie beneath the surface of every interaction. Moreover, people tend to assume that their interpretation of another person's way of speaking is the correct interpretation, whether or not that interpretation was the person's intent or not.

Differences in expectations and perceptions vary to some degree across a single language community, of course; but there are greater differences across different language communities. Of particular interest are two very different groups of language users: American Sign Language (ASL) signers and English speakers. The literature on ASL signers (Deaf people) suggests that they differ greatly from English speakers' (hearing people's) way of speaking. Their communication style has been termed *straight talk* (Mindess, 2006), *frank talk* (Lane, Hoffmeister, & Bahan, 1996), or *directness* (see, e.g., Roush, 1999). In fact, a common observation made among ASL signers is the following: DEAF/topic, BE-DIRECT. HEARING /topic, BE-VAGUE [*translation: Deaf people are direct, and hearing*

1

Transcription Notes 1

Common glossing conventions are used in this book to represent signing in the written form. Each capitalized word represents a single sign (e.g., DEAF) and hyphenated capitalized words also represent a single sign (e.g., BE-DIRECT). Underscoring signifies the scope of particular nonmanual signals that accompany the signed phrase, e.g., DEAF/topic, in which *topic* stands for *topicalization*, a nonmanual signal that includes features such as raised eyebrows that co-occur with the signs that are underscored (for more on such nonmanual signals see Baker-Shenk & Cokely, 1980; Bridges & Metzger, 1996; Neidle, Kegl, MacLaughlin, Bahan, & Lee, 2000; Valli, Lucas, & Mulrooney 2005). See Appendix I for a more complete list of transcription conventions used in this book.

(non-Deaf) people are indirect (or vague).] (See Transcription Notes (1).)[1]

Mindess and Holcomb (2001) report, for example, that the question of whether or not it is appropriate to ask a friend how much a car costs is viewed much differently by ASL signers than by English speakers. They report that ASL signers tend to ask the question directly, whereas English speakers (hearing people) tend to ask about the price in an indirect way or to avoid the question altogether. Mindess and Holcomb also report that ASL signers are more direct and English speakers more indirect when providing feedback, and when making comments about personal appearance. In addition, Mindess (2006) states that Deaf people are more direct when discuss-

---

1. The capitalized word *Deaf* is used to refer to the community of ASL signers who comprise American Deaf culture. When the lowercase word *deaf* is used, it is used to refer to being audiologically deaf. See *American Heritage Dictionary*, 2001; Padden & Humphrey, 1988, 2005; Wilcox, 1989; Woodward, 1982.

ing "pertinent information about their health, relationships, work, travel plans, and other significant aspects of life (p. 90)."

> One of the most frequently cited examples of directness [by ASL signers is] related to comments about appearance. This might include statements about weight loss or gain, hair change, clothes, looking older or just about anything that would look different from the last time one saw the other. (Roush, 1999, p. 36)

Such anecdotal and interview evidence is often cited to support the claim that culturally Deaf people are direct and hearing people are indirect.

Few researchers disagree with this characterization of ASL signers. A notable exception is Roush (1999) who argues that ASL signers do in fact use a few different strategies when making requests and rejections.[2] Nonetheless, Roush does not report any indirect requests or rejections, such as *Gee, it's hot in here*, as an indirect way to request that someone turn down the heat. Zimmer (1992) further reports:

> I have asked many Deaf people whether they would interpret a statement like "Gee it's hot in here" as a request. All of the Deaf people I asked told me that they would not interpret such a statement as a request. Interpretation of pragmatic meaning, then, is entirely dependent on knowledge of . . . cultural conventions. (p. 83)

However, Valli, Lucas, and Mulrooney (2005) state that such indirect pragmatic meaning can be conveyed in ASL, in that the utterance *It's hot in here* "can be used in ASL with similar results" (p. 155). Valli, Lucas, and Mulrooney also report that the question, HOME YOU/q [*translation: Are you going home?*], may be interpreted in one of three ways: (a) a request for information, (b) a request for a ride home, or (c) a complaint by a boss to an employee for leaving too early. Unlike the first interpretation (a), which is a direct request for information (*Are you going home?*), interpretations (b) and (c) are indirect because they imply an alternate interpretation based on the context in which they are signed, that is,

---

2. These include, for example, the use of yes/no-questions, the sign glossed as "WELL" (which Roush terms *5HPU*, '5' handshape palm up), and three specific nonmanual markers.

someone putting on a coat and getting ready to leave a meeting for the second interpretation or a boss seeing an employee trying to leave too early for the third interpretation (pp. 155–56). This example (HOME YOU/q) shows that ASL signers may well use indirect strategies. However, the status of indirect strategies in ASL is still in question, as more evidence is needed to determine what kinds of indirect strategies are used in ASL and under what conditions they may be used.

Stereotyping

The characterization of ASL signers as direct and English speakers as indirect may well be an overstatement, and this statement can best be categorized as *stereotyping* (which Roush, 1999, calls a *folk stereotype*). Stereotyping begins when a dichotomy is made between groups based on one particular dimension and when an exaggerated positive or negative value is associated with it. The result is a view of each group that is over simplistic. "Stereotyping is a way of thinking that does not acknowledge internal differences within a group, and does not acknowledge exceptions to its general rules or principles. . . . Stereotypes limit our understanding of human behavior and of intercultural discourse because they limit our view of human activity to just one or two salient dimensions and consider those to be the whole picture" (Scollon & Scollon, p. 169). Any comparison between language communities runs the danger of stereotyping.

This book is the result of my own interest and investigation into the language usage of ASL signers and English speakers. I am a native user of both ASL and English, in that my parents and two of my seven siblings are Deaf, and I am an ASL/English interpreter and interpreter educator. Although I have long recognized an overall difference between these two groups in terms of communication style, I have also noticed times when ASL signers were more indirect and times when English speakers were more direct. For example, an ASL signer may sign a statement one way with a friend and then sign the same statement to a new acquaintance in a different way. Such instances made me realize there is an inconsistency in what people assume about the communication styles of these two language communities and what actually occurs in face-to-face interactions.

Generalizations may certainly be made about a language community (e.g., being comparably more direct or more indirect), but such generalizations in and of themselves may limit one's ability to more deeply understand differences between language communities. When such dichotomies are not explored further, they have a life of their own and can quickly become a stereotype.

For instance, the fact that Chinese does not have words for *yes* and *no* has led to a stereotype about Chinese people. Amy Tan, the award-winning author, has said that she is worried "about the effect of one-dimensional statements on the unwary and the guileless. When they read about this so-called vocabulary deficit, do they also conclude that Chinese people evolve into a mild-mannered lot because the language only allowed them to hobble forth with minced words?" (Tan, 2004, p. 26)

One strategy to avoid stereotyping "is to use multiple dimensions to contrast cultures" (Scollon & Scollon, 2001, p. 175). This means when it comes to addressing the issue of stereotyping:

> The solution to the problem is twofold: comparisons between groups should always consider both likenesses and differences, that is, they should be based upon more than a single dimension of contrast, and it must be remembered that no individual member of a group embodies all of his or her group's characteristics. (Scollon & Scollon, 2001, p. 170)

Labeling ASL signers in America as direct as if they have no variation in communication style "does not adequately characterize the complexity and diversity of conversational styles which are used by its members" (Roush, 1999, p. 1).

Likewise, Amy Tan points out that Chinese people cannot be assumed to fit a particular mold:

> And how many tourists fresh off the bus have wandered into Chinatown expecting the self-effacing shopkeeper to admit under duress that the goods are not worth the price asked? I have witnessed it.
> "I don't know," the tourist said to the shopkeeper, a Cantonese woman in her fifties. "It doesn't look genuine to me. I'll give you three dollars."

"You don't like my price, go somewhere else," said the shopkeeper.

"You are not a nice person," cried the shocked tourist, "not a nice person at all!"

"Who say I have to be nice," snapped the shopkeeper. (Tan, 2004, p. 32)

ASL/English interpreters and interpreting students may find the feedback from ASL signers to be quite direct, but they may also be surprised at times when they ask an ASL signer for feedback on their interpreting work and the person says, "FINE+" [translation: *You did fine, really*], then they find out later that the person was unhappy with their interpreting work. (See Transcription Notes 2.) "But Deaf people are direct," they may say. "Why didn't they tell me directly?"

Like the Chinese storekeeper's reaction above, an ASL signer could well say, 'DIRECT/q. FOR+/wh-q' [translation: *Why should I be direct (with you)?*]. Recognizing that some general cultural tendencies may exist, the more intriguing question seems to be how and when Chinese speakers, ASL signers, and other language users alter their communication style at any given time.

In writing this book, I sought to look beyond the general classification of ASL signers as direct and English speakers as indirect by investigating relevant social variables in specific contexts, and by exploring the particular linguistic strategies ASL signers and English speakers employ when they interact in these contexts. At this level of analysis, a better understanding of the linguistic choices of these language groups can be revealed in their rich complexity.

Differences in communication styles between these two language communities are readily apparent when comparing the two groups; however, these differences, by and large, are oversimplified. Because

---

Transcription Notes 2

The symbol, +, indicates that the sign is repeated. The sign glossed FINE involves a single movement, whereas FINE+ is signed twice in quick succession.

much of the reporting to date is based on anecdotal evidence, there is little empirical data to clarify to what degree these two language groups are similar and different in terms of how they make language choices within particular face-to-face interactions. I use empirical data to go beyond these general cultural assumptions, and to investigate the domain of face-to-face interaction in which linguistic and cultural differences intersect in ways that are often misinterpreted or overlooked in cross-cultural communication.

In writing this book, I had three primary goals. First, I sought to go beyond the assumption that ASL signers are direct and English speakers are indirect. Second, I sought to clarify a specific area of cross-linguistic difference: politeness, and to explore two primary types of politeness and how the linguistic expression of politeness varies across languages. Third, I sought to report the findings of an investigation of the linguistic strategies used in various contexts by English speakers and ASL signers to express politeness concerns in face-to-face interaction.

This study, framed within politeness theory, includes new findings on the linguistic marking of politeness in ASL and English. These findings indicate that certain linguistic strategies are employed by both language groups, and that certain linguistic strategies differ due to different cultural expectations or due to differences that are language specific. The findings reveal an interaction between these strategies and certain social variables, as well as a complexity to face-to-face interaction within each language community that goes beyond simply being direct or indirect.

Key to understanding face-to-face interaction, and the linguistic expression of politeness in particular, is to recognize the process by which people interpret each other's utterances. At the heart of this level of communication is the distinction between *form* and *function*.

Form, Function, and the Interpretation of Utterances

People vary the way they express themselves based on the context in which they find themselves. For example, English speakers may say, "Do you have any salt?" in one context, "I think this needs a little salt," in another context, or "Hand me the salt," in yet another context. Although English speakers would consider all of these utterances to be requests to pass the salt, some of these utterances could be considered more polite than others. Politeness, and the interpretation of meaning more generally, involves a difference between form—what a person says—and function—what linguists refer to as the intent that the interlocutor is conveying in that particular context. These three examples all differ in form, in that different words and even different sentence types are used in each utterance, but all of them have the same function, or speaker's goal: to request that someone pass the salt.

Different functions may also be interpreted from a single form. For example, *It's cold in here* may be interpreted several ways. The addressee may interpret the speaker's intent, the *function,* as an effort to inform (*I want you to know it's cold in here*), to request (*I want you to make it warmer in here; it's too cold*), or to complain (*I want you to know I am not happy that it is too cold in here*).

In short, people do not always mean what they appear to say, in that form and function may differ greatly. Take, for instance, the comparable ASL and English utterances in Examples 1 and 2 below, which could be stated in the workplace. Although I have attempted to structure utterances in ASL and English using similar forms, some of the utterances may be incongruent with standardized ASL usage.

1. They will need that sent to them tomorrow.
   THEY(LEFT) NEED SEND-TO-LEFT TOMORROW/nod.
2. I was thinking you could send that to them tomorrow.
   COME-TO-MIND, YOU CAN SEND-TO-LEFT TOMORROW, CAN, YOU/nod.

On the surface, the speaker or signer of each of these utterances appears to be relating someone else's need in the first example and expressing one's own thoughts in the second. However, both of the utterances in English above may be interpreted as making a request for action, albeit indirectly, and the interpretation is made possible by one's social knowledge of language use, or implicature. This current study has sought to clarify if such ASL utterances have the same interpretation as the English utterances.

Another possible form used in making a request is the imperative form, which is both direct and unambiguous, as in Example 3 below.

3. Send that to them tomorrow.
   TOMORROW/topic, YOU SEND-TO-LEFT.

This utterance represents a matching of form and meaning, in that the imperative form is the unmarked form of a request for action: a command. Yet another form that is commonly used in requests is shown in Example 4.

4. Could you send that to them tomorrow?
   CAN SEND-TO-LEFT TOMORROW, YOU/q.

Note that this utterance is literally asking about the hearer's ability to send something tomorrow, but it too may be interpreted as a request. The utterances in Example 4 show a special, conventionalized

---

Transcription Notes 3

Signs that appear with a direction indicate the location in space used by the signer. For example, THEY(LEFT) is signed on the left and #SEND-TO-LEFT is signed toward the left. Again, the underscoring in this case indicates that nodding co-occurs with the entire utterance.

Transcription Notes 4

The abbreviation *q* stands for the yes/no-question marking in ASL. This marking is composed of raised eyebrows, leaning forward, and direct eye contact (see, e.g., Baker-Shenk & Cokely, 1980; Bridges & Metzger 1996; Neidle et al., 2000; Valli, Lucas, & Mulrooney, 2005).

Transcription Notes 5

The symbol, #, represents lexicalized fingerspelling, i.e., a fingerspelled item (a borrowing from written English) that has become lexicalized—or an independent word—in ASL (see, e.g., Baker-Shenk & Cokely, 1980; Battison, 1978; Valli, Lucas, & Mulrooney, 2005). The abbreviation *neg* stands for the negation marking in ASL (primarily a shaking of the head) and the abbreviation *rh-q* stands for the rhetorical question marking in ASL (raised eyebrows, a headshake, and a tilt of the head) (see, e.g., Baker-Shenk & Cokely, 1980; Bridges & Metzger 1996; Neidle et al., 2000; Valli, Lucas, & Mulrooney, 2005). The sign glossed as "WELL" is a naturally occurring gesture that is used in ASL and is made by holding out one or both open hands with the palms facing upward. See Figure 1.1 for an example of <u>"WELL"</u>/q.

---

form of indirectness that is a common form used in making requests (see chapters 2 and 3).

In addition, a variety of expressions may be used for rejecting a request. As with requests, the forms of rejections range from direct refusals (see Example 5) to indirect rejections (see Example 6).

5. No, I can't do that.
   <u>NO, CAN'T, I</u>/neg.
6. I wish I could, but I doubt it's going to be ready by tomorrow, so maybe we could get it out the day after.
   <u>WISH</u>/nod, #BUT <u>READY TOMORROW</u>/rh-q. <u>DOUBT, I</u>/neg.
   MAYBE TWO-DAYS LATER-ON, <u>"WELL"</u>/q.

All the requests in English above may be interpreted by the addressee as a request to send something the next day, and the rejections above may be interpreted as turning down that request. What differs greatly, of course, is *how* the requests and rejections

Figure 1.1. "WELL"/q

are made. Again, how the ASL utterances in particular would be interpreted by an addressee is in question, in that this is a new area of study.

An interlocutor may choose to alter the form of a request or a rejection for a few different reasons. For example, the interlocutor may alter the form to express (a) the degree of certainty or uncertainty about what is being said: *I will be there* vs. *I'll most likely be there*, (b) the degree of formality or informality of the situation: *Excuse me, but I have an obligation that cannot wait* vs. *See ya. Gotta go*, (c) surprise: *I see you're still here* vs. *Oh, you're still here!* or (d) politeness or impoliteness: *Could you help me out a second?* vs. *Don't just sit there!* It is this last dimension, politeness, that is the focus of this book. So, what is politeness exactly?

What Is Politeness?

People generally know politeness when they see it, but defining politeness is no easy task. ASL signers have likely seen the following in ASL: "POLITE/topic, NONE, YOU/neg" [*translation: You don't have any manners* or *How rude*] or "#RUDE INDEX!" [*translation: He is rude!* or *That was rude!*].[3] English speakers may also have heard similar expressions in English: *That was rude* or *Didn't his parents teach him any manners?* And, no doubt, the speaker and addressee understood why they considered that person to be rude, but they may not be able to put it into words. For example, they may think, "NOT NICE, INDEX/neg" [*translation: He wasn't being very nice*], but certainly being nice is different from being polite. For instance, if a person smiles a lot or gives someone an unexpected gift, that person would be considered nice, but not necessarily polite, per se. In fact, it may well be that people could be nice (pleasant or considerate) on the surface, but be quite impolite (lacking manners) in their intent. Politeness, then, is related to the notion of being nice in that both have to do with expectations regarding social behavior, but it differs in some respects, in that politeness is at least more specific.

Four Levels of Meaning

To understand politeness as it pertains to language usage, one must first look at how people communicate. In addition to function (e.g., to request, to compliment, to educate, to reject), there are at least three other levels of meaning that exist within any utterance. First, speakers convey *content*, which is the specific information expressed in an utterance.

Second, they signal how their current utterance relates to the preceding section of discourse (in a conversation or monologue) and/or the expectations for the forthcoming discourse. This level of discourse meaning is the *textual meaning*. For example, if a signer signs, "HANDWAVE", BE-DIRECT, BE-HONEST. FEEL NOT TRUE, INDEX/neg" [*translation: [Addressee's name], to be direct and honest, I don't feel that's true*], the person uses the sign, "HANDWAVE", to signal a desire to take a turn, and by the rest of the utterance signals that he is arguing for a different viewpoint by framing the discourse as a debate or serious discussion. So, in addition to content and function, speakers

---

3. INDEX is a pointing sign that may function as a pronoun, determiner, or adverb (of location) in ASL (see Baker-Shenk & Cokely, 1980; Neidle, Kegl, MacLaughlin, Bahan, & Lee, 2000; Valli, Lucas, & Mulrooney, 2005). No distinction is made among these functions in this book.

Transcription Notes 6

The sign glossed as "HANDWAVE" represents a sign that is used as a conversational opener (discourse marker) and has been glossed elsewhere in the literature as "HEY" (see, e.g., Baker-Shenk & Cokely 1980). The sign is produced by waving the hand up and down slightly toward the addressee, as shown in Figure 1.2.

---

express textual meaning: how the current utterance relates to the previous or upcoming discourse.

Third, interlocutors also communicate how a particular utterance relates to the social context of the moment. This level of meaning represents the intersection of language usage and *social meaning*, and is the level at which the linguistic expression of politeness takes place. Note that in the example above, the person begins the utterance with "HANDWAVE", BE-DIRECT, BE-HONEST. [*translation*: *[Addressee's name], to be direct and honest*] before delving

Figure 1.2. "HANDWAVE": hand waves up and down slightly

into the disagreement in order to prepare the addressee for the up-coming disagreement. Alternatively, the person could sign the dis-agreement outright without the introductory remark (i.e., "FEEL NOT TRUE, INDEX/neg" [*translation: I don't feel that's true*] or "NOT TRUE, INDEX/neg" [*translation: That's not true*]). Why an interlocutor uses one linguistic form or another depends on such social factors as the setting, the participants, the topic, and how the interlocutor perceives the speech act (e.g., the request or the rejection) will be received by the addressee. At this level of meaning, the linguistic form reflects how the participant perceives the social context and the participant's place in it.

In sum, there are at least four types of meaning conveyed in an utterance:

1. Content
2. Function (or Speaker's goal)
3. Textual meaning
4. Social meaning

Politeness is primarily concerned with social meaning and, specifically, the expectations of the participants in particular contexts. Social meaning is part of a speaker's *metamessage*: "what is communicated about relationships—attitudes toward each other, the occasion, and what we are saying" (Tannen, 1986, p. 16). The metamessage is often the implicit (unstated) message that the speaker intends to convey in an utterance.

The linguistic expression of social meaning varies by culture and context. For instance, English speakers who are members of main-stream U.S. culture would generally see the exchange in Example 7 below as very natural and socially appropriate.

7. **Context: Speaker A and Speaker B are friends, and are standing before a vending machine.**
   Speaker A: Hey, can I borrow a dollar?
   Speaker B: Sure. *(hands over a dollar bill)*
   Speaker A: Thanks. I'll pay you back tomorrow.
   Speaker B: No problem.

This short interaction is characterized by cooperation and makes use of conventions such as *thanks* (sometimes expressed as *thank you* in other contexts) and *no problem* (sometimes *you're welcome* or *that's okay* in other contexts). These discrete, often learned, polite forms of expression provide the glue for social interaction and they are not unlike the use of *gracias* [*thank you*] and *de nada* [*it's nothing*] in Spanish or THANK-YOU and FINE+ [*that's fine*] in ASL.

These conventionalized expressions are only a small part of the world of politeness, however. For example, each of the following is a possible way of expressing a request to borrow a dollar: *Got a dollar? Can I borrow a dollar? I was wondering if I could borrow a dollar, Give me a dollar,* and *I'm a dollar short.* All of these are options for the requester. The expression used at a particular time conveys what the speaker perceives as most appropriate given the setting and the relationship with the addressee, which shows that "sentences are not *ipso facto* polite, nor are languages more or less polite. It is only speakers who are polite, and then only if their utterances reflect an adherence to the obligations they carry in that particular conversation" (Fraser, 1990, p. 233).

These examples and the discussion thus far clearly place politeness in the domain of face-to-face interaction. Framed within this domain, the exact nature of politeness can be more fully explored. What does it mean to say someone is being polite at any particular moment? We now will explore two views of politeness: (a) the social norm view of politeness and (b) linguistic politeness.

Social Norm View of Politeness

Many books on good manners or social etiquette have been published. The purpose of these publications is to delineate prescribed rules of social behavior (i.e., they have taken the social norm view of politeness; Fraser, 1990). This level of politeness has also been termed *social politeness* (Janney & Arndt, 1992) and *polite behavior* (Watts, 1989, 1992). In this view, "a positive evaluation (politeness) arises when an action is in congruence with the norm, [and] a negative evaluation (impoliteness = rudeness) when action is to the contrary" (Fraser, 1990, p. 220).

Take, for example, the following excerpt from a book on etiquette by Judith Martin (1982), better known as Miss Manners:

Elbows
DEAR MISS MANNERS:
My home economics teacher says that one must never place one's elbows on the table. However, I have read that one elbow, in between courses, is all right. Which is correct?

DEAR GENTLE READER:
For the purpose of answering examinations in your home economics class, your teacher is correct. Catching on to this principle of education may be of even greater importance to you now than learning correct current table manners, vital as Miss Manners believes that is.

Elbows are banned during eating because of the awkward, crane-like motion it gives to the hand on the other end of the elbow, trying to get down to table level for food. Also it is a delightfully easy error to catch children in, whose other errors may be more subtle.

When one is not actually eating, it is still a good rule to keep one's arms close to the body, but a less formal posture, with one elbow parked close to the plate during a pause in the meal, is no longer punishable by hanging. (p. 128)

In Miss Manners' view, the world is composed of certain social rules of which one must be aware and which one must follow. Such rules as, Don't eat with your mouth full, Don't forget the magic word (i.e., Please), and Wait until all the guests are seated and served before beginning to eat are other social rules to which one is expected to adhere. Violation of these rules is considered rude.

Some examples in ASL of such polite behavior include actions that facilitate communication and promote group unity. The following, for example, would violate these social expectations: keeping a secret rather than letting the group in on something, turning one's back improperly to cut off communication, or leaving a social gathering too quickly rather than properly extending the good-bye. All of these behaviors would be considered rude by ASL signers (see Hall, 1989; Lane et al., 1996). In fact, "this basic rule [of sharing information and facilitating communication] also explains why some

behavior that is rude among hearing people, blunt speech and telling a secret, is not rude among . . . Deaf [people]" (Hall, 1989, p. 101).
The social norm view of politeness, then, is a reflection of the values
held by a particular community. One is expected to behave in ways
that reflect what is valued in the community. Thus, what is considered polite behavior regarding the issue of privacy differs between
English speakers and ASL signers because these two language communities value them in different ways.

Although the social norm view of politeness may appear to be
quite obvious and intuitive, one's face-to-face interactions and the
resulting perceptions of one's linguistic behavior are not so simple.
For example:

> [In] Garfinkel's experiments in the 1970s . . . students were instructed
> to behave 'more politely than usual' with their families and to observe
> the reactions. Most students equated increased politeness with in-
> creased formality, and reported that such increased unexpected formal
> behavior was interpreted as impoliteness, disrespect, or arrogance.
> (Fraser, 1990, p. 221)

In other words, striving to be overly polite in one's interactions may,
in fact, backfire.

Following a set of social norms is but one level of politeness. The
sample English utterances at the beginning of this chapter—such as
I was thinking you could send that to them tomorrow, *Send that to them
tomorrow*, and *Could you send that to them tomorrow?*—make it clear
that there is no explicit rule regarding which linguistic form to use
when making such requests in the workplace.

Linguistic Politeness

This book is focused on the type of politeness that occurs in everyday face-to-face interaction: *linguistic politeness*. Linguistic politeness
is concerned with the linguistic choices that interlocutors make and
has also been referred to as *interpersonal politeness* (Janney & Arndt,
1992) and *politic behavior* (Watts, 1989, 1992). Linguists have used
three approaches to explain how language users make linguistic
choices based on politeness concerns.

The Conversational Maxim View

The conversational maxim view (see, e.g., Fraser, 1990) uses Grice's (1975) Cooperative Principle as a starting point. Conversations require that the interlocutors cooperate by following certain unspoken guidelines, or maxims. Grice outlines four maxims that become the basis for face-to-face interaction, and these can be summarized as follows:

1. Maxim of Quantity—Say as much as is necessary, but not too much
2. Maxim of Quality—Be honest
3. Maxim of Relation—Be relevant
4. Maxim of Manner—Do not be ambiguous

Following these maxims allows for smooth interaction between interlocutors, and interlocutors generally only violate these maxims for the purpose of conveying alternate meanings. For example, a speaker may say, "I don't know that I can really help you out right now," to turn someone down instead of saying, "I can't help you." The latter utterance, of course, is direct and unambiguous, in that it matches form and function, and is clearly a rejection. It also does not violate any of the maxims. However, in the former utterance, the speaker is violating the Maxim of Quality (be honest). In that case, the speaker expects the addressee to recognize that the speaker is equivocating, thus violating this maxim, and therefore, the addressee is not to interpret the utterance literally. That is, when the speaker says, "I don't know that . . . ," the addressee realizes the speaker does indeed *know*, but is using this phrasing as an attempt to mitigate or soften the rejection.

Lakoff's (1973) Politeness Principle functions like the Cooperative Principle but is focused instead on the social relationship of the interlocutors. Lakoff stresses that "only by appeal to context [in which utterances are stated] could we account for the unacceptability under some conditions of sentences which under other conditions were unexceptional" (Lakoff, p. 292). The Politeness Principle is composed of three maxims:

1. Do not impose [do not intrude into other people's business]
   Example: *May I ask how much you paid for that vase, Mr. Hoving?*

2. Give options [let the addressee make his/her own decisions; leave options open for the addressee]
   Examples: *I guess it's time to leave.*
   It's time to leave, isn't it?
3. Make the hearer feel good—be friendly [create a sense of camaraderie and equality]
   Examples: Use compliments and nicknames (or direct communication).
   (Lakoff, pp. 298–302)

These three maxims attempt to capture how politeness is realized in face-to-face interaction when the speaker is making linguistic choices to appear polite. Each of these options functions at the level of social meaning. However, although these maxims capture the goals of a speaker, they lack specificity, in that they do not clarify *when* speakers use the maxims. It is not clear when a speaker would choose to not impose, to give options, or to make the hearer feel good, and yet, each would certainly have a different effect.

Leech (1983) has expanded on Lakoff's maxims and has proposed six interpersonal maxims: Tact, Generosity, Approbation, Modesty, Agreement, and Sympathy. By adding maxims, Leech has been able to capture a wider variety of options that speakers have for politeness purposes. In reality, it is not possible to capture all the ways in which a speaker may seek to be polite. However, some scholars see much promise to the conversational maxim view and suggest that perhaps a single Politeness Maxim should be included as part of the Cooperative Principle, and this maxim should be equal to the maxims of Quality, Quantity, Relation, and Manner (see, e.g., Fraser, 2005 for discussion).

In sum, the conversational maxim view has sought to identify various goals of speakers when they use linguistic politeness and to identify how these goals are accomplished. However, this approach lacks in specificity (why certain maxims are followed at certain times). Further the number of maxims needed to capture the goals of interlocutors may be too numerous and may indeed be too far-reaching (see, e.g., Fraser, 1990). At the same time, this approach does show that politeness functions at the level of social meaning much like conversational maxims function at the level of specific speech acts within conversation, in that violations of certain maxims cause the addressee to interpret an alternate meaning or metamessage. That is, violating a politeness maxim could be perceived as impolite or rude.

The Conversational Contract View

A *conversational contract view* of linguistic politeness has also been proposed (Fraser, 1990; Fraser & Nolen, 1981):

> Upon entering into a given conversation, each participant brings an understanding of the initial set of rights and obligations that will determine, at least for the preliminary stages, what the participants can expect from the other(s). During the course of time and because of a change in the context, the two parties may readjust just what rights and what obligations they hold towards each other. In other words, what counts as politeness is an on going negotiation. (Fraser, 1990, p. 232)

These rights and obligations vary partly due to conversational conventions (e.g., taking turns) and social institutions, both of which are seldom negotiable. They also vary partly due to the particulars of the situation, such as status, power, and the role of the participants, which are more likely to be negotiable (Fraser, 1990, p. 232). In this view, *politeness* is defined as the act of "operating within the then-current terms and conditions of the [conversational contract]" (Fraser, 1990, p. 233).

This view highlights the fact that linguistic politeness is far from static, in that what is considered polite at one point in face-to-face interaction may be interpreted differently at another point in the interaction. Stated another way: "The same politeness strategies are apt to encode different social and psychological meanings at any given point in verbal interaction" (Kasper, 1990, p. 205).

The conversational contract view clearly places politeness within the realm of the expectations in interaction, rather than something that is considered as an exception to normal interaction. However, it is less clear how speakers actually decide what linguistic devices to use during the "then-current terms and conditions" of the conversational contract.

What both the conversational maxim view and the conversational contract view have in common is an attempt to identify the motivation for politeness in face-to-face interaction. For the conversational maxim view, the motivation is defined as a list of speaker goals relative to the social dynamics of the moment, and for the conversational contract view, the motivation is to work within the expectations regarding the rights and obligations that the interlocutors hold toward each other. A third view, the face-saving view of politeness, is the most commonly held view of politeness among linguistic scholars.

The Face-Saving View of Politeness

The face-saving view of politeness has been the most influential in the field of linguistics, and is based on the notion that interlocutors strive to save face for themselves and others in face-to-face interaction (see, especially, Brown & Levinson, 1987, Scollon & Scollon, 2001; also see, e.g., Hickey & Stewart, 2005; Lakoff & Ide, 2005; Mey, 2003). Face, based on the work of Goffman (1967), is "the positive social value [or image] a person effectively claims for himself . . . by making a good showing for himself (or his group)" (p. 5). How this is accomplished varies from situation to situation, because people use different strategies depending on the context in which they find themselves. Brown and Levinson's (1987) face-saving approach to politeness, in particular, provides a detailed categorization of various linguistic strategies that speakers may use to save face for the speaker and/or the addressee.

Face can be understood to be of two kinds: (a) the desire to be unimpeded in one's actions and (b) the desire to be approved of (Brown & Levinson, 1987). Human beings communicate these two aspects of face to let others know that they either want approval or are expressing approval of others, and, at the same time, to let people know that, in certain respects, they do not want to be imposed upon or do not want to impose upon others.

Brown and Levinson (1987) use the term *positive politeness* for the type of politeness associated with showing approval and camaraderie, whereas others have used the term *involvement* (see, e.g., Scollon

& Scollon, 2001; Tannen, 1986). For the type of politeness associated with wanting neither to impose upon others nor to be imposed upon, Brown and Levinson (1987) use the term *negative politeness* and others use the term *independence* (Scollon & Scollon; Tannen, 1986). In this book, *involvement* refers to the type of face associated with expressing approval and showing camaraderie, and *independence* refers to the type of face associated with not wanting to impose.

An example of involvement strategies at work is when someone is excited about sharing some new pictures with a group of close friends. Each person contributes to the discussion in a very familiar way, most likely joking with each other, and feeling good about themselves and the interaction. In this example, what is stressed is what everyone has in common in the form of mutual approval and acceptance, and there is a strong sense of camaraderie.

Independence strategies are most readily seen among people who, for whatever reason, want to respect each other's individual boundaries, as in the case of making an important request of a superordinate, such as a new boss or foreign dignitary. When making a request in this type of context, the addressee's independence is foregrounded, and speakers making such a request are on their best behavior and try to not impose. In short, they generally follow social rules of decorum.

The primary focus of politeness theory over the past few decades has been on *face-threatening acts* (FTAs), which are threats to the addressee's, or the speaker's, face needs (Brown & Levinson, 1987). For example, a request may be an FTA because it is a threat to the addressee's independence (negative face needs), and a rejection (or refusal) may be an FTA because it is a threat to the addressee's involvement (positive face needs).

Although the Brown and Levinson (1987) view of politeness has been criticized for being overly pessimistic because it focuses on avoiding threats to the speaker's or addressee's face needs, in fact politeness strategies may also represent antithreats, or face-flattering acts (FFAs; Kerbrat-Orecchioni, 2005):

> Every speech act could, therefore, be described as an FTA, an FFA,
> or a compound of the two. In correlation, two forms of politeness

emerge from this theoretical base: *negative politeness* [independence], which involves avoiding or softening the formulation of an FTA (as a way of saying "I wish you no harm"); and *positive politeness* [involvement], which involves the production of an FFA, possibly reinforced (as a way of saying "I wish you well"). Seen from this vantage point, the ebb and flow of an exchange involves a constant and subtle swinging back and forth between FTAs and FFAs. (Kerbrat-Orecchioni, p. 31)

Both FTAs and FFAs are mitigated in face-to-face interaction. FTAs are often softened, or downgraded (e.g., *Do you want a little bit of sugar?*). However, FFAs tend to be reinforcing or upgraded (e.g., *Thank you so much*), but not downgraded, as in *Thank you a little bit* (Kerbrat-Orecchioni, pp. 31–32). It can also be said that "all acts can range on a contiuum with face threat occupying one end, and face enhancement the other" (Sifianou & Antonopoulou, 2005, p. 265).

Not all FTAs or FFAs have the same weight. Several factors determine the assessment of the seriousness of an FTA or FFA in a particular context. At least three factors determine to what degree speech acts such as requests and rejections are mitigated: (a) the Power relation (P) between the speaker and the hearer, (b) the relative Social Distance (D) between the speaker and the hearer, and (c) the Ranking (R) of the Imposition in a particular culture (Brown & Levinson, 1987, pp. 74-84). These factors provide the motivation for using more or fewer politeness strategies within a particular context.

In face-to-face interaction, speakers communicate messages about both involvement and independence, and addressees interpret the social meaning of these speakers. There is always the danger of misinterpretation, however:

> The danger of misinterpretation is greatest, of course, among speakers who actually speak different native tongues, or come from different cultural backgrounds, because cultural difference necessarily implies different assumptions about natural and obvious ways to be polite. (Tannen, 1986, p. 28)

That is, there is generally greater misinterpretation between language communities than within them. Different language communities not only often have different expectations regarding politeness (e.g., involvement vs. independence), they may also use different linguistic forms for these purposes.

The face-saving approach to politeness provides a framework that can be used to investigate how language users make linguistic choices based on this particular aspect of social meaning. Discussion in this book is therefore based on the following definition of *politeness:* the act of maintaining face for the speaker and/or the addressee, and is accomplished by using linguistic strategies either to mitigate a face-threatening act or to reinforce a face-flattering act.

Politeness as it pertains to language usage is more than following rules of etiquette or being nice. Language users have many linguistic options at their disposal. Based on specific aspects of the context, they use certain linguistic forms to convey content, function, and textual meaning, as well as social meaning. Politeness strategies are used to meet the needs for involvement or independence of the speaker and the addressee, and function at the level of social meaning. The relative risk to face (as either a threat or enhancement to face) is a factor in determining which politeness strategies to employ at any given time. The goal of the current study is to identify patterns in language use based on variables such as power (P), social distance (D), and ranking of imposition (R), and to go beyond a broad cultural categorization of a language community as direct or indirect (based on this one difference).

Three Levels of Analysis

Scholars tend to focus on one of at least three different levels of analysis in their investigations of the nature of linguistic politeness across languages and across language varieties. These three levels include (a) *culture,* (b) *discourse style,* and (c) *interaction.* In actuality, these levels of analysis often overlap and scholars usually work within at least two levels simultaneously. This section will review all three levels of analysis to clarify the distinctions among them and then will conclude with a brief discussion of the interactional approach used in this study and the benefits of this approach.

The Cultural Level of Analysis

Culture is a powerful vehicle used to transmit language, values, beliefs, and norms from one generation to the next. There are also different cultural expectations regarding what linguistic devices to use in the mitigation of speech acts, as well as different cultural views of face itself. The *cultural level of analysis* deals with such cultural differences.

For example, Mao (1994), who focuses on differences in Chinese and American notions of face, proposes an interactional construct to account for cross-cultural notions of face, which he calls *relative face orientation*. In short, there are two interactional ideals that may be more salient and sanctioned in a particular language community. These are *ideal social identity* and *ideal individual autonomy*. The ideal social identity

> motivates members of the community to associate themselves with others and to cultivate a sense of homogeneity. On the other hand, the "ideal individual autonomy" marks off a separate and an almost inviolable space, within which the individual can preserve and celebrate his or her freedom of action without fear of becoming an outsider. . . . Furthermore, these two ideals compete for saliency in a given speech community. (p. 472)

It has been proposed that the Chinese have more of an ideal social identity and Americans have more of an ideal individual autonomy (see Gu, 1990; Mao).

Katriel (1986) is also interested in the level of cultural analysis, particularly Israeli culture (Sabra culture), in which *dugri* (straightforward) speech entails being sincere, assertive, matter-of-fact, natural (simple and spontaneous), and terse. This way of speaking is in great contrast to that of American English speakers. "Americans tend to interpret the paucity of politeness formulas [expressions] in Israeli speech as rudeness, and Israelis tend to experience the standard American use of these conventions as a mark of insincerity" (Katriel, p. 2).

To better understand these different underlying perceptions of politeness at the cultural level of analysis, Blum-Kulka (1997) compares politeness as it is realized in Chinese culture and in Israeli culture along the dimensions of sincerity and truthfulness.

> For the Chinese, sincerity seems a matter of symbolic persuasion, a necessary outward show, whereas actual truthfulness is waived in service of the principle of polite modesty (cf. Leech, 1983). The Israeli cultural notion of *dugriyut* (literally "straightforwardness") as studied by Katriel (1986) involves no contradiction in marrying sincerity and truthfulness with politeness; redress to self and other's face might be expressed by stating sincerely the truth of a critical, threatening act. Cultural interpretations of face constituents should therefore be considered seriously in discussions of the universality of politeness systems. (p. 143)

It is at the level of cultural difference that we can best recognize such key differences in expectations regarding politeness. As with other cultural values and norms, certain dimensions of politeness may be more salient in one culture than another, as in the case of ideal social identity versus ideal individual autonomy and truthfulness versus sincerity in the examples above.

Such cultural dimensions help explain utterances such as, *I don't know if I can make it, but I'll try,* in an American English speaker's response to an invitation to an event. Some foreigners are surprised to learn that this statement is intended to be taken as a rejection (no) because these foreigners may assume that truthfulness (being honest) has more of a priority than sincerity (seeming to be genuine and polite) in such a context. Conversely, in some cultural groups even hinting that one cannot attend an event would be offensive and cause the addressee to lose face. Furthermore, in some cultures saying the rejection outright would be considered the most appropriate and least offensive response. Which linguistic option is used is largely influenced by underlying cultural norms regarding the mitigation of threats to involvement and independence, as well as the view of face itself.

Some of these generalizations based on cultural differences are enlightening. At the same time, the cultural level of analysis may risk creating or perpetuating stereotypes if they are taken at face value. Another level of analysis looks more closely at specific linguistic tendencies of a language community.

The Discourse Style Level of Analysis

Members of a language community share tendencies regarding discourse patterns that may differ markedly from those of other language communities. Some scholars, such as Tannen (1986) and Scollon and Scollon (2001), have focused their analysis on the level of discourse style.

Scollon and Scollon (2001) focus their attention on discourse systems that differ between Chinese culture and American culture, and apply their findings to Eastern and Western cultures more generally. Such differences include whether or not the speaker begins with the main point (a deductive rhetorical pattern: X because of Y) or ends with the main point (an inductive rhetorical pattern: because of Y, X). In some cultures such as in the United States, if you say something first, it is given special attention; and in some cultures such as in China, if you say something last, it is given special attention. Such differing discourse expectations can cause problems in cross-cultural communication. Interlocutors can leave a conversation with quite different understandings of what was being said based on the discourse system (discourse style) each was using.

Scollon and Scollon (2001) propose two types of face politeness systems that they call involvement and independence, which correspond in many respects to Brown and Levinson's (1987) positive politeness and negative politeness (discussed above). See Figure 1.3 for a summary of these two face politeness systems, their relationship to deductive and inductive rhetorical strategies, their emphases, and the speaker's motive for each.[4]

These differences in discourse systems are of particular interest to Scollon and Scollon because in the East "hierarchy in relationships is much more consciously observed than it is in the west [sic]" (p. 93), which results in these different discourse systems, and this difference in discourse systems may result in cross-cultural misinterpretation.

Tannen (1986) is also interested in the discourse style level of analysis, which she terms *conversational style*. Unlike Scollon and

---

4. Also see Scollon and Scollon (2001) for a discussion of corporate discourse, professional discourse, generational discourse, and gender discourse.

Rhetorical Strategy	Face Politeness System	Emphasis	Speaker's Motive
DEDUCTIVE (topic-first)	INVOLVEMENT	-what the participants have in common	-does not want to assert independence -is willing to be accepted in common membership
INDUCTIVE (topic-delayed)	INDEPENDENCE	-independence of the participants	-does not wish to impose on another -does not want to assume the listener will automatically agree

Figure 1.3. Topic and face—Two discourse systems. Scollon and Scollon's two discourse systems represent two face politeness systems, each of which has a different emphasis and results from a different speaker's motive.
(Summarized from Scollon & Scollon, 2001, pp. 86–99)

Scollon (2001) whose work focuses on differences across cultures, Tannen's (1986) work has been focused on differences in conversational styles within the same culture. Her most noted work has been with sociolinguistic differences between male and female conversational styles in the United States. Tannen (1990) has proposed that men tend to use the language of exclusion, in which they tend to emphasize autonomy and independence and to downplay their intimate relationships. In contrast, women tend to use the language of inclusion and connection, in which they are more likely to play up intimacy and relationships. Tannen (1990) states:

> If women speak and hear a language of connection and intimacy, while men speak and hear a language of status and independence, then communication between men and women can be like cross-cultural communication, prey to a clash of conversational styles. Instead of different dialects, it has been said they speak different genderlects. (p. 42)

See Figure 1.4 for a summary of men's and women's conversational styles.

Even within one language or language variety, some diversity exists regarding the discourse patterns used by speakers. First, not all speakers may use the same discourse pattern, as Tannen (1990)

POLITENESS—IT'S HOW YOU SAY IT

	Tend to use a system of:	And engage in:
Women	INTIMACY, a system of symmetry which involves networking with close friends, minimizing differences, trying to reach consensus, and avoiding seeming superior	RAPPORT-TALK (private speaking), which is used to establish connections and negotiate relationships
Men	INDEPENDENCE, a system of asymmetry which involves maintaining separateness and difference (autonomy), establishing and maintaining status in a hierarchical social order	REPORT-TALK (public speaking), which is used to preserve independence and negotiate and maintain status in a hierarchy

Figure 1.4. Men and women—Two conversational styles. Tannen contrasts the conversational styles of men and women by identifying differing (a) systems of symmetry or hierarchy and (b) types of talk in which each engages.
(Summarized from Tannen, 1990, pp. 23–95)

states regarding men's and women's conversational styles: "Though all humans need *both* intimacy and independence, women *tend* to focus on the first and men on the second" (p. 26) (emphasis added). Second, speakers are members of more than one linguistic group. In other words, "in any particular communicative situation, the participants will simultaneously be members of various discourse systems" (Scollon & Scollon, 2001, p. 261), so speakers by and large use a combination of discourse styles.

The discourse style level of analysis allows some generalizations to be made about the language usage of specific language communities. Whether based on culture, gender, or some other common feature, these tendencies reflect general discourse patterns that are identifiable to a particular group. There is yet one more level of study, which is the level of analysis used in this book.

The Interactional Level of Analysis

The focus of this book is on the *interactional level of analysis*. This level of analysis is reflected in the work of those involved in the Cross-Cultural Speech Act Realization Project (Blum-Kulka, House,

& Kasper, 1989), in which the focus is on contextual factors and their effect on the linguistic decisions made by members of a linguistic community when engaging in specific speech acts such as requests, rejections, apologies, and criticisms. This level of analysis provides a more detailed account of linguistic differences than the other two levels of analysis because the research concentrates specifically on how speakers of a language alter their way of speaking based on the particulars of a situation, the current interaction, and the specific speech act.

The variables of power (P), social distance (D), and ranking of the imposition (R) are used by researchers at the interactional level of analysis to identify patterns in linguistic strategies. By providing participants with different discourse contexts and altering these variables, researchers are able to identify such patterns in language use. This is the approach used in the current study.

It may be difficult at times to separate the three levels of analysis, especially because it is sometimes difficult to discuss one level without mentioning the others; however, the focus of each varies considerably. At the level of interaction, the primary focus is not on cultural tendencies or even shared discourse patterns of a language group, but rather on the specific devices that are used in particular kinds of contexts. However, the other two levels of analysis provide the basis for initiating an interactional investigation, and the results of an interactional study have implications for the other levels of analysis as well. The focus of an interactional level of analysis is on how speakers handle certain speech acts within face-to-face interaction. This is the level of analysis that is used in this book to investigate the specific area of managing requests and rejections in ASL and English.

See Figure 1.5 for a visual representation of the three levels of analysis.

Each of the levels of analysis offers a different lens through which we may view and examine language usage. The cultural level provides the widest scope in that it investigates broad, cultural tendencies, such as a cultural identity, or the ranking of such values as sincerity and truthfulness. The discourse style level provides an intermediate view by exploring tendencies based on discourse patterns

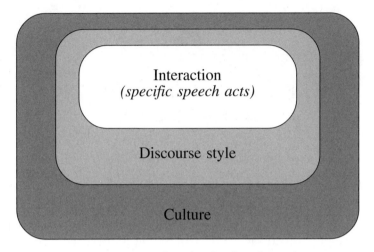

Figure 1.5. Three levels of analysis.

(e.g., discourse systems and conversational styles). The interactional level provides a close-up view of language usage, in that it involves detailed examination of the specific linguistic strategies used in varying contexts by members of a language community.

The observation at the cultural level in the literature is that ASL signers tend to be direct (forthright) and English speakers, comparatively, tend to be more indirect (evasive). This observation, along with anecdotal evidence, has perhaps led to the assumption and perception that each group has a different discourse *style*: being direct and indirect, respectively. This book is an exploration of the interactional level to determine to what degree this assumption is true.

2

EXPLORING LINGUISTIC STRATEGIES

An addressee may feel imposed upon when asked to do something. This is because inherent in a request is the implication that the addressee should be cooperative and should comply with the request. It can be difficult to say, "No," unless the request truly seems unreasonable. At the same time, the person who is making the request does not want to seem to impose unduly on the addressee. In such request-response adjacency sequences, the speaker and the addressee risk losing face. Speech acts, such as requests and rejections, have the potential to cause the speaker or the addressee to lose face (in terms of involvement or independence), and people usually want to save or maintain face.

Therefore, speakers typically mitigate such speech acts as requests and rejections by altering their linguistic form in some way. For example, if someone needs help with moving several large piles of books, he may say, "Could you help me out a second?" This particular request is mitigated by using a conventionalized form of making a request: using a question form (rather than a command) and a subjunctive modal (*could*) as well as hedging on the amount of time needed to move the books. Obviously, moving the books will take more than a second, but the speaker is well aware that he is imposing on the independence of the addressee, so hedging on the time needed to complete the act is a way of downplaying the request.

Responding affirmatively to a request is not usually an issue, as that would meet with the expectations and promote involvement. Ignoring the request would certainly be inappropriate. The expectation at the *textual level* is that a request will be acknowledged or responded to in some way, usually by being accepted or rejected.

If the addressee does not want to comply or is not able to comply with a request, the addressee may find that turning down a request in some situations is dicey at best. There is a constant pull toward maintaining solidarity and cooperation on the one hand and a pull toward maintaining independence on the other. So the person turning down the request may say something like, "Sorry. I'm kind of busy right now. Maybe Suzie could help you out." In this example, the speaker is using an apology, a statement about being busy which provides a reason for noncompliance, and a suggestion that the requester ask someone else. All of these linguistic strategies serve to mitigate the rejection by showing both cooperation (involvement) by making a suggestion and independence by apologizing and providing a reason (a type of indirect apology).

So, how do we know how and when to use such strategies to convey linguistic politeness? These strategies are certainly not contained in a grammar book. Grammar books focus on form (i.e., structure), but this use of language occurs at the level of *social meaning*. Neither the *content* (information expressed in the utterance), per se, nor the *function* is altered by how the request or rejection is made; rather, only the social meaning is affected. Social meaning is a vital component of every conversation and plays out at the metamessage level: what the person is saying about the relationship and the social context (Tannen, 1986).

There are situations such as emergencies in which content is more important than politeness concerns or other social meaning. In such cases, a request may be made outright. For example, someone may yell, "Get out of here!" when there is a fire. There are also some situations such as arguments in which speakers may show little to no regard for the face-needs of the addressee. At times, some of these speakers may apologize later for this lack of regard. Conversely, some speakers may, in fact, go out of their way to embarrass, annoy, or taunt the addressee in certain situations.

In addition, sometimes a switch to either involvement strategies or independence strategies may be used for the purpose of irony, social effect, or humor. For example, a friend or sibling may say something like, "Come over here, you nitwit!" In many situations, such a comment would make the speaker or the addressee lose face, but in some situations, the wording of this utterance would signal camaraderie and would convey the social meaning of involvement: *I can tease you and call you a name, and because we are so close, there are no hurt feelings; we can laugh about it because we know it is all in fun.*

Most interactions proceed without much effort because both inter-locutors engage in the social use of language, and mitigate threats to involvement and independence. This process is like a dance, with both speakers doing their part to make the interaction work smoothly by expressing this type of social meaning—knowing when to use involve-ment strategies and when to use independence strategies, and when to mix up the strategies for certain effects.

Cross-linguistic requests and rejections

Some of the linguistic strategies used across languages to mitigate requests and rejections downplay the request or rejection (when it is perceived as a face-threatening act [FTA]) and others enhance or upgrade the request or rejection (when it is perceived as a face-flattering act [FFA]). Some strategies convey the social meaning of politeness at the expense of clarity, whereas others do not. However, they all serve the language user by helping to maintain face and to match the expectations of the moment.

Direct Requests and Rejections

The purpose of a request is to elicit action from the addressee and the purpose of a rejection is to turn down a request. For example, if the addressee has the speaker's book and the speaker wants the addressee to hand it back, the speaker may use a direct request, such as *Give me my book,* which is a clear, unambiguous statement that matches the imperative form (command) and function (to elicit action). Likewise, an example of a direct rejection would be, *No, I'm not giving it to you.*

People do not generally use only direct requests and rejections, however. That is to say, people do not always state literally what they mean, at least not those who are in touch with the social fabric of society. A direct request and a direct rejection are generally made in those contexts in which the threat to face is minimal and in which the people are perceived as so close to each other that making the request or rejection does not threaten face. Consider the appropriateness of the direct rejections in the interchanges shown in Examples 1, 2, and 3:

1. **Context: A teenager (T) and parent (P) at a department store**
    T: Want to grab something to eat?
    P: No.
2. **Context: A supervisor (S) and an employee (E) during a supervisory meeting**
    S: Could your department increase productivity by 5%?
    E: No.
3. **Context: Two strangers (S-1 and S-2) on the street**
    S-1: Can you tell me how to get to State Street?
    S-2: No.

Of these three interchanges, a direct rejection seems to be socially appropriate only in Example 1. This is because the parent is a family member of higher social status, and because going out to lunch after being at a department store is not a large request to make of someone. In short, little is at stake and a straightforward rejection by a parent in this case is acceptable.

The direct rejections in the other two examples, however, seem inappropriate. It is generally inappropriate for an employee (subordinate) to say no outright to a supervisor (superordinate) in reply to what appears to be a very important request as in Example 2. The expectation in this case is that the employee would do *face-work,* that is, would give more of an explanation for the rejection, or mitigate the rejection in some way (e.g., *I can see what we can do, but I can't promise anything*). Face-work becomes crucial when there is potentially an increased threat to face. Likewise, when a stranger asks someone for directions (as in Example 3), it is generally considered inappropriate in English to just blurt out a direct rejection (*No*).

Rather, the person is expected to do some face-work. The expectation is that the person should say something like, "Sorry. I'm kind of in a hurry right now. You'll have to ask someone else."

In short, a speaker uses direct requests and rejections under certain circumstances (see, e.g., Brown & Levinson, 1987; Scollon & Scollon, 2001). In general, such direct speech acts are made in discourse contexts in which the speaker knows the addressee, as when speaking with a friend, family member, or well-known acquaintance; the speaker has a higher status or perhaps an equal status with the addressee, such as being the addressee's boss, parent, or sibling; and the speech act does not impose too much on the addressee, such as asking a person to do a minor task or a task that is expected as part of the addressee's role. For example, a direct request may be used by a parent asking a child to remove her homework from the kitchen table before dinner or by a boss asking an employee to write a short report that is part of the employee's regular job responsibilities.

Conversely, speakers are less likely to use direct requests and rejections with strangers or people they know less well, with people of higher status or power, or when making a difficult request or rejection. As discussed in chapter 1, social situations are complex and a speaker has many options other than simply to be direct.

Although language users employ a variety of strategies including direct requests and rejections, some researchers have suggested that some language communities are more direct overall than other language communities. As mentioned in chapter 1, Isreaelis are known for their directness, whereas the Chinese are known for their indirectness (Katriel, 1986; Blum-Kulka, 1997), and ASL signers have been reported to be more direct than American English speakers (e.g., Lane, Hoffmeister, & Bahan, 1996; Mindess, 2006).

Mindess (2006) posits that the Japanese are extremely indirect whereas Americans (English speakers) are more direct, and furthermore, that Deaf Americans (ASL signers) are more direct than American English speakers, and that Israelis are even more direct and the most direct of these four language communities (p. 89). She reports that

Israelis get right to the point, even if they have a negative comment. In a business situation where Americans might preface a criticism with a softening phrase such as "It seems to me that . . ." or "You might want to consider . . . ," many Israelis would say directly, "This part of your project is impractical" or "These dates on your timeline are impossible." (Mindess, 2006, p.85, citing Shahar & Kurz, 1995, pp. 123–127)

Likewise, Lane et al. (1996) report the following for American English speakers and ASL signers:

In hearing society, especially in more formal situations, it is considered rude to come directly to the point and state it explicitly. The hearing student dissatisfied with a grade, for example, is more likely to say to the teacher, "Excuse me, I would like to talk with you about a grade," than "You gave me a C. Why?" Hinting and vague talk in an effort to be polite are inappropriate and even offensive in the Deaf-World. (p. 73)

These examples clearly show the contrast between these language communities. At the same time, given that both ASL signers and English speakers are less direct than Israelis overall, there must be some ways in which they are both less direct than Israelis. That is, ASL signers and English speakers are not always as direct or indirect in the ways suggested in the literature.

Claims regarding the relative directness of other languages have been made in the literature. For example, speakers of German are also noted for their directness and explicitness when compared to speakers of some other languages such as British English and American English. It has been noted that the requests, apologies, and complaints of German speakers tend to focus more on content than social meaning and to introduce topics explicitly without much small talk or warm-up talk (House, 2005). Such talk is used for social purposes rather than to convey content per se, and is used less often in German.

For instance, in the German translation of Michael Bond's *A Bear Called Paddington* (*Paddington unser kleiner Bär*) the following sequence of phatic moves [i.e., warm-up moves] in the original—"Hallo Mrs. Bird," said Judy, "It's nice to see you again. How's the rheumatism?" "Worse than it's ever been," began Mrs. Bird—is simply omitted. (House, p. 20)

Although the warm-up talk sounds perfectly natural in English, it was simply considered unnecessary in the German translation.

Furthermore, a German speaker may utter "an unmitigated 'No, this is not true' . . . rather than 'you must forgive me but this is simply not true'" (House, 2005, p. 22). Germans "are more likely to say what they mean, to prefer clear topics, to prefer detailed instructions and timetables, and to avoid ambiguity" (House, p. 22). This shows that notions of politeness are based in part on relative cultural values, and can be highlighted when contrasting one language community's expected discourse style with another.

Some generalities can be made about regional differences in Europe as well (Hickey & Stewart, 2005). In Southern countries, such as Portugal, Spain, and Greece, the focus is on close social relationships and frankness, so involvement or camaraderie reigns supreme (Araújo Carreira, 2005; Hickey, 2005; Sifianou & Antonopoulou, 2005; Terkourafi, 2005). Conversely, Northern countries, such as Finland and Norway, tend to be more independence-oriented and favor more indirect or evasive strategies (Fretheim, 2005; Yli-Vakkuri, 2005), with Scandinavian politeness highly characterized by thanking (Fredsted, 2005; Fretheim, 2005). This is unlike Greece, where thanking, as well as apologizing, is infrequent, and even considered unnecessary or offensive, in close relationships or with family members because of the high value given to involvement (Sifianou & Antonopoulou, 2005). France, a more centralized country, seems to share many of the characteristics of both its Northern and Southern neighbors (Kerbrat-Orecchioni, 2005). Switzerland, on the other hand, has a politeness ethos as a whole that is more characterized by independence and autonomy despite the fact that it has four official languages (German, French, Italian, and Romansh); is influenced by France, Italy, and Germany; and is culturally diverse (Manno, 2005).

There is also an East-West distinction that can be made in Europe (Giles et al., 1992, as cited in Keevallik, 2005; Hickey & Stewart, 2005). Western countries tend to be more focused on the independence or avoidance aspect of relationships, as with Great Britain in which independence strategies such as hedging and indirectness are common (Stewart, 2005). Eastern countries are more focused on information than on relationships, as with Estonia. "Estonians seem to focus more on content than relationships in communication. Directness need not be offensive or impolite" (Keevallik, p. 214).

Similar claims have been made for other languages as well. For example, Blum-Kulka & House (1989) report that, based on their research regarding requests in five language groups, Argentinian Spanish speakers are more direct than Hebrew speakers, and Australian English speakers are the most indirect, with Canadian French speakers and German speakers falling between these two extremes. Likewise, Le Pair (2005) reports that Spanish speakers use more imperatives (commands) than Dutch speakers.

Language communities have general cultural tendencies regarding involvement and independence, which is especially evident when comparing Asian languages and Western languages. Asian languages tend to be more indirect, whereas Western languages tend to be more direct. In actuality, however, one finds both involvement and independence strategies "are used in both Asian and western [sic] communities. . . . In other words, where people are in close relationship to each other and of relatively equal status, in both east and west the normal pattern is the deductive pattern [i.e., the topic-first rhetorical style, which is a more direct, involvement style]" (Scollon & Scollon, 2001, p. 95). For example, it is common for friends in Taiwan and Hong Kong to use more involvement strategies in conversations with friends, and it is common for friends in the United States to use more independence strategies when requesting a big or embarrassing favor, such as asking to borrow a large sum of money. In short, some language communities prefer directness in more contexts than others due to cultural values and norms; however, language users also alter their way of speaking based on particular contexts.

Direct requests and rejections can be made in some contexts to reflect the expectations regarding politeness concerns. Conversely, in other contexts, they may signal that the speaker is uncouth. It is assumed that the addressee is attending to social meaning and, therefore, the speaker is perceived as either sending the metamessage, *We both know I can just request this (or turn the request down)*, or the metamessage, *I know it is awkward to request this (or turn the request down), but I don't care.*

Social meaning is generally conveyed at the unconscious level, but it forms the basis of our judgments about people's social competence with language. Whereas direct requests and rejections may be confined to specific situations or may occur more often in some language communities than in others, requests and rejections are often mitigated in other ways. In fact, some requests and rejections are quite subtle and may be conveyed only through hints.

Indirect Requests and Rejections

Some requests and rejections do not appear on the surface to be such. Rather, they only hint at the fact that a request or rejection is being made. In these contexts, the speaker hints at the speech act by making a comment about the discourse context and the addressee is expected to interpret the hint as a request or a rejection. The following are examples of indirect requests from Weizman, (1989, p. 123): *I have so much work to do* (i.e., leave me alone); *It's cold in here.* (i.e., close the window); *Are you going home now?* (i.e., I want a ride); and *The kitchen is a bit of a mess* (i.e., clean up the kitchen).

Indirect requests (requestive hints) are characterized by a high deniability potential by the speaker and the addressee because of their dependence on context for interpretation. For example, for all of the indirect requests above, the speakers could say that they meant the comment literally or said it for some other reason but did not intend the comment to be a request. For example, the speaker who uttered the sentence, "I have so much to do," could say that she was relating how much work she has to do because she wanted support or she just wanted to share that fact. She could deny that her intent was to request that she be left alone. With no overt request, speakers can back out of the request and say they meant something else, which makes an indirect request inherently less of a face-threat.

EXPLORING LINGUISTIC STRATEGIES

Regardless of where indirect requests are used, these hints work by violating one of the four conversational maxims proposed by Grice (1975), as discussed in chapter 1 (Quantity, Quality, Relation, and Manner). When a speaker violates one of these maxims, the addressee sees a conflict between what was said and what was meant and interprets the utterance to mean something other than its literal meaning.

A clear example of an indirect request is a statement such as *We're out of paper again* as a way of requesting that an office worker restock paper in the office. Certainly, the addressee does not respond to this statement as though no action is expected, but rather either acts on the request, or responds by making a comment that clearly indicates compliance or understanding.

This indirect form of requesting more paper (by making a statement) works in the following way:

1. The statement violates the Maxim of Relation (be relevant), in that it is clear in the context that the speaker is not merely making a statement about being out of paper for no reason at all.
2. The addressee recognizes that the statement is not to be taken at its face value and is intended to relate in some way to the current situation.
3. The addressee therefore interprets the statement as a request since keeping the office stocked with paper is the part of the addressee's office responsibilities, and responds accordingly.

In this way, the function (making a request) is interpreted as intended and, additionally, the utterance is understood to convey the metamessage: *I'm being considerate by not asking outright* (i.e., respecting the addressee's independence).

When a speaker violates a conversational maxim by making an indirect request or rejection, the addressee knows that the speaker means something other than what is being said, and the addressee looks to the discourse context to determine that meaning. For example, if a speaker asks, "Are you going home now?" of someone who is putting on a jacket and leaving a meeting, there is again a clear violation of the Maxim of Relation. In a context where the speaker has asked for a ride home in the past, the question is taken to be a request for a ride home.[1]

Indirect requests have been reported to occur relatively infrequently, for example, based on discourse completion tests, a low incidence of 2% to 8% has been reported for English, German, French, Hebrew, and Spanish speakers (Blum-Kulka & House, 1989). However, at least one study (Rinnert & Kobayashi, 1999) shows that hints comprised over 50% of the requests for Japanese speakers and English speakers working in a university office setting (58% and 54%, respectively). Rinnert and Kobayashi explain, "The frequent use of hints in our naturally occurring data is due in part to the fact that the participants can derive the pragmatic clarity fairly easily, 'within reasonable limits' (Blum-Kulka, 1987: 141). In this case, many hints in such settings may cease to be 'off record' [i.e., indirect]" (p. 1191) because they have become conventionalized. Rinnert and Kobayashi explain that in contexts such as this university office setting in which roles are clear, the participants attempt to build solidarity by using such strategies as making a personalized statement (e.g., *I have a need for . . .* as opposed to *I want . . .*) and minimize status difference to maintain a more reciprocal relationship (i.e., acting as though the participants are equals). In naturalistic settings, the speakers have the complete context and may indeed use indirect requests more frequently in certain settings than has been previously reported. The degree to which indirect requests are used in naturalistic settings still needs to be investigated.

Indirect rejections, like indirect requests, violate Grice's (1975) conversational maxims to imply a rejection. For example, a person could say, "I wish I could, but I'm booked all day that day," in response to a request to attend a meeting on a particular day. The speaker is not overtly turning down the request, in that the person does not actu-

---

1. As mentioned in chapter 1, Valli, Lucas, & Mulrooney (2005) have reported that this type of indirect request—HOME YOU/q [*translation: Are you going home?*—is used in ASL.

ally say no, but rather states a desire to comply with the request (*I wish I could*) and then provides a reason for not being able to comply (*I'm booked all day that day*). In this request-response adjacency sequence, the speaker is expected to either accept or reject the request, but does neither outright. Therefore, given the Maxim of Relation (be relevant), the addressee takes this effort to be cooperative (*I wish I could*) and the explanation of a conflict in scheduling (*I'm booked all day that day*) as a rejection. Indirect rejections often work by identifying "extenuating circumstances [that] prevent compliance, e.g., 'I have to work then'" (Turnbull & Saxton, 1997, p. 159).

In short, utterances such as, *It's cold in here*, and, *I have to work then*, may be used to indirectly make a request or a rejection (respectively). Such utterances are often ambiguous, leaving the speaker an opportunity to deny that a request or rejection is being made, and, therefore, are less of a threat to face.

There is also a special type of indirect request that has become more standardized and is so common that, although indirect, is less dependent on the social context for interpretation. This type of request is called a *conventionally indirect request*.

Conventionally indirect requests

There is a common requestive form that is neither direct nor truly indirect, but rather is a specific type of indirect request that is so common in languages that it is immediately understood to be a request because it has become a conventionalized way of making a polite request. In conventionally indirect requests, the speaker often makes the request in the form of a question, as in *Could you hand me my book?* In this case, the speaker is not actually requesting that the person hand over the book, but rather is asking if the person is *able* to hand over the book (*Could you—?*). By implication and by social convention, the addressee knows that the intent is not to question one's ability, but rather is a request to do something.

There are actually at least three different kinds of *conventionalized indirectness* (Rinnert & Kobayashi, 1999). As in the example above, the speaker may ask if someone is *able* to comply (*Could you—, Can you—*). The speaker could also ask if the addressee is *willing* to comply (*Do you mind*—, *Would you be willing to*—) or has the *desire* to comply (*Do you want*—?). Likewise, the speaker can make a conventionally indirect request by claiming one's own ability (*I was thinking I could*—), willingness (*Let's*—), or desire (*I'd like to*—) to engage in an act.

A French customer sometimes asks for a baguette at a bakery by saying, "*Je voudrais X*" (I would like X) (Kerbrat-Orecchioni, 2005), which is an example of a conventionally indirect request of the desire type. Certainly saying, "I would like—," in many contexts would not be considered a request. For instance, saying, "I would like to be a linguist someday," when discussing future goals would not be considered a request, but rather a statement about one's ambitions. However, the expression, "I would like—," is clearly taken as a polite request in the context of a customer addressing a clerk.

Brown and Levinson (1987) claim that off-record (i.e., indirect) requests, such as *This needs a little salt* as a request for someone to pass the salt, are used to redress greater threats to face than are conventionalized indirectness forms, such as *Can you pass the salt?* However, Blum-Kulka (1987) found that in her study of Hebrew and English speakers, both groups rated conventionally indirect requests as the most polite, followed by indirect requests (hints), with direct requests being considered the least polite by both groups. She explains this ranking (which differs from Brown and Levinson's proposed ranking) in this way: "Thus the most polite way of making a request is by *appearing* to be indirect without burdening the hearer with the actual cost [extra work] of true indirectness" (pp. 143-144). In short, for both groups, statements such as *Could you pass the butter?* would seem more polite than *I'm out of butter*, which in turn would seem more polite than the direct request (command), *Give me the butter*. This study shows that increased indirectness does not necessarily correspond to increased politeness.

The use of directness, indirectness, and conventionalized indirectness are examples of strategic moves a speaker makes to mitigate requests and rejections. However, a speaker may also use an entirely different type of linguistic strategy: *social indexing*.

Social indexing

The devices used to accomplish linguistic politeness can be understood to be one of two primary types: *strategic politeness* or *social indexing*. Strategic politeness (Kasper, 1990)—also termed *volition* (Hill, Ide, Ikuta, Kawasake, & Ogino, 1986; Ide, 1989; Ide, Hill, Carnes, Ogino, & Kawasake, 1992) and *instrumental politeness* (Gu, 1990)—involves changing the wording (form) of a speech act due to politeness concerns. For example, a speaker may make a request by saying, "Could I look at your book for a second?" instead of "Give me your book."

The other kind of linguistic strategy, *social indexing*, is less concerned with changing the wording of an utterance and is more concerned with indicating one's social standing. Social indexing (Kasper, 1990)—also termed *discernment* (Hill et al., 1986) and *normative politeness* (Gu, 1990)—is more concerned with following group norms than attending to individual face needs.

Japanese is an example of a language in which social indexing is an important feature. Japanese makes use of certain honorifics and verb endings to signal formality level. In such languages, the social standing is conveyed as a necessary part of the message, and in itself conveys the standing of the people and, thus, serves a politeness function. The form of the request (e.g., being direct or using conventionalized indirectness) is less important than including such honorifics and verb endings, which are an essential part of the language.

To better understand the nature of social indexing, see the English sentence and a Japanese sentence with comparable meaning in Example 4 below.

4. **Comparable sentences in English and Japanese (from Ide, 2005, pp. 51-52)**
   Mary gave me the book. (English)
   Kono hon kure ta no yo. (Japanese)

   [<u>Gloss</u>: THIS BOOK BE-GIVEN PAST 'nominalizer particle' 'final particle']

Two key differences can be noted in these two utterances. The first has to do with the overt expression of the subject (Mary), object (the book), and indirect object (me) in the English sentence. Whereas all of these features are expressed explicitly in the English example, neither the subject nor the indirect object is overtly stated in the Japanese utterance. The subject and indirect object are assumed to be already understood in the context and so they are not expressed as part of the utterance in Japanese.

A second difference is the use of the two particles at the end of the Japanese utterance. The particle, *no*, "indexes the speaker's identity as a sweet female. Another sentence final particle 'yo' at the end of the utterance asserts the speaker's attitude toward the information" (Ide, 2005, p. 52). Neither of these is expressed in the English utterance, which is less concerned with social indexing and more concerned with expressing factual information. The Japanese utterance does not convey some information that is already understood (the subject and indirect object), but does express contextual information (by using the particles *no* and *yo*).

> The practice of polite behavior according to social conventions is known as *wakimae* in Japanese. To behave according to *wakimae* is to show verbally and non-verbally one's sense of place or role in a given situation according to social conventions. (Ide, 1989, p. 230)

Such social indexing is key to expressing politeness concerns in languages such as Japanese.

The difference between the English and Japanese utterances reflects a major difference between high-context communication and low-context communication. High-context (HC) communication occurs when

> most of the information is either in the physical context or internalized in the person, while very little is in the coded, explicit, transmitted part of the message. A low-context (LC) communication is just the opposite; i.e., the mass of the information is vested in the explicit code. (Hall, 1976, p. 79)

The English utterance is an example of a LC message, whereas the Japanese utterance is an example of a HC message. The English utterance objectively conveys all the components of meaning and the context of the utterance becomes secondary, whereas the Japanese utterance leaves some information unstated (the subject and the indirect object) and foregrounds the social context of the utterance.

"There is no neutral predicate form in Japanese for the proposition sentence 'Today is Saturday.' One has to make obligatory choices for the predicate forms among plain, polite or super-polite honorific forms according to the context of speaking" (Matsumoto, 1989, as cited in Ide, 2005, p. 56). Thus is the nature of HC communication: the context is a key component of the message.

The view of face in language communities that practice *social indexing* and in language communities that practice *strategic politeness* differs. Asians are familiar with the concept of face, and

> will recognize the term *mianai* in Mandarin (*minji* in Cantonese, *mentsu* in Japanese, *chae myon* in Korean), where it carries a range of meanings based upon a core concept of 'honor', but perhaps the way it is used in contemporary sociolinguistics and sociology will be somewhat different. . . . Within sociological and sociolinguistic studies face is usually given the following general definition: *"Face is the negotiated public image, mutually granted each other by participants in a communicative event."* In this definition and in the work of sociolinguists the emphasis is not so much on shared assumptions as it is on the negotiation of face. For our purposes we want to keep both aspects of face in mind. We believe that while there is much negotiation of face in any form of interpersonal communication, participants must also make assumptions about face before they can begin any communication. (Scollon & Scollon, 2001, pp. 44-45)

Both strategic politeness and social indexing reflect shared assumptions and the negotiation of face in interaction.

Language communities vary in the degree to which they use strategic politeness and social indexing, and tend to use one strategy type more than the other. For example,

> Japanese polite linguistic expressions . . . tend to reflect more discernment politeness [social indexing], as opposed to English polite expressions, which reveal more use of volitional politeness [strategic politeness]. (Rinnert & Kobayashi, 1999, p. 1175)

This distinction is largely an East-West distinction, in that many oriental languages, such as Chinese and Japanese, make use of social indexing. Mao (1994) states, for example, that Chinese politeness has some similarities to social indexing (discernment) in Japanese, but differs in that politeness in Chinese occurs more at the discourse level than at the morphological and lexical level (e.g., honorifics and verb endings).

Languages may be said to be on a continuum between strategic politeness and social indexing, with many Eastern languages on the social indexing end of the continuum and many Western languages on the strategic moves end of the continuum.

The informal/formal (T/V) distinctions in some languages such as French (*tu/vous*) and Spanish (*tú/usted*) reflect this type of social indexing but to a lesser degree (see Barke & Uehara, 2005). Although true social indexing is characteristic of Eastern languages more than Western languages, there is some social indexing that is accomplished by such linguistic forms. The word *tú* in Spanish, for example,

> is used among relatives, friends, colleagues, young people and others of equal 'status', whether acquainted or not, while [*usted*] prevails in formal situations or among strangers of, say, 50 upwards who do not envisage having any personal relationship with one another. The usage is not necessarily reciprocal: older persons may use *tú* with youngsters, who in turn use *usted* [with them]. (Hickey, 2005, p. 319)

If unsure whether to use *tú* or *usted*, the first-person plural pronoun may be used to avoid the formal/informal dichotomy, as in *¿Cómo estamos?* [*How are we?*].

Although there is a popular view that French behavior is highly influenced by a sense of hierarchy, "situations where an asymmetric use of the pronoun of address (*tu-vous*) serves to express a hierarchical relationship are becoming very rare" (Kerbrat-Orecchioni, 2005, p. 41). Rather, this distinction is generally used symmetrically (among relative equals) to express distance or familiarity. In fact, in symmetrical relationships, "the number of situations in which one chooses to use *vous* rather than *tu* is greater in France than in most neighbouring countries" (Kerbrat-Orecchioni, p. 41).

There has also been a change in the use of the T/V distinction across several languages. For example, it has been reported that younger generations use the T/V distinction less often and tend to use the T form more often in contexts in which older generations would use the V form (see Haumann, Koch, & Sornig, 2005; Keevallik, 2005; Manno, 2005; Nekvapil & Neustrupny, 2005).

Other verb forms and pronouns, and certain forms of address, also serve a politeness function in some languages (see Huszcza, 2005; Haumann et al., 2005; Terkourafi, 2005; Yli-Vakkuri, 2005). Some of these forms are more common in some languages than others. For example, "in contrast to usage in Germany, titles and honorifics are still a prominent and specific characteristic of formal conversation in Austria" (Haumann et al., 2005, p. 87), and "traditional Polish 'titlemania' is . . . gradually decreasing and Polish is moving towards a more . . . grammaticalised system of honorifics" (e.g., the use of special verb forms) (Huszcza, 2005, p.233).

In addition to linguistic forms that express strategic politeness or social indexing, speakers may also use nonlinguistic forms of expression. These include *paralinguistic features* such as rhythm, stress, volume, and intonation, and *nonverbal cues* such as body language and eye contact.

Paralinguistic and nonverbal cues

Changes in paralinguistic features (or prosody), such as rhythm, stress, volume, and intonation, can affect the addressee's interpretation of a speaker's utterance. Such changes can affect the social meaning of an utterance, and have a role in making requests and rejections. For example, compare the request, *I'd like you to . . . uh . . . come in early next week . . . if you can*, with the request, *I'd like you to come in early next week, okay?*

> Whereas words convey information, how we speak these words—how loud, how fast, with what intonation and emphasis—communicates what we think we're doing when we speak: teasing, flirting, explaining, or chastising; whether we're feeling friendly, angry, or quizzical; whether we want to get closer or back off. In other words, how we say what we say communicates social meanings. (Tannen, 1986, p. 16)

In terms of politeness, one's speech rate, stress, volume, and intonation pattern can have either an involvement function or an independence function.

For example, a change in stress and intonation can indicate an exaggerated interest as in *What a fantástic gárden you have!* (Brown & Levinson, 1987, p. 104), and these devices can be used to exaggerate one's appreciation when making a request, as in *It would be wónderful if you could help me finish wrapping thése présents!* The stress, intonation, and speech rate indicate involvement (by upgrading the interest).

Conversely, note the tentativeness, as conveyed by both the speech rate and the use of *uh*, in the following request: *I'd like to ask you . . . if you could . . . uh . . . help me out a second.* The hesitancy indicates a desire to not impose and most likely mitigates a higher level of imposition. Also, compare the two following utterances: *I don't mean to impose . . . but could you possibly . . . lend me a hand?* (said at a slower rate or with some hesitancy) and *Hey, Joe, help me out here a second!* (said without hesitancy). The metamessage of each utterance is quite different: *I am trying not to impose* is the metamessage in the first instance and *I'm assuming cooperation* in the second. Generally, more hesitation indicates a greater degree of imposition, and a lack of hesitation indicates a lesser degree of imposition.

Note the difference in social meaning between the two following rejections: *No, I can't go*, and *Oh, I wish I could . . . but I'm just too swámped right now . . . uh . . . maybe néxt time.* The paralinguistic features signal a different amount of reluctance in each of these rejections. The first rejection is a direct rejection uttered with little pausing. The second rejection, however, makes use of stress and extensive pausing to indicate reluctance in making the rejection. In each case, paralinguistic features convey the relative weight of imposition, and clearly convey the social meaning of involvement or independence in the second. Paralinguistic features can either upgrade the effect of a speech act, as with the stress in *maybe néxt time*, or downgrade the effect of a speech act, as with the hesitation in *Oh, I wish I could, but I'm, uh. . . .*

In addition, some nonverbal features, which are neither linguistic (features of the language) nor paralinguistic (related to prosody) are associated with face-work. For example, an increase in eye contact is sometimes associated with face-work, and, for some language users, a headshake occurs when downgrading (downplaying) the request, as if a negative response is anticipated (see Fredsted, 2005). Verbal hedges, such as *could*, *maybe*, and *perhaps*, are also used to downgrade, but:

> Perhaps most of the verbal hedges can be replaced by (or empha-sized by) prosodic or kinesic means of indicating tentativeness or emphasis. The raised eyebrow, the earnest frown, the *umms* and *ahhs* and hesitations that indicate the speaker's attitude toward what he is saying, are often the most salient clue to the presence of an FTA [face-threatening act], even cross-culturally. (Brown & Levinson, 1987, p. 172)

Nonverbal cues and paralinguistic features of the utterance, along with other linguistic features, communicate how the speaker per-ceives the weight of the threat to face in the particular context, and whether involvement or independence is being foregrounded.

Other Strategic Moves

Other linguistic strategies are used to mitigate requests and re-jections across languages. These *strategic moves* represent a sampling of the other types of linguistic features that are used cross-linguistically to accomplish strategic politeness.

Some languages are known for using certain *ritualized forms* of politeness such as *please*, *thank you*, or other phrases. Children in the United States, for example, are encouraged to use *please* and *thank you*, to be seen as polite. Although linguistic politeness goes well beyond using such ritualized forms, these forms do perform a face-saving function. These forms convey the following social meaning: *I am being considerate* or *I am being polite*.

However, not all languages use such forms to the same degree. German speakers, as discussed above, use little ritualized language or small talk. In fact, there is no equivalent for the term *small talk* in German (House, 2005). This is not to say that Germans never use ritualized expressions or small talk at all, but rather that they are used much less often by German speakers when compared to speak-ers of other languages, such as French, for example.

Some languages are noted for their use of ritualized language. Take, for instance, the following utterances, which are the most commonly heard types of requests in the transactional interchanges in small French shops, such as bakeries: *Donnez-moi X s'il vous plait* (Give me X if you please) or just *s'il vous plait* (if you please), *Je voudrais X* (I would like X), *Je vais prendre X* (I'm going to take X), or *Vous avez X?* (Have you got X?) (Kerbrat-Orecchioni, 2005). These *ritualized forms* are so common that it is unusual to hear other expressions of request by customers in these settings.

Another strategic move that is used to make requests has been termed *mitigated directness*. Mitigated directness uses the structure of an imperative but also includes a key word or phrase that mitigates the force of the request (Blum-Kulka, 1997). Blum-Kulka (1997) found in her investigation of the parental directives of Jewish Americans, native Israelis, and Israeli Americans (i.e., American-born Israeli families of European origin), that in about half the directives parents used a command to make the directive (direct request). However, these parents also used such internal mitigators as endearments (e.g., *sweetie*), nicknames, and changes in point-of-view (e.g., *Let's . . .*), as well as affect; and external mitigators such as making a prerequest (e.g., *Can I ask you something?*) and making an appeal to reason (e.g., *We need . . .*). The internal mitigators—such as pet names and affect— reflect the need for involvement, and the external mitigators—fore-warning that a request is coming and appealing to reason—reflect the need for independence. Such is the nature of such close relationships; there is a unique balance that is maintained between involvement and independence. Blum-Kulka reports that mitigated directness is the second most used strategy in the data.

Likewise, although a French person may use a command when ordering a baguette, the direct request is invariably mitigated by using the phrase, *s'il vous plait* (if you please) (Kerbrat-Orecchioni, 2005). *S'il vous plait* softens the force of the command, and reflects the appropriate social meaning.

Modals may also function as a strategic move. Modals, such as *could, can,* and *have to,* are often used in requests and rejections. The use of modals are widely used in conventionalized indirect requests (e.g., *Could you hand me that pencil?* or *Would you like to go out to lunch?*). Modals often appear in rejections as well. Turnbull and

Saxton (1997) found that 75% of rejections contained at least one modal and 33% contained two or more modals (e.g., *I don't really think I can*; *I won't be able to*; *I can't*—; or *I have to work then*).

Some modals also express pessimism. Note the difference between *Can you lend me your car?* and *Could you lend me your car?* The subjunctive modal, *could*, conveys a sense of pessimism that is not conveyed by *can* (see Brown & Levinson, 1987). The pessimism expressed by such subjunctive modals downgrades the imposition created by a speech act.

Hedges also strategically serve to downgrade the imposition. Hedges include such expressions as *perhaps, maybe, if you can*—, *sort of*, and *I was wondering if you would*—, as in *Perhaps you could give them a call* or *If you can help them out, that would be great.*

Lexical items such as *little*—as in *I need a little help here* or *I'm a little late, so I can't do that right now*—are used to minimize requests and rejections in many languages. The adjective, *petit*, in French, for example, not only conveys size, it also has a ritualized function of conveying social meaning, as in Example 5.

5. <u>Context</u>: **A customer (C) is making a request of a butcher (B) (from Kerbrat-Orecchioni, 2005, p. 39).**

   C: *je voudrais un petit bifteck*

   [*translation*: *I'd like a little steak*]

   B: *un gros?*
   [*translation*: *A large one?*]

   C: *moyen*
   [*translation*: *medium-sized*] ·

In Example 5 above, the lexical item, *petit*, is being used to mitigate the threat to independence associated with making a request. According to Kerbrat-Orecchioni (2005),

> It is worth noting that these minimizers also turn up, with approximately the same value, in other Romance languages, such as Italian and Spanish; but in these languages, they most often take on a morphological form [diminutive suffix]. In French, minimization involves lexical choice. (p. 39)

In Spanish, for instance, *Espere un momentito [Wait just a second]* is preferred to *Espere un momento [Wait a moment]* in stores and public places because the diminutive form, *momentito*, conveys politeness, whereas *momento* does not (Mendoza, 2005, p. 168). "Thus the question *¿Quiere que le ponga más pollito?* 'Do you care for some more chicken?' is likely to elicit a reply that contains a diminutive as well: *Bueno, deme un poquito* 'Alright, just a little bit'" (Mendoza, 2005, p. 168).

Greek makes use of such diminutive suffixes to indicate smallness as well. As with the French and Spanish examples above, Greek diminutives are used not only to indicate size, but to also convey social meaning. It has been reported that diminutives in Greek are used only in relatively informal contexts and carry an informal, involvement function (Sifianou & Antonopoulou, 2005; Terkourafi, 2005).

A common strategic move used by American English speakers in rejections is to make a *positive remark* before engaging in a rejection. A study by Takahashi and Beebe (1993) found that a typical American pattern in a professor-to-student correction is (a) to use a positive remark, such as *That was very good* or *That was a great account*, (b) to say, "but," and then (c) to make the correction. In Takahashi and Beebe's study, 64% of the American English speakers used this strategy, unlike the Japanese speakers who used this strategy only 13% of the time. The distribution of softeners, such as *I think that was . . .* were more common in American English professor corrections of students; however, these softeners were more common in Japanese student corrections of the professor (Takahashi & Beebe). Both positive remarks and softeners mitigate the threat associated with the correction (a type of rejection).

Another linguistic form that strategically mitigates threats to face is a *surprise* or *warning marker*. Anything that would be unexpected, or a surprise, for a hearer is a potential threat to the addressee's face-needs. Because of this, Hickey (1991) proposes that a speaker may use a surprise or warning marker, such as *actually* or an expression such as *I am sorry to have to tell you this*, before making the rejection, to warn of the upcoming face-threat associated with the rejection. The speaker may also apologize immediately after making the rejection.

There are many other politeness strategies that are used to mitigate rejections. For example, Turnbull and Saxton (1997) propose at least five classifications of rejections in English that range from *direct rejections* to stating *extenuating circumstances* for not being able to comply:

1) *Negate request*—a direct *No* response [a direct rejection]
2) *Performative refusal*—use of a verb of negation such as *I better* say *no,* or *I think I'll* pass
3) *Indicate unwillingness*—a statement about not being interested or willing to grant the request, e.g., *I really don't think I want to . . .*
4) *Negated ability*—a statement about not being able to grant the request, e.g., *I can't go* or *I won't be able to . . .*
5) *Identify impeding event/state*—extenuating circumstances prevent compliance, e.g., *I have to work then.* (pp. 158-159)

Of these five categories, the negated ability and identify impeding event/state types of rejections are by far the most used in Turnbull and Saxton's (1997) two studies of rejections.

Blum-Kulka (1997) has proposed four categories for the parental refusals of children's requests in Jewish American, native Israeli, and Israeli American families:

1) *Agreements*—unambiguous cooperative reply (e.g., *We'll go there again, absolutely*)
2) *Conditional agreements*—specification of a condition or a delay (e.g., *As long as you don't . . .* or *Not now . . . after dinner*)
3) *Noncommittals*—a clarification statement, metacomment, or joke—as a preparation for disagreement (e.g., *What for?*)
4) *Disagreements* (with or without an account)—an unambiguous negative reply (e.g., *No, you can't*) or a statement that nullifies the request (e.g., *No, [he or she] does not need that*) (pp. 172–173)

The distribution of these strategies differs for the three groups studied, showing clear cultural preferences. Jewish Americans have a preference for agreements in making rejections, native Israelis have a preference for disagreements in rejections, and Israeli Americans have a preference for noncommittal responses. Blum-Kulka reports, "In all groups, parents provide accounts, delay compliance, and hedge, but at least part of the time, and especially in the Israeli families, they also just say no" (1997, p. 171).

There are many strategies used to make requests and rejections cross-linguistically. This section has highlighted major linguistic strategies that have been discussed in the literature. Some strategies primarily serve a social indexing function and others primarily serve a strategic politeness function. In addition, some strategies are linguistic, and others are paralinguistic or nonverbal; however, they all function to mitigate threats to involvement or independence in face-to-face interaction.

For the current study, I investigated the linguistic strategies used to mitigate requests and rejections in ASL and English.

The Study: DCTs in ASL and English

The goal of the current study was to investigate the relationship between contextual factors and the politeness strategies used to address requests and rejections in ASL and English. A discourse completion test (DCT) was developed of the kind originated by the Cross-Cultural Speech Act Realization Project for requests and apologies (Blum-Kulka, House, & Kasper, 1989).

The Discourse Completion Test

A DCT provides discourse contexts to which the participant is to respond, such as the following: "A student asks his roommate to clean up the kitchen [that] the latter had left in a mess the night before" (Blum-Kulka, House, & Kasper, 1989, p. 14). The purpose of the stimulus in this particular example is to elicit a response regarding a request (a threat to the addressee's independence) and, specifically, to focus on two potential variables that could affect the weight of the request and, hence, the linguistic strategies the speaker may use: the social distance and the power relationship. Other cases call for a response to discourse contexts in which there is greater social distance as when talking to strangers, or a different power relationship as when an employee addresses a boss.

The DCT in this study was designed to elicit participants' intuitive politeness strategies for making requests and rejections in different discourse contexts. Of the three variables (power, ranking of imposition, and social distance), only power (P) and ranking of imposition (R) are variables in the stimulus discourse situations. Because social distance (D) has been the most disputed factor in determining the weight of imposition, I designed the DCT for the current study specifically to control for social distance. Studies show that social distance may need to be further broken down into, at least, the social dimension of *familiarity* and the psychological dimension of *affect*—especially *liking*, which has been shown to be significant in a speaker's increased use of politeness (Kasper, 1990; Meyer, 1994). That is, not only do changes in familiarity (social distance) and status (power relations) affect the linguistic strategies one uses, but whether or not the speaker likes the addressee also has an effect. To control for social distance (D), the participants were told that the person to whom they were speaking in the DCT was someone they knew well, got along with, and liked. In addition, the Deaf participants were told that both signers in the contexts provided were culturally Deaf (i.e., STRONG DEAF) and were fluent ASL signers (STRONG #ASL).

Development of the DCT

Twelve work-related discourse contexts were devised by using a two-step process. The first step in the development of the DCT was to have five ASL signers and five English speakers rank various discourse contexts. The English speakers and ASL signers in the developmental stage were all working professionals. In addition, all of the ASL signers had attended residential schools for deaf students, and four of the ASL signers were ASL instructors[2].

Some 50 contexts involving requests and rejections in random order were signed in ASL to the ASL signers, and the English speakers read these contexts in English on index cards. First, each of the participants ranked the requests on a 5-point Likert-type scale ranging

---

2. The five ASL signers in the developmental stage of the study did not have Deaf parents; whereas, all of the ASL signers in the final study did. Because of the limited number of potential participants who were native ASL signers (Deaf people with Deaf parents), those with Deaf parents were retained for the final study.

from *very easy* to *very hard* to ask, and ranked the rejections on a 5-point Likert-type scale from *absolutely no concern at all* to *very concerned* about how they would be perceived (e.g., as putting off the person or upsetting the person). Only those contexts for which at least 8 of the 10 DCT development participants ranked the discourse context the same were used in the final ASL and English versions of the DCT. That is, at least 4 ASL signers and 4 English speakers had to rank these factors the same. Further, the item was included only if the remaining participant's ranking differed from the other participants' ranking by no more than one number on one factor. These responses resulted in the discourse contexts that comprised the final version of the DCT that was completed by a separate group of participants.

This developmental step enabled me to make the contexts as culturally equivalent as possible and to predict with more accuracy the native participants' perception of the contexts in the final DCT. That is to say, if members of these two different linguistic groups rank a request or rejection equally, then it increases the likelihood that the final participants would perceive the contexts in at least the same range that was intended, which would allow for a more reliable comparison.

Second, the participants in the DCT development stage were given a range of statuses (e.g., child/parent, male/female, Deaf/hearing) and roles (e.g., parent/child, professional/the professional's supervisor, coworker/coworker) in random order, and asked to compare the roles and statuses with regard to power. The purpose of this comparison was to ascertain whether or not these ASL signers and English speakers ranked the following roles as expected: a professional's supervisor as +Power (+P), the supervised professional as –Power (–P), and coworkers as =Power (=P), and that was indeed the case.

Based on the results of the developmental study, the discourse contexts were divided into two categories, requests and rejections, in a random order with regard to the ranking of imposition. (See Hoza (2004) for further discussion of developing DCTs for cross-linguistic studies.) See Appendix II for the discourse contexts in their entirety.

Participants

Of the participants who completed the final DCT, 4 were native English speakers and 7 were native ASL signers. A native speaker/signer is defined as someone who is born to parents who use that language and who has used the language since birth. All of the native English speakers were hearing, did not have any deaf relatives, and did not know ASL. All of the native ASL signers used ASL as their primary language, were both culturally Deaf and audiologically deaf, as were their parents (and in some cases, their siblings). Among the English-speaking participants, 2 were male (1 in his mid-30s and 1 in his mid-40s) and 2 were female (1 in her low-40s and 1 in her mid-40s); and 3 held Master's degrees and 1 had approximately two years of college, but no college degree.

Among the ASL signers, 6 were female and 1 was male. The females consisted of a college student in her mid-20s, a teacher in her mid-30s, and 4 social service professionals in their low to mid-40s. The male was a teacher in his mid-30s. The college student was pursuing a Bachelor's degree, the 2 teachers held Master's degrees, and of the social service professionals, 3 held Bachelor's degrees and 1 had some college but did not have a degree. All of the (Deaf and hearing) participants lived in New England and were of European descent.

Administration of the DCT

The final discourse contexts were assumed to be either relatively easy or difficult based on the rankings they received in the developmental stage. However, to ensure that the final participants themselves perceived the contexts in the same way, prior to the elicitation of linguistic data, the participants in the final DCT used a 3-point scale to rank the requests and rejections with regard to level of difficulty (1 = *easy*, 3 = *difficult*), level of obligation on the addressee's part to comply with the request (1 = *feeling of obligation*, 3 = *no feeling of obligation*), and the level of likelihood that the addressee will comply with the request

(1 = *likely,* 3 = *not* likely). This was done to verify these participants' own individual rankings, so that the linguistic data could be interpreted as the utterance was intended by the participant.

ASL signers viewed videotaped stimulus material in which I signed each discourse context in ASL. English speakers read aloud the situations that were written in English on index cards.

In an effort to make the contexts more natural, all elicited responses involved the participant and I engaging in a role play, in which I played the part of the addressee. All interviews were videotaped and all responses were transcribed for analysis.

Data Analysis

The requests and rejections elicited from the DCT were first grouped by how they were ranked by the participants on the three factors of difficulty, obligation, and likelihood. The results of these groupings were compared for the ASL signers and the English speakers. The groups were generally in agreement, except for a few unique instances. These instances are discussed in subsequent chapters.

Politeness strategies from Brown and Levinson's (1987) extensive list of politeness strategies (see Appendix III) were identified in the ASL and English DCT data, and trends were discovered based on their interaction with the factors of power and ranking of imposition.

Limitations of the Study

The findings of the DCT used in this study reveal some newly discovered linguistic strategies that are used in the mitigation of requests and rejections in ASL and English. The findings reveal striking similarities and differences between these two language communities; however, the findings should not be overgeneralized. The results are limited in at least two respects.

First, the results of a DCT may be prototypical in nature because the language samples are dependent on self-reporting on the part of the participants. The data of the DCT allow for the identification of key linguistic features, but further study needs to be conducted to elaborate on the distribution of linguistic strategies in various natural settings. The goal of the study was to determine the inter-action between two variables (power and ranking of imposition) and specific politeness strategies used. Although the study has revealed key linguistic features used to mitigate requests and rejections in ASL and English, and shown interactions with the power variable and ranking variable, the question of which of these strategies are used most often in specific real-world contexts still needs to be in-vestigated.

The results of this study have been shared and reviewed with hundreds of ASL signers and English speakers through personal communication, workshops, and presentations throughout the United States. These people have confirmed the findings of this study, in that they recognize the strategies as occurring in natural settings. However, the generalizability of these findings is limited because the participants of this study were White professionals in New England and predominantly female. Many of these same strat-egies are likely used by other groups of ASL signers (e.g., those who live in different regions of the United States or belong to different ethnic groups), but the distribution of them may vary.

Second, although I have Deaf parents and two Deaf siblings and I am a native user of both ASL and English, I am not audiologically deaf. Because I conducted the elicitations for the DCT, my status as a hearing child of deaf adults (CODA) could have an effect on the re-sults of the study. Baker-Shenk & Cokely (1980) propose a model that shows four avenues to membership in the Deaf culture, one of which is one's audiological status, which "is not available, by definition, to hearing people" (pp. 54-58). The other avenues are political, social, and linguistic. There is some disagreement in the literature regarding the membership status of hearing CODAs in Deaf culture (see Lane et al., 1996, pp. 374-375; Preston, 1994, pp. 220-224).

Neidle, Kegl, MacLaughlin, Bahan, and Lee (2000) address the issue of how to best achieve natural elicitations from native ASL signers. They stress the importance of selecting Deaf, native ASL-signing in-formants, and of ensuring that the elicitations be "carried out via native or near-native signing elicitors" (p. 21). They also stress that attention needs to be paid to "setting up the context of the elicitation and the task itself in such a way as to minimize the likelihood of code-switching and interference from the majority language and to maximize natural signing" (p. 21). This study sought to reduce these unwanted effects in two ways. First, the Deaf participants and I engaged in a conversation in ASL before the elicitations began. Second, the participants were reminded several times during the elicitation of the discourse context they were to envision, that is, both signers in the discourse contexts were STRONG DEAF and STRONG #ASL, and they were encouraged to picture someone they knew who embodied these features.

In sum, the data reveal tendencies in the language use of ASL signers and English speakers. However, the data need to be understood within the context in which the elicitations took place: the nature of the participants, the background of the person who did the elicitation, and the limitations of the contexts themselves. The findings show definite trends in the strategies used, as well as some variation based on the variables of power and ranking.

Conclusion

The design of a DCT requires special consideration. Because its purpose is to compare the linguistic strategies used by two different language groups, I emphasized ensuring that both language groups ranked discourse contexts similarly. However, researchers must bear in mind the danger of overgeneralizing where and when the linguistic features revealed in the study may be used in real-life situations.

3

REQUESTS IN ASL AND ENGLISH

Human beings who are engaged in conversation not only convey content and relay goals (functions), they also negotiate the interaction (convey textual meaning) and usually strive to present themselves as socially competent communicators by employing politeness strategies as needed. Linguistic politeness is like a dance. Just as we prefer to dance with someone who knows how to dance and who does not step on our toes, we prefer to have conversations with people who convey the social meaning we expect. When someone meets our expectations in a situation, we don't typically notice it or think about it. However, when someone seems to be an incompetent communicator and loses face for themselves or for us, it can be quite awkward.

What constitutes being socially competent in terms of social meaning varies across cultures. As noted in chapter 2, many strategies are available to language users when making requests and rejections. Some language communities may expect more direct strategies overall and others may expect more indirect strategies overall, but language users learn the metaphorical dance of their particular language community. They know how to use the various strategies for the desired effects.

This is true for English speakers and ASL signers as well, as is evidenced by the results of the DCT. The DCT results for requests are reported in this chapter and the results for rejections are reported in chapter 4. These findings indicate that both language groups share many of the same politeness strategies; however, the distribution of certain strategies (i.e., when they are used) varies in some important respects for each language group. In addition, some strategies are not shared by the English speakers and ASL signers, and some language-specific forms are unique to each language.

Shared Politeness Strategies

Ten politeness strategies are shared by both language groups in the request data: the direct strategy of (a) using an imperative form (command); the independence strategies of (b) being conventionally indirect, (c) question, (d) hedge, (e) being pessimistic, (f) minimize the imposition, and (g) apologize; the involvement strategies of (h) giving or asking for reasons, and (i) offer/promise; and the indirect strategy of (j) violating Relevance maxim, that is, give hints. See Appendix III for a list of these strategies ordered by category.

Use an Imperative Form (Command)

When contrasting a straightforward command such as *Send that to them tomorrow* and TOMORROW/t, SEND-TO-LEFT, YOU, with conventionalized indirectness such as *Can you send that to them tomorrow?* or CAN SEND-TO-LEFT TOMORROW, YOU/q, it is clear that the latter example requires the speaker or signer to go to more of an effort to make the request and for the addressee to go to more of an effort to interpret the intent of the speaker or signer. In contrast, commands do not make use of redress or mitigation, and may be interpreted as requests unambiguously and without any extra effort.

The DCT request data includes three instances in which a command is used. The distribution of commands is quite clear: The supervisor (+P) is the only person who uses a command in both the ASL and English request data. Out of the 42 elicited requests in ASL (7 participants each signing 6 requests), 2 involve the use of a command by the supervisor, and out of 24 elicited requests in English (4 participants each signing 6 requests), 1 involves the use of a command by the supervisor. See the two ASL commands in Examples 1 and 2.

1. <u>Context</u>: **A supervisor (S) requests that an employee make an initial call to a potential new consumer.**
    S: "HANDWAVE"/oh, recent/cs, I RECEIVE WRITING.
    CL-B(nondominant hand)'holding memo', INDEX-CL-B/oh.
    NEW CONSUMER, USE^AGENT,[1] INDEX-CL-B. **YOU FOLLOW-UP,**
    CALL-LEFT, WHAT's-UP/tight lips.

---

1. This signer produces an initialized sign, CONSUMER, immediately followed by the sign, USE^AGENT.

[*translation*: Oh, I just received this memo. It's concerning a new consumer. **Follow up on this, give them a call, and let me know what happens.**]

2. **Context**: A supervisor (S) requests that an employee complete a big project much earlier than expected.

   S: "HANDWAVE"/*polite grimace (pg)*, REALLY SORRY/tight lips INFORM-YOU/*pg*. RECENT/*cs inform-me/pg* /browraise, headshake. MAYBE YOU NOT HAPPY HEAR INDEX-DOWN— HEAR INDEX-DOWN[2]/neg, INFORM-YOU/tight lips. INFORM-YOU, ONE-MONTH ASSIGNMENT, THAT, YOU/t, MOVE-BACK TWO-WEEKS, "WELL"/nose wrinkle, tight-lips-to-the-side, YOU FINISH IN TWO-WEEKS, "WELL". SORRY/tight lips. NEED/pg PROGRESS, TIME NEAR/tight lips HOLIDAY, MUST TAKE-OPPORTUNITY/tight lips PROGRESS TWO-WEEKS/pg BEFORE EVERYONE-LEAVE VACATION, "WELL"/bt,tight-lips-to-the-side.[3]

   [*translation*: Hey, I'm really sorry to tell you this. It's something I just heard. Maybe you won't be happy to hear this, but let me tell you. The one-month assignment is being pushed back to 2 weeks, so, well, **finish it in 2 weeks.** Well, sorry. You need to speed it up because it's close to the holidays, so it has to be done before everyone leaves on vacation, so I guess that's it.]

Although the actual request itself (the head request) in each of these examples is expressed as a straightforward command, the requester engages in other face-work elsewhere in the request, especially in the difficult (+R) request in Example 2. In both of these instances in which a command form is used, the supervisor employs politeness strategies elsewhere in the request. As would be expected, the supervisor in the easy (–R) request (Example 1) uses little mitigation. The supervisor gives a reason and uses a nonmanual modifier (NMM) when making the easy (–R) request, but the supervisor uses extensive mitigation when making the difficult (+R) request

---

2. The phrase HEAR INDEX-DOWN is signed a second time due to a production error.

3. This variation of *tight lips* (i.e., *tight-lips-to-the-side* produced with the lips tensing to one side of the mouth) occurs four times in the request data and is further discussed in chapter 5.

(Example 2). In the difficult request, the supervisor apologizes, warns of the upcoming threat to face, and uses more intensive NMMs (such as *tight lips, politeness grimace, body teeter;* see chapters 5 and 6 for a detailed analysis of these nonmanual features).

As with the ASL examples, the command form in the English example includes mitigation of other types, as shown in Example 3.

3. <u>Context</u>: **A supervisor (S) requests that an employee make an initial call to a potential new consumer**

  S: [Name], I-that new referral that we talked about, that I gave you yesterday, I-you know, if you haven't followed up on that, **please call that person** because we really need to connect them to services, um, because they've been made eligible, we really, um, need to bring them in.

Although the head request appears in the form of a command in this instance, it is mitigated by the word *please*. Additionally, there are other strategies the supervisor employs, such as addressing the employee by name (an involvement strategy which will be addressed below) and by giving a reason.

The request data of both languages do not include even one instance of an entire request made without redress. The commands

---

Transcription Notes 1

Several nonmanual modifiers (NMMs) co-occur with particular phrases in Examples 1 and 2, e.g., *oh, cs, tight lips, polite grimace* (*pg*), and *body/head teeter* (*bt*). NMMs are unique to signed languages and appear primarily on the mouth to modify, or alter, the meaning of the utterance. Chapters 4 and 5 review in more detail five NMMs that are associated with politeness strategies, including *tight lips, pg,* and *bt*, which are shown in Figures 3.1, 3.2, and 3.3. The symbol, CL-B, signifies a classifier that resembles an (open) B handshape and is used here to represent the memo, to which the signer points (indexes). In addition, the caret symbolizes a compound sign: USE^AGENT.

Figure 3.1. tight lips

Figure 3.2. polite grimace (pg)

Figure 3.3. body/head teeter (bt): body teeters from side to side

in both the ASL and English data are made by the supervisor, whose role it is, in part, to assign duties to subordinates. That is, only supervisors are licensed to make such requests given their role and obligations. Crucially, commands in the DCT data do not occur in requests made by coworkers (in the =P contexts) nor in requests made by the employee of the supervisor (in the –P contexts) for either the ASL signers or the English speakers in these work-related contexts.

Although no commands were used by coworkers or employees in the discourse contexts in this DCT, in real-life situations, coworkers and employees may use commands in work settings. Further study of different kinds of requests could further elaborate under what conditions (if any) commands may be used by native language users of equal status or by a subordinate to a superordinate. It would seem feasible, for instance, that certain simple (–R) requests, in particular, could elicit a command with or without other types of mitigation.

There may also be discourse contexts in which a supervisor would use an unmitigated command without other mitigation. For example, it seems that if a supervisor meets with an employee every week to request that the employee call potential consumers, a command may be used (e.g., *Give this person a call, too* or CALL-LEFT INDEX-paper [_translation_: *Call the person listed here*]).

Be Conventionally Indirect

Both the ASL signers and the English speakers use conventionalized indirectness (CI) more than any other independence strategy. However, the data indicate that the distribution of CI type used by each language group varies considerably.

CI relates to the hearer's ability, willingness, or desire to engage in or approve of the requested act (Rinnert & Yobayashi, 1999). When using CI, speakers either claim, suggest, or question their own ability, willingness, or desire (e.g., *I'd like to—*) or that of the addressee (e.g., *Can you—?*) to engage in an act. See Table 3.1 for examples of these different types of conventionalized indirectness in English and ASL.

REQUESTS IN ASL AND ENGLISH

Table 3.1 Examples of Three Types of Conventionalized Indirectness
in English and ASL

Types of conventionalized indirectness	English	ASL
Ability	Can/Could you—?	CAN—/q.
	I was wondering if you could—.	I WONDER, CAN YOU—/q.
	You can/could just—.	YOU CAN—/nod.
Desire	I want you to—.	I WANT YOU—.
	I would like you to—.	YOU WANT—/q.
	Do you want to—?	
	Would you like to—?	
Willingness	Will/Would you—?	WILL—, YOU/q.
	Would you mind—?	DON'T-MIND—/q.
	Let's—. May I—?	WHY^NOT—/q.
	Why don't we—?	

CI represents a compromise between two opposing tensions, which it encodes (see Brown & Levinson, 1987, pp. 130-136): (a) the desire to give the speaker an out by being indirect and (b) the desire to go on record as having the speech act unambiguously attributed to the speaker.

The result is a contextually ambiguous meaning that is conventionalized, or standardized, to the point that it is readily understood. That is, due to its conventionality, the hearer immediately interprets the function as a request and the social meaning as polite.

For instance, Example 4 is taken from an interaction that was overheard at a bookstore; note the use of CI which is highlighted in bold type.

4. **Context: A young assistant manager (M) and a young
   clerk (C) are standing behind the register.**
   M: **Do you want to** go to the back room and throw out
      those empty boxes?
   C: I don't *want to*, but I *will*.

In this example, the intent of the assistant manager is clearly a CI request for action, although the form of the request is a yes/no question regarding the desire of the addressee to do the act. By questioning the addressee's desire, the speaker intended, by implication, that the question be interpreted by the addressee as a request. The clerk's response captures the irony between what people say and what they mean. In this situation, after the clerk made this comment, he nevertheless headed toward the back room to comply with the intended request.

In addition, a precondition request, such as *Do you have a pencil?*, that may be used in English to make a request for a pencil, is also considered conventionally indirect. Such forms are so transparent in their implicature (in this case, the implication of wanting to borrow a pencil) and are so standardized that they are immediately taken to be requests and, thus, are conventionally indirect. Example 5 shows this type of CI, which was caught on videotape prior to one of the ASL DCT elicitations:

5. **Context: The researcher has just asked the participant to sign and print the participant's name on an informed consent form.**
   Participant: PRINT, FINE/tight lips,nod. (*leans forward*) HAVE PEN, HAVE PEN, YOU/q.

   [*translation*: *Print there; sure, fine. Do you have a pen—do you have a pen?*]

Although such requests may appear to be indirect requests, they are so standardized that they are readily interpreted as polite requests and, therefore, should be considered conventionalized indirect requests.

As seen here, CI is used in both ASL and English; however, ASL and English request data differ in the distribution of CI by type. The most common type of CI used in the ASL request data is the willingness variety. In fact, the DON'T-MIND [*don't mind*] sign is used in 70% (28 out of 40) of the head requests in ASL (e.g., DON'T-MIND BORROW FIFTY DOLLAR/tight lips,q [*translation*: *Could I borrow 50 dollars?*], and DON'T-MIND WORK-IT-OUT, CALL, WORK-IT-OUT NEW CLIENT, YOU, "WELL"(1-hand)/pp,q,nod /q [*translation*: *Could you call this new consumer and work this out, could you?*]). There is also one instance of another willingness form of CI that does not use the DON'T-MIND

Transcription Notes 2

The gloss DON'T-MIND is used here as it is used elsewhere in the literature. It represents a sign that is produced with the index finger moving two times from the nose outward in front of the face (see Figure 3.4). However, the true semantic value, and pragmatic and syntactic functions of this sign may not be accurately captured by the gloss. Further research is needed to flesh out its meanings and functions. For example, in requests it seems to resemble, in meaning and function, the compound sign FOR^ME [*translation: for me*] in ASL, which is sometimes used to ask someone to do a favor (see Smith, Lentz, & Mikos 1992).

Figure 3.4. DON'T-MIND: beginning and end of sign

sign, and that is I BORROW PEN/q [*translation: Borrow your pen?*].

The other type of CI used in the ASL request data is of the ability variety. For example, I/pg,[4] POSSIBLE I WEDNESDAY INDEX-RIGHT+/t, POSSIBLE, IF CAN/cond, OFF I INDEX-RIGHT WEDNESDAY, "WELL"

---

4. The nonmanual marker, pg (polite grimace), is used to mitigate more severe threats to face (see chapter 6).

Transcription Notes 3

The sign glossed QUESTION-MARK(wiggle) and often shortened to QM(wg) represents a unique tag question used in ASL to stress the question much like "You're going, <u>aren't you?</u>" in English (see, e.g., Baker-Shenk & Cokely, 1980; Neidle et al., 2000; Valli, Lucas, & Mulrooney, 2005).

<u>*(1-hand)/tight lips*</u> /q [<u>*translation*</u>: *Is it at all possible for me to have that Wednesday off, do you think?*]; <u>YOU CAN PROGRESS FINISH, CAN YOU, QUES-TION-MARK</u>(wiggle)(nondominant hand)/pg.q [<u>*translation*</u>: *Do you think you could manage to get all the work done, do you think you can?*]. Note that in each instance the signer is questioning the ability of the addressee to do, or approve of, the act.

The distribution of the willingness (DON'T-MIND) CI forms and the ability (CAN) CI forms differ in ASL, and there are no occurrences of the desire (WANT) CI forms in the ASL request data. The willingness form (DON'T-MIND) occurs in both easy (–R) requests and difficult (+R) requests, and accounts for all of the 19 forms of CI in easy (–R) requests (of the 21 easy requests). The other two instances in easy (–R) requests in the ASL request data are the one case in which the signer uses a command (Example 1 above) and one instance in which a joke is used to make a request (discussed below).

In contrast, the ability CI forms only occur in difficult (+R) contexts in the ASL request data and account for about half (11 out of the 21) incidents of CI in these contexts. The other 10 are instances of willingness CI. See Table 3.2 for the distribution of CI by type in the ASL request data.

Although ASL signers use CI of willingness (DON'T-MIND) throughout the requests, and use CI of either ability or willingness in difficult (+R) requests, the English speakers use the willingness type of CI only two times in the English request data and, then, only in easy (–R) requests.

Table 3.2 The Distribution of Conventionalized Indirectness by Type
in the ASL Request Data

	Willingness	Ability	Desire
Easy requests (–Ranking)	19/21	0/21	0/21
Difficult requests (+Ranking)	10/21	11/21	0/21

Note. The total given in each cell in the table is for all 21 requests (i.e., each cell represents the number of occurrences out of 21 easy and difficult, respectively, requests).

In the English request data, the two expressions, *Would you mind—?* and *Do you mind—?* are used when asking the supervisor to pass one's pen and when asking to borrow a pen from a coworker, respectively. CI of ability is by far the most used in the English request data and is used in 16 of the 24 elicited requests. These occur in all of the contexts and take the form of such expressions as *Could I? I was wondering if I could (possibly)—*, and *Can I—?* There are also two instances of CI of desire in the "requesting the day before Thanksgiving off" (–P, +R) context in the English request data (e.g., *I would really like to—*). The distribution of CI types in the English data, which appears in Table 3.3, differs substantially from the distribution CI types in the ASL data.

This difference in CI type between the two language groups may well reflect a difference in *relative face orientation* (Mao, 1994) between these ASL signers and English speakers. Given that willingness CI

Table 3.3 The Distribution of Conventionalized Indirectness by Type
in the English Request Data

	Willingness	Ability	Desire
Easy requests (–Ranking)	2/12	8/12	0/12
Difficult requests (+Ranking)	0/12	8/12	2/12

Note. The total given in each cell in the table is for all 12 requests (i.e., each cell represents the number of occurrences out of 12 easy and difficult requests, respectively).

may be geared more toward cooperation and one's social identity as a member of a group, and ability CI may be geared more toward autonomy and individual identity (as an independent actor), this possible cultural difference in relative face orientation may account for the marked difference in the distribution of the type of CI (willingness, ability, or desire) used in the request data of the ASL signers and the English speakers.

Question

The question strategy in a request involves the use of a yes/no question (e.g., _DON'T-MIND I BORROW_/_tight lips_ #PEN/q or _Can I borrow your pen?_). The question strategy occurs in all but three requests in the ASL request data—for both easy and difficult requests. The question form is plainly a predominant feature of ASL requests in the data. The three exceptions to using a yes/no question include the two instances of the commands used by the supervisor (in +P contexts), discussed above, and the other instance involves the use of the DON'T-MIND sign, but in this particular instance the signer does not use the yes/no-question grammatical marking (raised eyebrows, direct eye gaze, and a lean forward) in making the request. The request appears in the "asking the supervisor to pass one's pen" (–P, –R) context: DON'T-MIND GIVE-ME, INDEX PEN [_translation:_ _Could you give me my pen._]. Because this request is devoid of the grammatical yes/no-question marking, it comes across as being a bit closer to a command, and yet the threat to face is mitigated by the DON'T-MIND sign. The implication is that the request will be acted upon without much question and that the request will not be perceived as much of a threat to the addressee's sense of independence. This lack of question marking appears notably in an easy (–R) request.

The distribution of the question strategy in the English request data differs from that of the ASL request data. The distribution of the question strategy differs for easy (–R) and difficult (+R) requests. First, as in ASL data, the question strategy is used in all easy (–R) requests in the English data except the one command used by a supervisor. See Example 6 for some examples of the question strategy in English.

6. **The question strategy in the English request data**
   E = employee, C = coworker, and S = supervisor

   E: Can you just hand me that pen?
   C: Do you mind if I borrow your pen?
   S: Could you give them a call please and, um, let me know how that works out?
   E: Oh, [name], could you give me my pen please?

Unlike the ASL distribution of question, there are only 3 instances of the question strategy in difficult (+R) contexts in the English request data (out of the 12 elicited difficult requests). For example, this strategy is used in one instance by the employee in the "requesting the day before Thanksgiving off" (–P, +R) context: "Oh, um, I forgot to ask you. Could I have tomorrow off?" and in one instance by the supervisor in the "requesting an employee to complete a big project" (+P, +R) context: ". . . is it possible for us to get this done in two weeks? . . ." See Table 3.4 for the distribution of the question strategy in the English request data.

In the "complete a big project sooner than expected" (+P, +R) context, the tendency is for the supervisor to use an indirect request (in three of the four instances) in the English data. However, with the other difficult requests—the "requesting the day before Thanksgiving off" (–P, +R) context and "asking to borrow $50" (=P, +R) context—the most common strategy is to use CI, but without forming it as a question. Instead, as shown in Example 7, the speakers

Table 3.4 The Distribution of Questions in the English Request Data

	Employee's request (–Power)	Coworker's request (=Power)	Supervisor's request (+Power)	**Total:**
Easy requests (–Ranking)	4/4	4/4	3/4	11/12
Difficult requests (+Ranking)	1/4	1/4	1/4	3/12
Total:	5/8	5/8	4/8	

Note. N = 4 native English speakers, 24 DCT ratings (6 ratings per participant). Total occurrences of questions reported over total number of elicitations (4 participants per discourse context).

use an embedded question (I wonder *if I could*—) or make a statement related to their own desire (*I'd like to*—).

7. **Examples of not using the question strategy in the English request data**

   E = employee, C = coworker

   C: I'm wondering if you could borrow . . . uh . . . lend 50 dollars to me until next pay period.

   E: [*Name*], I was wondering if I—if I could possibly, um, take the day before Thanksgiving off.

   E: I know that I didn't get a chance to ask you this before, [*name*], but I would really like to have the day off before Thanksgiving.

   C: I'm wondering if you could lend me 50 dollars, until payday.

   E: Uh, [*name*], I'd like to ask if I can have the day before Thanksgiving off.

Again, these forms appear almost exclusively in two difficult (+R) requests: the "requesting the day before Thanksgiving off"(–P, +R) context and the "asking to borrow $50" (=P, +R) context. This is unlike the ASL signers who use the question strategy in almost all instances across the board, for both easy (–R) and difficult (+R) requests.

In the few instances in which the phrase I WONDER is used in the ASL requests, the signer customarily uses a question form (i.e., in all but one case which is discussed below), e.g., I WONDER CAN I BOR-ROW, "WELL", FIFTY DOLLAR/q [*translation: I wonder if I could borrow, well, 50 dollars?*]. This seems to be a grammatical difference between English and ASL, in that in English the embedded question (I wonder *if I could*—) appears as part of the head sentence as a statement; whereas, in ASL this type of embedded *question* appears in the *question* form (with accompanying yes/no-question marking) (see Neidle, Kegl, MacLaughlin, Bahan, & Lee, 2000, pp. 189-190). However, the clause containing the sign, WONDER, may or may not appear with the yes/no-question marking, as in this one instance in the data: I WONDER CURIOUS/tight lips, THINK POSSIBLE BORROW 50 DOLLAR/q [*translation*: *I was just wondering, do you think it's possible that I borrow 50 dollars?*].

The signers use the question form in three of the four instances in which embedded requests occur. In the one exception, a participant makes the request without the use of a question form (in the difficult [+R] request of a coworker): I WONDER I CAN BORROW FIFTY+ FOR INDEX-LEFT EXPEND-LEFT [*translation*: *I wonder if I could borrow 50 dollars because I need it for some expenses I have*]. This lack of grammatical marking in the embedded question may be the result of the casual register assumed between coworkers, although such lack of marking needs further study.

A *tag question* is a short question, such as #OK/q [*okay?*], that follows a statement to change the statement into a question or follows a question to stress the question. In addition to the question strategy, tag questions also are used in the ASL data. In contrast, no tag questions are used in the English data.

For the ASL signers, nine tag questions occur in three specific contexts: in both supervisor (+P) contexts and in the "asking to borrow $50" (=P, +R) context. Only the tag question #OK/q (two such instances) is used by the supervisor in the easy (–R) context ("call a new consumer"). However, a greater range of tag questions is used in the two relevant difficult (+R) contexts (i.e., by the coworker and supervisor). These contexts include the following tag questions: CAN/q [*can you?*], QM(WG)/q (QUESTION-MARK (wiggle)/q) [*right?* or *don't you think?*], and #OK/q [*okay?*].

The tag #OK/q is the only tag question used by the supervisor (+P) in the easy (–R) request data. The supervisor uses this particular tag (#OK/q) to soften a command by questioning the addressee's willingness in easy (–R) requests. CAN/q, of course, questions the addressee's ability, which allows the supervisor to be definitive in the difficult (+R) request by first using a command, then softening the request by using CI to ask about the employee's ability to do the act. In this way, the supervisor can take both a superordinate stance (by using a command) and a less imposing, more cooperative, stance

Table 3.5 The Distribution of Tag Questions in the ASL Request Data

	Employee's request (−Power)	Coworker's request (=Power)	Supervisor's request (+Power)	**Total:**
−Ranking ('easy' requests)	0/7	0/7	2/7	2/21
+Ranking ('difficult' requests)	0/7	3/7	4/7	7/21
Total:	0/14	3/14	6/14	

Note. N = 7 native ASL signers, 42 DCT ratings (6 ratings per participant). Total occurrences of tag questions reported over total number of elicitations (7 participants per discourse context).

(by using a form of CI) in difficult (+R) requests. The unique form, QM(wg)/q, stresses the question at hand, so it can be used to question ability, willingness, or desire. In the data, however, this particular tag question is only used in difficult (+R) requests in which the head request is expressed as an *ability* CI form, e.g., YOU CAN PROGRESS FINISH, CAN YOU, QM(wg)(nondominant hand)/pg,q [*translation: You can work to complete it on (on time), can't you (don't you think)?*]. In this instance, the supervisor is using two tag questions (CAN YOU and QM(wg)) to mitigate the difficult (+R) request. See Table 3.5 for the distribution of *tag questions* in the ASL request data.

Hedge

The independence strategy of hedging is defined as using either the sign "WELL" or the sign POSSIBLE in ASL, and this strategy only appears in difficult (+R) requests in ASL.

Although the sign "WELL" often occurs at the beginning of the utterance, it also appears elsewhere in the sentence (e.g., midsentence and at the end of the sentence), as shown in the following examples:

The use of "WELL" in requests
1) REALLY I, "**WELL**", OVERWHELMED, MANY CLIENTS, LIST/pg
   (*indirect apology* by giving an overwhelming reason)

   [*translation: Actually, I am . . . well . . . overwhelmed with my long list of consumers . . .*]

Transcription Notes 4

The sign "WELL" is a natural gesture that is used in ASL to hedge or to indicate reluctance. The sign is produced by extending one or both hands palm up (usually) to the side(s) of the body. See Figure. 3.5. See Roush (1999) for a typology of five meanings this sign can convey in ASL conversations.

Figure 3.5. "WELL"/q

2) **"WELL"**, KNOW-THAT/tight lips I HAVE-TO WORK ON THANKSGIVING, **"WELL"** (*indirect apology* by admitting the impingement)

[*translation*: Well, I . . . uh . . . know that I need to work because of Thanksgiving, uh . . .]

3) **"WELL"**, SORRY/pg-frown (*direct apology*)

[*translation*: Well, I'm so sorry . . .]

4) NEXT-WEEK/CS FRIDAY PAY CHECK/t, WILL PAY #BACK, **"WELL"**/ pp (*offer, promise*)

[*translation*: I'll pay you back when we get paid next Friday, so . . .]

"WELL" is most often accompanied by an NMM to mitigate it further, although there are instances in which "WELL" appears without an accompanying NMM.

There is another type of hedge that appears in the ASL data, which can best be termed a hedge/tag question, in that the "WELL" sign—which serves to hedge the request—appears as a tag question with yes/no-question grammatical marking (<u>"WELL"</u>/q). The hedge/tag question appears in only difficult (+R) requests in ASL, in which one would expect more hedging of this sort.[5]

The hedge/tag question in ASL (<u>"WELL"</u>/q) is used to mitigate the head request in many difficult (+R) requests (in 13 instances). It is also used to mitigate an offer/promise (two times) and an indirect apology (one time) in the "requesting the day before Thanksgiving off" (–P, +R) context.

Both hedges and hedge/tag questions function to provide extensive face-work in ASL. Although tag questions of any sort do not appear in the English data, other forms of hedging are used in the English request data and these hedges have both a different form and a different distribution from the hedges in ASL.

In contrast to the distribution of hedging in ASL in which it appears in only difficult (+R) requests, the hedge strategy appears in all of the contexts in the English request data. Hedges in English are defined as the following lexical items: *just, could, would, possible,* and *possibly.*[6] Hedges appear in all of the difficult (+R) requests, with the exception of three instances of indirect requests by the supervisor (see below). Hedges also appear in easy (–R) requests (2 out of 4 instances in all three easy [–R] discourse contexts). Some examples of the use of hedging include "Can you **just** hand me that pen? . . .";
" . . . **could** you **just** call this person and find out what they're— what type of services they're looking for?"; "I **would** really like to

---

5. Hedge/question tags are not included in Table 3.5 (tag questions) because there is nothing comparable in the English request data.

6. As discussed in chapter 2, the modals, *could, would,* and *possible,* are considered to be the manifestation of two strategies: hedge and be pessimistic (Brown & Levinson, 1987).

borrow 50 bucks **if possible**," and "**Would** you—**would** you mind passing me the, uh, pen?"

Both the form and the distribution of hedges in ASL and English differ. For coding purposes, ASL hedges are considered to be the signs "WELL" and POSSIBLE, and English hedges are considered to be the lexical items *just, could, would,* and *possible/possibly.* Only lexical items are coded as hedging.

Other types of hedging, most notably changes in paralinguistic features such as hesitations and nonverbal cues such as body language are evident in the data, especially in difficult (+R) requests; however, these features are not coded in the data as hedges. This is because although a speaker's hesitations may signal *hedging,* there may be other reasons for the hesitations. For example, the speaker may be trying to get a word out or may be thinking about how to state the request. Therefore, only hedging expressed overtly in such lexical items as *could* and "WELL" are coded as hedging. The analysis of the DCT data did not include either paralinguistic features or nonverbal cues. Other types of possible forms of hedging in ASL, such as certain NMMs in ASL that indicate reluctance, are also not coded as hedging in this study. Likewise, the use of such fillers as *um* or *uh* in English, are not coded in the data as hedges. It is important to note, however, that both the English speakers and the ASL signers do tend to hesitate more in difficult (+R) contexts.

The lexical items coded as hedges appear in only difficult (+R) requests in ASL, and appear in both easy (–R) and difficult (+R) requests in English. If one considers some NMMs (all except the *politeness pucker*) to be hedges, then both languages would have a similar distribution. However, further research in the area of hedging in ASL is needed.

One difference worth noting between these NMMs in ASL and lexical items such as *just* and *could* in English is where they appear in requests. Although these English lexical items appear almost exclusively in the head request, NMMs appear not only in head requests, but may co-occur with a variety of politeness strategies such as the *apologize* and *offer/promise* strategies (see chapters 5 and 6).

Be Pessimistic

The be pessimistic strategy, in keeping with Brown and Levinson (1987), is defined as specific lexical items that express pessimism in each language. These include POSSIBLE and MAYBE in ASL and *would, could, if possible,* and *possible/possibly* in English. As with hedges, only lexical items were coded for the be pessimistic strategy.

This strategy—in the form of POSSIBLE and MAYBE—occurs in the ASL request data in two instances. One instance occurs in the "asking to borrow $50" (=P, +R) context: "HANDWAVE", I WONDER CURIOUS/tight lips, THINK **POSSIBLE** BORROW FIFTY DOLLAR/q [*translation: [Name], I was wondering if you think it'd be possible for me to borrow 50 dollars?*]. The other instance of this strategy occurs in the "requesting the day before Thanksgiving off" (–P, +R) context. See Example 8.

8. **Context: An employee (E) at a grocery store requests the day before Thanksgiving off.**

    E: I/pg, **POSSIBLE** I WEDNESDAY INDEX-RIGHT+/t, **POSSIBLE, IF CAN/cond,** OFF I INDEX-RIGHT WEDNESDAY, "WELL"(1-hand)/ tight lips /q. SUPPOSE YOU **(roleshift)** HAVE-TO/pg,cond, I **WILLING/pp**. YOU HAVE OTHER PEOPLE COVER ME, "WELL"/tight lips(1-hand, nondominant hand, move forward) /q, **POSSIBLE, "WELL"(some circular movement)/ (slight rocking)bt** /tight lips,q.

    [*translation: I—is it is **possible** that I could have Wednesday off, you think? If you say I have to work, I certainly will. But **maybe** other people could cover for me, do you think? Do you think there is **the remotest possibility?**]

In this example, the employee is hoping to get the day off, but is communicating to the supervisor that she is pessimistic about the outcome of the request. This pessimism is expressed by the repetition of the sign, POSSIBLE, and the one instance of the give deference strategy in the request data: "SUPPOSE YOU (roleshift) HAVE-TO / pg,cond, I WILLING/pp" [*translation: If you say I have to work, I certainly will*]. The signer acknowledges that the supervisor has the ultimate say in the matter, and states a willingness to comply with the supervisor's decision. The give deference strategy is not used in the English request data and is discussed below.

The be pessimistic and give deference strategies are also used in a spontaneous example produced by a participant when explaining that she would alter the request depending on who the addressee was. She states that she would sign the following request to borrow $50 from a coworker whom she does not know as well, which makes the request a greater threat to face: #IF NOT/neg,cond, I UNDER-STAND+/pp. #IF NO-TO-ME/neg,cond, UNDERSTAND+/pp [*translation: If not, I certainly understand. If you have to tell me, "No," I'll understand*].

In contrast to the low frequency of the be pessimistic strategy in ASL, it appears in 16 of the 24 rejections in the English data. The following lexical items were coded as be pessimistic in English: *would, could, if possible,* and *possible/possibly* (see Brown & Levinson, 1987). See below for a discussion of this difference and how the two languages use this strategy to much the same degree, albeit through different forms.

This strategy appears in all six contexts in the English request data, but primarily in four contexts. See Table 3.6. The distribution suggests a sensitivity of this strategy to power and ranking values. In sum, the employee (–P) uses this strategy in making requests of the supervisor (7 out of 8 such requests). Although employees use

Table 3.6 The Distribution of Be Pessimistic in the English Request Data

	Employee's request (–Power)	Coworker's request (=Power)	Supervisor's request (+Power)	**Total:**
Easy requests (–Ranking)	3/4	1/4	3/4	7/12
Difficult requests (+Ranking)	4/4	4/4	1/4	9/12
Total:	7/8	5/8	4/8	

Note. N = 4 native English speakers, 24 DCT ratings (6 ratings per participant). Total occurrences of be pessimistic reported over total number of elicitations (4 participants per discourse context).

the be pessimistic strategy in both easy and difficult requests over-all, coworkers use this strategy more often in difficult (+R) requests, and the supervisor uses this strategy more often in making easy (–R) requests of the employee.

The supervisor uses the be pessimistic strategy in making easy (–R) requests of the employee in 3 out of 4 instances in the English request data, which is surprising. The data indicate that in these three instances, the supervisors use the modal *would* or *could*. That is, the pessimism expressed in these forms is apparent when con-trasted with the nonsubjunctive forms of these modals: *will* and *can*. In fact, *would* and *could* account for most of the instances of this strategy in the English request data. With the exception of the lexi-cal items, *possible* and *possibly*, which are used exclusively in difficult (+R) contexts (in four instances), all other occurrences of be pessi-mistic are realized as a subjunctive form of a modal.

Brown and Levinson's (1987) definition of be pessimistic has im-plications for what is reported in English and ASL due to a differ-ence in the languages. The frequent use of this strategy by these English speakers (16 out of 24 requests, compared to the 2 instances of the strategy in the ASL data) may well be a distortion due to cod-ing differences. This coding difference, in fact, allows us to observe a unique language difference between ASL and English.

The comparable forms that express pessimism in ASL are POSSIBLE and MAYBE; however, these ASL lexical items seem to have a much greater sense of pessimism to them than subjunctive modals in En-glish. Although other forms (i.e., *if possible* and *possibly*) are associ-ated with this strategy in English and are closer to the degree of pessimism expressed in the ASL forms, the modals occur much more frequently in the English data (*could, would, I'd,* [i.e., *I would*]). The forms, *if possible* and *possibly/possible*, are used one time and three times, respectively.

Although it is true that *could*, for example, conveys a sense of pessimism, it certainly does not convey the degree of pessimism that these last two forms convey. These forms are closer to what is coded in the ASL data. In fact, some NMMs seem to express a degree of pessimism (see chapter 6), so the be pessimistic strategy may, indeed, be quite common in ASL requests. The use of NMMs, then, appears to be a language-specific expression of pessimism, in that when these NMMs are used within a request (e.g., CAN . . . /pg), there is less of an expectation of a likelihood of compliance.

Minimize the Imposition

The strategy, minimize the imposition, is defined as downplaying the seriousness of the face-threat. An example of this in everyday conversation is saying, "This will only take a second," to downplay the amount of time involved in completing a requested act. The distribution of the minimize the imposition strategy differs between the two language groups in the study.

The minimize the imposition strategy is used seven times in the ASL request data and all of these overlap with the offer/promise strategy and are restricted to the "asking to borrow $50" (=P, +R) context. For example, UNDERSTAND+/browraise, NEXT-WEEK PAY CHECK, I EXPEND-YOU #BACK [*translation:* Understand that when I get my paycheck next week, I'll pay you (right) back]; NEXT-WEEK/CS FRIDAY PAY CHECK/t, WILL PAY #BACK, "WELL"/pp [*translation:* When we get our paychecks next Friday, I will pay you back, no problem]. This promise to pay the money back next Friday is used by all seven ASL signers in this context, and is coded as both *offer/promise* and *minimize the imposition* because it functions both as a promise to reassure the addressee and as a way of minimizing the request.

The minimize the imposition strategy is used five times in the English request data. Three appear in the "asking to borrow $50" (=P, +R) context, and two appear in the "asking to borrow a pen" (=P, –R) context. In each instance, the speaker again combines the offer/ promise and the minimize the imposition strategies. See Examples 9 and 10.

9. **Context: A coworker (C) asks to borrow a pen from another coworker.**

C: Geez, [*name*], I would really like to-to note this in my schedule and, unfortunately, I didn't bring a pen. Could I borrow yours **for a moment? I'll return it to you as soon as I'm done.**

10. **Context**: **A coworker (C) asks to borrow $50 from another coworker.**

> C: Oh, I was going to get—I told you before, um, before lunchtime here, that I wanted to talk to you about something, and recently I've come across a need for, uh, some extra money: 50 dollars. And I don't like going to people about it, but, uh, I was wondering if you could possibly give me a loan for $50, and **I'll pay you back, you know, with the next paycheck**. Uh, I don't like asking people, but-but a need has come up and I really, you know, really could use your help.

In the English request data, this minimize the imposition strategy occurs in both the easy request and the difficult request made by the coworker (=P); whereas, in the ASL request data, it only occurs in the difficult (=P, +R) request made by the coworker. It is likely that cooperation between two employees who are ASL signers is more likely assumed (and, therefore, face is less threatened) than is the case with two English-speaking coworkers, so an easy request does not need to be as mitigated. This may well be an example of a cultural difference between the two language communities.

Apologize

The independence strategy, apologize, is divided into two different categories for purposes of analysis: (a) *indirect apology*, which involves implying an apology by expressing regret, and (b) *direct apology*, which involves using a direct, on-record apology: saying, "sorry," or signing, "SORRY." In addition, the indirect apology strategy is further divided into three subcategories, which will be explained below: (a) *admit the impingement*, (b) *indicate reluctance*, and (c) *give overwhelming reasons* (see Brown & Levinson, 1987). Apologies of both types occur more often in difficult (+R) requests than in easy (–R) requests, but the distribution across the power values differs for these ASL signers and English speakers.

In the ASL request data, indirect apologies occur 26 times in difficult (+R) requests (out of the 21 difficult requests), in that indirect

Table 3.7 The Distribution of Indirect Apology in the ASL Request Data

	Employee's request (–Power)	Coworker's request (=Power)	Supervisor's request (+Power)	**Total:**
Easy requests (–Ranking)	1/7	6/7	5/7	12/21
Difficult requests (+Ranking)	11/7	5/7	10/7	26/21
Total:	12/14	11/14	15/14	

Note. N = 7 native ASL signers, 42 DCT ratings (6 ratings per participant). Total occurrences of indirect apology reported over total number of elicitations (7 participants per discourse context).

apologies are sometimes used more than once in a single difficult (+R) request and 12 times in easy (–R) requests (out of the 21 easy requests), as shown in Table 3.7. Three examples are (a) I/pg SEEM I MESS-UP BUDGET, I/tight lips [*translation:* I seem to have miscalculated my budget, seriously]; (b) [I NEED TO] SHOP THANKSGIVING/pg, "WELL"/pg-frown [*translation:* [I need to shop] for Thanksgiving, so, well—]; and (c) KNOW-THAT NEAR THANKSGIVING TOMORROW [*translation:* I know it's the day right before Thanksgiving]. The first two examples of indirect apologies are of the give overwhelming reasons type and the third example is of the admit the impingement type. In fact, the sign, KNOW-THAT, is commonly used in ASL in indirect apologies of the admitting the impingement type.

Unlike the overwhelming reasons given in difficult (+R) contexts, almost all of the reasons given in easy (–R) contexts are basic reasons, or background contexts and are considered instances of the involvement strategy of giving reasons (rather than indirect apologies). Most of the easy (–R) requests are of this sort (e.g., I NEED #PEN. *DON'T-MIND*/tight lips GIVE-ME/q [*translation:* I need a pen. Mind handing me yours?]) although there are some exceptions to this, in that some indirect apologies also occur in easy (–R) contexts (see Table 3.7). These reasons have been coded as indirect apologies due to the overwhelming reasons given, for example:

(a) COME-TO-MIND, DARN-IT[7]/pg, I BETTER JOT-DOWN ADDRESS BEFORE I MIND^DISAPPEAR /th [_translation:_ I just remembered something. Darn it. I better jot down this address before I forget it]; (b) I, OH-I-SEE/pp, PURSE/t, LOSE PEN. I THINK MY DAUGHTER TAKE-IT/th [_translation:_ Oh, I see. Actually, I've lost my pen; it's not in my purse. I think my daughter took off with it.] In both of these examples, the amount of explanation is greater than merely expressing the need for a pen and, therefore, is more of an indirect apology (see Brown & Levinson, 1987).

The other type of indirect apology, admit the impingement, occurs in only two contexts: the "requesting the day before Thanksgiving off" (−P, +R) context (five times) and the "complete a big project much earlier" (+P, +R) context (four times). Note that this type of indirect apology only occurs in difficult (+R) requests by the employee or the supervisor.

Unlike indirect apologies, direct apologies explicitly redress the threat to the addressee's independence by using an unambiguous apology: signing, "SORRY." There are two instances of the direct apology strategy (SORRY) in the ASL request data. Both occur as part of the supervisor's request that the employee finish a big project much earlier than expected (the +P, +R context).

In the English request data, the indirect apology strategy occurs in every request in the difficult (+R) requests made by the coworker (=P) and the employee (−P) (and sometimes is used twice within the same difficult (+R) request). This differs from the ASL request data, in which the greatest frequency occurs in difficult (+R) requests made by the employee (−P) and the supervisor (+P). The indirect apology strategy is also used one time in each of the other contexts in the English request data, as shown in Table 3.8.

English examples of the indirect apology strategy appear in Example 11.

---

7. The sign glossed DARN-IT is produced by hitting the 'fist' (or 'S') handshape of the dominant hand sharply against the palm of the nondominant open hand ('open B' handshape).

Table 3.8 The Distribution of Indirect Apology in the English Request Data

	Employee's request (–Power)	Coworker's request (=Power)	Supervisor's request (+Power)	**Total:**
Easy requests (–Ranking)	1/4	1/4	1/4	3/12
Difficult requests (+Ranking)	1/4	6/4	5/4	12/12
Total:	2/8	7/8	6/8	

Note. $N = 4$ native English speakers, 24 DCT ratings (6 ratings per participant). Total occurrences of indirect apology reported over total number of elicitations (4 participants per discourse context).

(11) **Examples of the indirect apology strategy in English**
C = coworker, S = supervisor

> S: I know that it's an onerous task.
> [admit the impingement]
> C: I hate to ask you this.
> [indicate reluctance]
> S: Some things have come up. The director has come up with a change in deadline.
> [give an overwhelming reason]

Note that all three types of indirect apologies appear in the data (and in the examples above).

The use of a direct apology (saying, "sorry") occurs only once in the English data, and that is when the employee says, "Oh, I'm sorry," before the head request in the "asking the supervisor to pass one's pen" (–P, –R) context. In contrast to this one direct apology in the English request data, indirect apologies appear rather frequently in these work-related contexts.

Give (or Ask For) Reasons

In the ASL request data, the involvement strategy, give reasons, occurs in all 3 of the easy (–R) request contexts, and occurs in 13 out of the 21 easy requests. Of the remaining 8 easy requests, 6 do not use give reasons at all, and the other 2 involve indirect apologies of the give overwhelming reasons type, as discussed above. The give reason involvement strategy gives the addressee the context for the request although the reason is not overwhelming as with indirect apologies. Given the high frequency in the ASL data of give reasons in easy (−R) requests and indirect apologies by giving overwhelming reasons in difficult (+R) requests, giving reasons seems to play a more central function in ASL requests than it does in English requests.

The strategy, give reasons, also appears primarily in easy (−R) requests in the English request data, but also appears one time in one difficult (+R) request: "asking to borrow $50" (the (=P, +R) context). This instance is given as Example 12.

12. **Context: A coworker (C) asks to borrow $50 from another coworker.**
    C: Geez, [*name*], I'm really uncomfortable asking this question. But **something's come up** and, um, I need to ask a big favor. I'm wondering if you could lend me 50 dollars, until payday.

As can be seen in this example, the need itself is secondary to the other face-work the speaker engages in. For example, the speaker uses indirect apologies (*I'm really uncomfortable asking this question* and *I need to ask a big favor*), as well as using conventionalized indirectness (*if you could*), and by hedging and being pessimistic (*I'm wondering if you could*—). That is, although the imposition is seen as high, the participant does not use the reason itself as an overwhelming motivation for the request.

The other reasons used in the English request data are more straightforward, and appear exclusively in easy (−R) requests. See Example 13.

13. **Context: A supervisor (S) requests that an employee make an initial call to a potential new consumer.**
    S: Um, we—**we just got a phone call for information and referral.** Um, could you just call this person and find out what they're—what type of services they're looking for?

In the English request data, the give reasons strategy is most used by the supervisor in the "call a new consumer" (+P, –R) context. In this context, it is used in 3 of the 4 requests. It is also used once in the "asking the supervisor to pass one's pen" (–P, –R) context and two times in the "asking to borrow a pen" (=P, –R) context. Although the English request data is small and one must be careful about overgeneralizing, it is clear that give reasons is used less often in the English data than in the ASL data.

Offer/Promise

The involvement strategy, offer/promise, appears in the ASL request data nine times, as has been discussed, in that seven of these instances overlap with the independence strategy, minimize the imposition. This strategy is used exclusively in two difficult (+R) requests: (a) the "asking to borrow $50" (=P, +R) context when the signer promises to pay the person back the next payday, and (b) the "requesting the day before Thanksgiving off" (–P, +R) context when the employee offers possible solutions for getting coverage for that day. See Table 3.9 for the distribution of the offer/promise strategy in the ASL request data.

The offer/promise strategy appears seven times in the English request data and is most often associated with difficult (+R) requests. Of these, four appear in coworker (=P) requests. Three occur in the "asking to borrow $50" (=P, +R) context and one occurs in the

Table 3.9 The Distribution of Offer/Promise in the ASL Request Data

	Employee's request (–Power)	Coworker's request (=Power)	Supervisor's request (+Power)	Total:
Easy requests (–Ranking)	0/7	0/7	0/7	0/21
Difficult requests (+Ranking)	2/7	7/7	0/7	9/21
Total:	2/14	7/14	0/14	

Note. $N = 7$ native ASL signers, 42 DCT ratings (6 ratings per participant). Total occurrences of offer/promise reported over total number of elicitations (7 participants per discourse context).

"asking to borrow pen" (=P, –R) context, as was discussed above. As with the ASL offer/promise strategy, these are also coded as the independence strategy, minimize the imposition.

This strategy also occurs two times in the "complete a big project much earlier" (+P, +R) context and one time in the "requesting the day before Thanksgiving off" (–P, +R) context. In these cases, however, the strategy is not also coded as minimize the imposition. For example, in the "complete a big project much earlier" discourse context, the supervisor offers the following: "I will work with you to try and help you accomplish this," and in the "requesting the day before Thanksgiving off" scenario, the employee suggests (after making the request): "I was wondering if there's any—you know, if there are other people that could cover for me, and [I could] have that day off?" See Table 3.10 for the distribution of this strategy in the English request data.

Although both the ASL signers and the English speakers use offer/promise primarily in difficult (+R) requests, especially in co-worker (=P) requests, they differ in that the English speakers also use the strategy in the difficult request made by the supervisor (+P, +R).

There is one example of the use of offer/promise in the English request data that particularly stands out, because it is an indirect offer/promise. See Example 14.

Table 3.10 The Distribution of Offer/Promise in the English Request Data

	Employee's request (–Power)	Coworker's request (=Power)	Supervisor's request (+Power)	Total:
Easy requests (–Ranking)	0/4	1/4	0/4	1/12
Difficult requests (+Ranking)	1/4	3/4	2/4	6/12
Total:	1/8	4/8	2/8	

Note. $N = 4$ native English speakers, 24 DCT ratings (6 ratings per participant). Total occurrences of questions reported over total number of elicitations (4 participants per discourse context).

14. **Example of an indirect strategy being used for offer/promise**

Context: A coworker (C) asks to borrow $50 from another coworker.

C: Geez, [*name*], I hate to ask you this, but, um, I really need to borrow—I'm looking to borrow money at this point, and I don't know if you have any, but if you do, I would really like to borrow 50 bucks if possible. **I know we don't get paid until next Friday, but I'm in true need.** (*pragmatic implication*: *I will pay you next Friday [because we both know I'll have the money then]*)

This example is interesting for a two reasons. First, the highlighted clause encodes both an involvement strategy, offer/promise, and an independence strategy, be pessimistic, with this second strategy also being conveyed elsewhere in the example. The example shows how complex language is and how pragmatic information such as that expressed by politeness strategies can be conveyed in a variety of ways. Second, on the surface, this clause seems to be stating a fact— acknowledgement that payday is next Friday— however, both the speaker and the hearer know, by implicature, that the speaker's metamessage is a promise to pay back the money on Friday. In short, the promise is made indirectly.

Violate Relevance Maxim—Give Hint (Indirect Request)

The ASL signers and the English speakers differ in their use of indirect requests. The indirect requests in the English request data are used in three of the four supervisor's difficult (+R) requests: "complete a big project much earlier" (the +P, +R context). See Examples 15 and 16.

15. **Context: A supervisor (S) requests that an employee complete a big project much earlier than expected.**
S: [*Name*], you know that, um, job I gave you to—the other day to do—do in a month? Well, unfortunately, I have to be the bearer of bad tidings, and **I'm going to need that in two weeks**. I know that it's an onerous task, and I'm here to really talk about what the barriers

would be for you to accomplish that, 'cause this is not a decision of my making. This is a have-to. Um, so I'm—I will work with you to try and help you accomplish this. But it's not a choice, unfortunately.

16. **Context: A supervisor (S) requests that an employee complete a big project much earlier than expected.**
    S: [*Name*], um, there seems to be a little problem on that project that, um, we talked about. Um, I know that I told you that it's due at the end of [*month*], well, it's really mid-[*month*] now, **so that cuts you down to 2 weeks**. How do you think that plays out?

In these (+P, +R) requests, the addressee is dependent on contextual knowledge to interpret these utterances, that is, they are not overt requests. In the first example, the fact that the supervisor states the need to have the project in 2 weeks implies that the employee must finish it in 2 weeks, and therefore this utterance is interpreted as a request. In the second example, the fact that the supervisor announces the new deadline also implies a request because it is the employee's deadline that has been changed. That is, the supervisor has the authority to change deadlines and the employee has the responsibility to complete the project. An announcement regarding the change in deadline is interpreted to be a request that the employee meet the new deadline. In contrast, the supervisor's (+P) head requests in the ASL request data either involve a command or a question form (i.e., using conventionalized indirectness or a tag question).

Only one instance of an indirect request strategy occurs in the ASL request data, and that is Example 17, in which the signer makes a joke to make the request.

17. **Context: An employee (E) asks the supervisor to pass one's pen.**
    E: I SICK-OF-IT, YOU STEAL MY #PEN, INDEX(nondominant hand). STEAL, YOU, "WELL"(1-hand, nondominant hand, movement forward), [*smiling*].

[*translation:* I hate that. You stole my pen; you took it!]

In Example 17, the signer is violating both the Manner maxim (do not be ambiguous) and the Relevance maxim (be relevant). The Quality maxim is violated in that the signer signs the request with a serious facial expression, then smiles jokingly. This joke works as an indirect request on a few different levels. First, the joke is made in an ironic manner, which signals that there is to be an alternate interpretation of the utterance. Second, the joke itself works by violating the Relevance maxim, that is, the addressee must use contextual cues to determine the signer's true meaning because the addressee has not truly stolen anything. The joke implies that the signer is making a request that the addressee give the pen back because people prefer to have stolen items returned and, therefore, the addressee interprets the utterance as a request. Third, using a joke is also an involvement strategy and conveys a sense of closeness or camaraderie.

In sum, indirect requests are not used in the ASL request data, except in this one instance of a joke. This suggests that ASL signers may use other types of indirect strategies in making requests, such as indirect apologies; but either ASL signers do not use indirect strategies in the head request (other than CI) or it may be that the DCT contexts did not capture them. In contrast, the English speakers clearly do make indirect requests in the English request data.

The request data indicate major differences in how ASL signers and English signers make requests in the workplace. ASL signers lean toward two strategies in making requests: (a) CI expressed in a question form and (b) direct requests (only by the supervisor and mitigated by other strategies). English speakers tend to use three strategies in making requests: (a) CI as well, but often not in a question form in difficult (+R) requests; (b) direct requests (by the supervisor only, in 1 instance out of 4 in the request data); and (c), unlike ASL, indirect requests (supervisor only) in the difficult (+P, +R) request. There is only one instance of an indirect request by an ASL signer and that is the use of a joke by an employee in the "asking the supervisor to pass one's pen" (–P, –R) context.

This difference in the use of indirectness is telling. Although the numbers are small, this difference does indicate a preference on the part of ASL signers for conventionally indirectness or direct requests over indirect requests. Independence seems to be stressed by the supervisor in the English requests, in that indirect requests are motivated by the desire to not impose (independence); whereas, involvement seems to be stressed in the one indirect request made by the employee, in that the involvement strategy, joke, presupposes a sense of camaraderie.

Politeness Strategies that Are Not Shared

Six politeness strategies used to mitigate requests are not shared by these two language groups. Very few instances of the politeness strategies associated with requests appear in one language but not in the other. In fact, of the 42 elicited ASL requests and the 24 elicited English requests, the requestive strategies that are not shared appear only one or two times in each language. Because of the low incidence of these strategies, it is unclear if they indicate real differences in trends between the two language groups. The requestive strategies found in English only are: (a) state the FTA as a general rule; (b) presuppose/raise/assert common ground; and (c) include both speaker and hearer in the activity. The requestive strategies found only in ASL are: (a) give deference, (b) joke, and (c) violate Quality maxim—be ironic. (See Appendix III for a complete list of strategies in order of their categories.)

State the FTA as a General Rule (English Only)

The independence strategy, state the FTA as a general rule, is used by one of the English speakers in the "complete a big project much earlier" (+P, +R) context. The supervisor states the following as part of the request: "The [director] has come up with a change in deadline." This general statement is used to clarify the need for the change in deadline. This strategy, although not a general rule in the strictest sense, is being used to communicate that this is something out of the control of the supervisor and the employee. They must abide by the decision, which in essence is a general rule or obligation.

Just as the give deference strategy reflects the nature of the asymmetrical relationship between the employee and supervisor, the use of the strategy, state the FTA as a general rule, also reflects the nature of this asymmetrical relationship. In such a relationship, there are certain inherent obligations, such as following rules and following edicts from above.

Presuppose/Raise/Assert Common Ground and Include Both Speaker and Hearer in the Activity (English Only)

Two involvement strategies are used in the English request data that are not used in the ASL request data: presuppose/raise/assert common ground and include speaker and hearer in the activity. Both of these strategies appear in the "complete a big project much earlier" (+P, +R) context. See Example 18, in which both strategies appear.

18. <u>Context</u>: **A supervisor (S) requests that an employee complete a big project much earlier than expected.**
    S: [*Name*], we, uh, you know when we met the other—the other day about this [*particular*] project, remember? And I know, you know, we had a month to do that. Well, something's come up. Um, a budget—we have a major budget restriction. We need to get this thing done within 2 weeks. Now I know this is not a month, **we're talking 2 weeks now, uh, I'm sure you have some concerns**, and **I'm going to work with you on those, but, um, it will be important for us to get this thing done within 2 weeks**.

In this example, the supervisor acknowledges the hearer's concerns, i.e., uses the presuppose/raise/assert common ground strategy, with such phrasing such as *Now I know* and *I'm sure you have some concerns*. In addition, the supervisor uses the include speaker and hearer in the activity strategy by using the plural first person pronouns, *we* and *us*. The supervisor also uses the offer/promise strategy discussed previously (*I'm going to work with you on this*), which also presupposes/raises/asserts common ground. Supervising employees involves more communication strategies than simply giving mandates. In this example, the supervisor mitigates the request by using involvement strategies. The supervisor shows support and tries to work with the employee in making the request to hand in the project 2 weeks earlier than previously arranged.

Give Deference (ASL Only)

The independence strategy, give deference, can best be described as an acknowledgement of the addressee's superior position and a humbling of one's own. This strategy is used only one time by an ASL signer and does not appear in the English request data at all. This ASL signer uses this strategy in the "requesting the day before Thanksgiving off" (–P, +R) context, in which the ASL user signs, "SUPPOSE YOU (roleshift) HAVE-TO/pg,cond, I WILLING/pp" [*translation*: *If you say I have to work, I certainly will*]. The ASL signer in this case is acknowledging the supervisor's position to make the ultimate decision, and by using this comment, expresses deference and respect for that position.

Joke (ASL Only)

One of the ASL signers uses the involvement strategy of a joke when making a request in the "asking the supervisor to pass one's pen" (–P, –R) context, and this request is also coded as the indirect strategy of hinting (see Example 17 above). After signing this utterance, the participant reports that this is how this request could be signed to someone with whom one is very close.

Humor provides a great bond; it also reflects a certain level of common background and even intimacy. This strategy uses that connection or involvement to make the request. At the same time, this strategy is decidedly indirect, in that no overt request is made. This is the only instance of an indirect request in the ASL request data.

Violate Quality Maxim—Be Ironic (ASL Only)

The use of a joke by the ASL signer to make an easy (–R) request of the supervisor uses not only that strategy, but also uses the strategy of violate the Quality maxim—be ironic. The signer smiles jokingly when signing this request (YOU STEAL MY #PEN [*smiling*]), which is more of an accusation in terms of form. The addressee, however, would immediately recognize that the signer does not mean this utterance literally and would recognize the joke as an indirect request.

The indirect requests made in the English request data occur in the context involving a supervisor's difficult request of an employee (+P, +R). However, this one indirect request in the ASL data involves an easy request made by an employee of the supervisor (–P, –R). In addition, the indirect requests in English employ many linguistic strategies—mostly independence strategies—in making the request. In this indirect request in ASL, the involvement strategy of joke, and the strategy of violate the Quality maxim—be ironic, are accomplished in the same utterance.

Other Strategies Used to Mitigate Requests

Additional strategies that are not identified by Brown and Levinson (1987) are used by the ASL signers and English speakers in the DCT data, and most of these strategies are language specific. Three of these strategies appear in the ASL data and four in the English data. Two of these strategies appear in both ASL and English: (a) PLEASE (in ASL) and *please* (in English) and (b) "*HANDWAVE*" (in ASL) and *naming* (in English). One other strategy appears only in the ASL DCT data: *NMMs*; and two other strategies appear only in the English data: *preparatory statement* and *surprise expression* (however, the ASL data may include a strategy comparable to surprise expression).

PLEASE (ASL) and *Please* (English)

The sign PLEASE in ASL and the word *please* in English appear in the request data, but are not included in Brown and Levinson's (1987) list of politeness strategies. The sign PLEASE occurs five times in the ASL data and is used only by the employee and supervisor with each other. The employee uses it twice in the easy (–R) request, and the supervisor uses it twice in the easy (–R) request and once in the difficult (+R) request. This sign seems to reflect the social roles each participant is playing (superordinate and subordinate). Notably, PLEASE is not used between coworkers or by the employee in the difficult (+R) request in the data.

The word *please* appears with greater frequency in the English request data (29% vs. 12% in the ASL requests), but otherwise has a similar distribution in the English requests, with one notable exception. As in ASL, most of the instances of *please* in the English request data (6 of the 7 instances) occur in the easy (–R) requests between the supervisor and the employee: in the supervisor's request to the employee (two instances) and the employee's request to the supervisor (four instances). Unlike PLEASE in ASL, however, *please* in English is used in the "asking to borrow $50" (=P, +R) context; this is the only occurrence of *please* in a coworker (=P) context in the DCT data. Otherwise, PLEASE and *please* are used exclusively in requests made by the supervisor (+P) and the employee (–P) in the request data, making the distribution similar for the two language groups, although the frequency is higher in the English requests.

"HANDWAVE" (in ASL) and Naming (in English)

The sign "HANDWAVE" in ASL (see Figure 3.6) and the act of naming the addressee in English have a similar function in the two languages. Although the forms are much different, both serve to get the attention of the addressee.

Naming has three functions in English: (a) to get a person's attention, (b) to show a connection with the person and serve an involvement function, and (c) as a discourse marker to introduce a new topic. Most likely the second and third usages were intended by the speakers, because the role plays involved making the requests in the middle of a conversation. The fact that names are used relatively often in the English data (one to three times per context) and across the board is worthy of note.

The strategy of naming is not used by the ASL signers, in that one does not address the addressee by name in ASL. Rather, an ASL signer may use a "HANDWAVE", or other strategy, to get the addressee's attention rather than signing the person's name. ASL names—commonly called name signs—are used when discussing people in third person (see, e.g., Supalla, 1992); however, a person's name sign is not used directly to get the person's attention or in addressing a person in conversation. Rather, the signer will wave a

Figure 3.6. "HANDWAVE"

hand in the person's line of vision or gently tap on the addressee's shoulder to establish and maintain eye contact. It is the maintained eye contact that makes it clear that the two are engaged in conversation (see, e.g., Baker, 1977). As with naming in English, the "HANDWAVE" sign is commonly used in the ASL requests. In fact, it is used to begin half of the elicited requests in ASL (21 of the 42 ASL requests). In the ASL request data, the "HANDWAVE" sign also functions as an involvement strategy and serves as a discourse marker to introduce a new topic.

NMMs (ASL Only)

NMMs are linguistic markers that occur on the mouth or involve the body and head. They are unique to signed languages such as ASL, appear frequently in the request data, and serve both independence and involvement functions (see chapters 5 and 6). NMMs function in ASL requests in at least two ways. First, some of them may express reluctance, pessimism, and possibly hedging, as discussed above. Second, some of them may also express surprise when they co-occur with the "HANDWAVE" sign at the beginning of a request (see surprise expression below).

Preparatory Statement (English Only)

Another form that appears in the English request data that does not appear in the ASL request data is the preparatory statement strategy. In this strategy, a statement such as *I forgot to ask you* or *I know I didn't get a chance to ask you this before*, prepares the addressee for a change in topic and for the forthcoming threat to independence associated with the request (see, e.g., Hickey, 1991). Preparatory statements are used three times in the English request data and appear in only two difficult (+R) requests: the "requesting the day before Thanksgiving off" (–P, +R) context and "asking to borrow $50" (=P, +R) context. Preparatory statements provide additional face-work to help prepare the addressee for a difficult (+R) request, and the supervisor does not engage in this type of face-work, which would be expected due to the his or her higher status (+P).

Surprise Expression (English Only?)

Another form used in the English elicitations is surprise expression. These forms are interjections such as *oh* or *geez* and occur at the beginning of the request. Some examples include: "Geez, [name], I would really like to note this in my schedule and, unfortunately, I didn't bring a pen" and "Oh, I'm sorry. Can you just hand me that pen?" These forms do not appear in any supervisor (+P) contexts, but they appear one to three times in the other contexts. In short, surprise expressions occur only in employee (–P) and coworker (=P) contexts, particularly in the "asking the supervisor to pass one's pen" (–P, –R) context and the "asking to borrow a coworker's pen" (=P, –R) context, with three occurrences in each of these contexts, and appear more often in easy (–R) requests. See Table 3.11 for the distribution of surprise expression in the English request data.

Like surprise expressions in English, the "HANDWAVE" sign also occurs at the beginning of requests in ASL. As stated above, "HANDWAVE" is used to begin 21 of the 42 elicited requests in ASL. The use of "HANDWAVE" and the accompanying NMM help to frame

Table 3.11 The Distribution of Surprise Expressions in the English Request Data

	Employee's request (–Power)	Coworker's request (=Power)	Supervisor's request (+Power)	**Total:**
Easy requests (–Ranking)	3/4	3/4	0/4	6/12
Difficult requests (+Ranking)	1/4	2/4	0/4	3/12
Total:	4/8	5/8	0/8	

Note. N = 4 native English speakers, 24 DCT ratings (6 ratings per participant). Total occurrences of surprise expressions reported over total number of elicitations (4 participants per discourse context).

the type of face-work that is forthcoming and is used to mitigate the threat to face associated with the request. Over half of these co-occur with a NMM.[8] Two occur without any NMM and the others occur with other mouthing. These other mouthed expressions include *oh* (four instances) or *ah* (two instances), and there is one instance of a surprise look. Some of these forms (e.g., *oh* and *ah*) seem more surprise-like, but do not occur as often as either the surprise expressions in English or the NMMs in ASL.

Although both surprise expressions in the English data and "HANDWAVE" (and the accompanying NMMs) in the ASL data frame the face-work that is forthcoming, surprise expressions are more restricted than the use of "HANDWAVE" in two ways. First, the "HANDWAVE" and accompanying NMMs express a wider range of imposition (small to extreme) rather than just mild surprise or reluctance as is the case with the surprise expressions. Second, "HANDWAVE" occurs at least once in all of the contexts except the "asking to borrow a pen" (=P, –R) context, which represents a different distribution than that of the surprise expressions in the English data.

---

8. These NMMs are *tight lips, polite grimace (pg), polite grimace-frown (pg-frown)*, and *body/head teeter (bt)*, with seven requests making use of the *tight lips* marker. See chapters 5 and 6 for a detailed account of these NMMs.

Conclusion

The requestive strategies used by the ASL signers and English speakers in the DCT data (based Brown and Levinson's [1987] strategies) fall within a limited set, and include direct requests, involvement strategies, independence strategies, and indirect strategies for both language groups. Although many of these strategies are used similarly by both language groups, some differ in their distribution. For example, true cases of direct requests do not occur in the request data, in that when commands are used, the requests are always mitigated by other means; and although indirect requests are commonly made by supervisors in the difficult (+R) requests in English, no indirect requests are made by ASL signers in the supervisor's (+P) requests.

The distribution of shared strategies differs in many respects, e.g., the distribution of the question strategy in ASL and English. Although strategy types were often shared, as with the case of CI, the

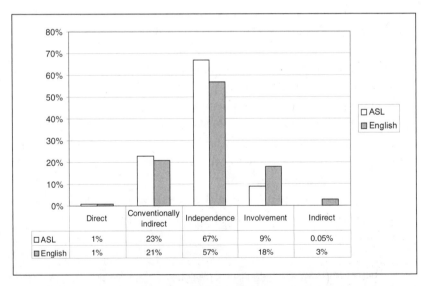

Figure 3.7. Distribution of Politeness Strategy Types for ASL
and English Requests

realization of specific types of CI—as with the willingness and ability varieties of CI—was shown to have quite different distributions in the ASL and English data. In the instances in which a strategy is used by one language group and not the other, the strategy always has a very low incidence, which shows that the language users, overall, use the same range of strategies in these work-related discourse contexts. In addition, some language forms, such as naming and "HANDWAVE", are unique to each language. See Figure 3.7 for the distribution of the major politeness strategy types used to mitigate requests in the ASL and English request data.

4

REJECTIONS IN ASL
AND ENGLISH

Turning down a request can threaten a relationship and one's involvement because the interlocutor may be seen as uncooperative. Of course, not all rejections have the same effect. If someone makes an outlandish request, you can usually feel confident saying no. There is usually little threat to face or to the relationship for rejecting such a request. However, if someone asks you to pass the salt that is sitting right beside you, saying no can seem antisocial; the request seems simple enough, so the rejection would seem quite odd. As a rule, difficult requests make for easier rejections and easy requests make for more difficult rejections.

Shared Politeness Strategies

The strategies used in rejections in the DCT data comprise a more limited set than those used in making requests. Six politeness strategies are shared by both language groups in the mitigation of rejections[1]: the independence strategies of (a) hedge, (b) apologize; the involvement strategies of (c) presuppose/raise/assert common ground, (d) offer/promise, and (e) give (or ask for) reasons; and the indirect strategy of (f) violate Relevance maxim—give hint.

---

1. The category of direct strategies is not listed here because there is only one instance of a direct rejection and that is in the ASL rejection data, and it is discussed later in this chapter.

Hedge

The hedge strategy is defined as "WELL" in ASL and specific phrases such as *I don't know that I would be able to* . . . in English. The function of such expressions is to soften the rejection.

Hedging occurs 64 times total in the ASL DCT data, but 3 times as often in difficult (+R) rejections (48 instances) as in easy (–R) rejections (16 instances), showing a strong tendency toward difficult (+R) contexts. This strategy is used more than any other in the ASL rejection data and is often used two or three times in a single difficult (+R) rejection.

There are only two instances of a hedge/tag question, "WELL"/q, in the ASL rejection data. This strategy, which appears in the form of a question, is used to mitigate an offer/promise, as in the following: CAN YOU GIVE-RIGHT OTHER PERSON DO, "WELL"/*tight lips* /q [*translation: Could you have someone else do this, do you think?*]. All of the other hedges appear as declaratives rather than as question forms. "WELL" appears with a variety of strategies, and most often appears with reasons (24 instances) and the head rejection, where the speaker overtly turns down the request in the rejection (13 instances). It also occurs with the opening, a direct apology (SORRY), and offer/promise. It is clear that the sign, "WELL" (with appropriate nonmanual modifiers; NMMs), is an important and prevalent component of many rejections in the data, especially difficult (+R) rejections. See Table 4.1 for the distribution of hedge ("WELL") in the ASL rejection data.

Table 4.1 The Distribution of Hedge in the ASL Rejection Data

	Employee's rejection (–Power)	Coworker's rejection (=Power)	Supervisor's rejection (+Power)	Total:
Easy rejections (–Ranking)	5/7	4/7	7/7	16/21
Difficult rejections (+Ranking)	19/7	16/7	13/7	48/21
Total:	24/14	20/14	20/14	

Note. N = 7 native ASL signers, 42 DCT ratings (6 ratings per participant). Total occurrences of hedge reported over total number of elicitations (7 participants per discourse context).

Table 4.2 The Distribution of Hedge in the English Rejection Data

	Employee's rejection (–Power)	Coworker's rejection (=Power)	Supervisor's rejection (+Power)	**Total:**
Easy rejections (–Ranking)	1/4	0/4	0/4	1/12
Difficult rejections (+Ranking)	2/4	0/4	0/4	2/12
Total:	3/8	0/8	0/8	

Note. N = 4 native English speakers, 24 DCT ratings (6 ratings per participant). Total occurrences of hedge reported over total number of elicitations (4 participants per discourse context).

Independence strategies are used little in the English rejection data, as is the case with hedges, which appear only three times in the English rejections. For coding purposes, hedging in the English data is defined as such phrases as *I don't think I can . . . right now, I don't know that I would be able to . . .*, and *you know*. Hedges occur only in the employee's (–P) rejections: once in the "turning down the supervisor's request to serve on the sunshine committee"[2] (–P, –R) context and twice in the "turning down the supervisor's request to call a potential new consumer" (–P, +R) context. See Table 4.2. This small number of occurrences of the hedge strategy is in contrast to the hedging that occurs in most of the ASL rejections, especially in the difficult (+R) rejections. In addition, the expressions associated with hedging in English are used exclusively in the employee's (–P) rejections, which shows a sensitivity to deference for the supervisor.

Apologize[3]

The independence strategy, apologize, appears throughout the ASL rejection data as a direct apology in the form of the sign SORRY. It is

2. A sunshine committee is a volunteer social committee at a place of employment that collects a small amount of money from employees and uses those funds to purchase special gifts or flowers for special events such as weddings, funerals, and the like.

3. No attempt has been made to differentiate indirect apologies from the give reasons strategy in the ASL and English rejection data. Because of the large number and variety of reasons given in rejections, indirect apologies that involve giving a reason are grouped with the give reasons strategy, which is discussed below.

REJECTIONS IN ASL AND ENGLISH

Table 4.3 The Distribution of Apologize in the ASL Rejection Data

	Employee's rejection (–Power)	Coworker's rejection (=Power)	Supervisor's rejection (+Power)	**Total:**
Easy rejections (–Ranking)	2/7	3/7	2/7	7/21
Difficult rejections (+Ranking)	3/7	5/7	5/7	13/21
Total:	5/14	8/14	7/14	

Note. N = 7 native ASL signers, 42 DCT ratings (6 ratings per participant). Total occurrences of apologize reported over total number of elicitations (7 participants per discourse context).

used in every context (from two to five times), but occurs nearly twice as many times in difficult (+R) contexts as in easy (–R) contexts (13 times and 7 times, respectively). See Table 4.3 for the distribution of this strategy in the ASL rejection data.

The apologize strategy in the English data involves using the direct form *sorry* and occurs only two times, appearing once in each of the coworker (=P) contexts ("turning down a coworker's request to go out to lunch" and "turning down a coworker's request for a ride to the garage"). As with the independence strategy of hedge, the English speakers use the independence strategy, apologize, in a very limited context; whereas, both apologies and hedges are used in every context in the ASL rejection data (although the apologize strategy appears less frequently than the hedge strategy). The limited distribution of the apologize strategy in the English rejection data appears in Table 4.4.

Table 4.4 The Distribution of Apologize in the English Rejection Data

	Employee's rejection (–Power)	Coworker's rejection (=Power)	Supervisor's rejection (+Power)	**Total:**
Easy rejections (–Ranking)	0/4	1/4	0/4	1/12
Difficult rejections (+Ranking)	0/4	1/4	0/4	1/12
Total:	0/8	2/8	0/8	

Note. N = 4 native English speakers, 24 DCT ratings (6 ratings per participant). Total occurrences of apologize reported over total number of elicitations (4 participants per discourse context).

Presuppose/Raise/Assert Common Ground

The involvement strategy, presuppose/raise/assert common ground, is realized in the rejection data as a positive statement about the signer's willingness, pleasure, or desire to comply with the request. See Example 1 for a list of some of these positive (common ground) statements in ASL.

1. **Examples of presuppose/raise/assert common ground used in making rejections**

    (a) NICE, FINE(wiggle), BUT . . .

    [_translation_: That'd be nice, great in fact, but . . .]

    (b) I DON'T-MIND/pp, LIKE T-O/nod, BUT . . .

    [_translation_: I wouldn't mind. I'd like to, but . . .]

    (c) I ENJOY/pp, BUT . . .

    [_translation_: I'd really enjoy that, but . . .]

    (d) _WANT/pp_ OUT LUNCH/nod, BUT . . .

    [_translation_: I'd like to go out to lunch, but . . .]

    (e) I ENJOY/nod. I CAN'T/neg.

    [_translation_: I'd enjoy that, (but) I can't.]

This strategy has a different distribution in the ASL data than it does in the English data. In ASL, half of the instances occur in the "turning down the supervisor's request to serve on the sunshine committee" (–P, –R) context. In this context in particular, the employee is less obligated to comply with the request but wants to maintain a good relationship with the supervisor.

This strategy typically occurs at the beginning of the rejection before the head rejection. In fact, 8 of the 10 instances in ASL occur either at the beginning of the response or immediately after the opening in which the signer typically signs "WELL".

See Table 4.5 for the distribution of this strategy in the ASL rejection data. Note that most of the ASL signers use this strategy in the "turning down the supervisor's request to serve on the sunshine committee" (–P, –R) context, but it is actually used at least once in

Table 4.5 The Distribution of Common Ground in the ASL Rejection Data

	Employee's rejection (–Power)	Coworker's rejection (=Power)	Supervisor's rejection (+Power)	Total:
Easy rejections (–Ranking)	5/7	2/7	1/7	8/21
Difficult rejections (+Ranking)	0/7	1/7	1/7	2/21
Total:	5/14	3/14	2/14	

Note. N = 7 native ASL signers, 42 DCT ratings (6 ratings per participant). Total occurrences of common ground reported over total number of elicitations (7 participants per discourse context).

every context except the "turning down the supervisor's request to call a potential consumer" (–P, +R) context.

Example 2 shows some instances of this strategy from the English rejection data.

2. **Examples of using the strategy, presuppose/raise/assert common ground, in English rejections**

C = coworker; E = employee

C: I'd love to do that, but . . . [*invitation to lunch*]

E: I would like to. I think it's a—it's a really nice thing we have, the sunshine committee; however, . . . [*sunshine committee*]

C: Normally, [*name*], I would, but my problem is that . . . [*ride to the garage*]

Like the ASL rejections, the English rejections have a higher incidence of the presuppose/raise/assert common ground strategy in the "turning down the supervisor's request to serve on the sunshine committee" (–P, –R) context. However, it is also used in the two rejections made by the coworker, the two (=P) contexts, and is used once by the supervisor to "turn down the request to attend a last-minute meeting" (the (+P, –R) context). See Table 4.6.

The fact that the English speakers use this strategy in most coworker (=P) contexts indicates a stronger tendency for the English speakers to address threats to involvement of a coworker by using

Table 4.6 The Distribution of Common Ground in the English Rejection Data

	Employee's rejection (−Power)	Coworker's rejection (=Power)	Supervisor's rejection (+Power)	**Total:**
Easy rejections (−Ranking)	3/4	4/4	0/4	7/12
Difficult rejections (+Ranking)	1/4	3/4	1/4	5/12
Total:	4/8	7/8	1/8	

Note. N = 4 native English speakers, 24 DCT ratings (6 ratings per participant). Total occurrences of common ground reported over total number of elicitations (4 participants per discourse context).

a positive statement (presupposing/raising/asserting common ground) than is the case for the ASL signers. It may well be that ASL signers are more likely to assume common ground (a shared identity) with a Deaf coworker and so this strategy is used less often to mitigate a rejection of a coworker's request.

In addition, for both the ASL signers and the English speakers, the supervisor is less likely to use the presuppose/raise/assert common ground strategy. This low incidence by the supervisor reflects the supervisor's status and the fact that the supervisor can generally assume the cooperation of the subordinate.

Offer/Promise

The involvement strategy, offer/promise, also figures heavily in rejections. This strategy represents an effort to cooperate and occurs in all of the discourse contexts in both the ASL and the English rejection data.

In the ASL data, the offer/promise strategy comprises four types. First, the signer may offer to engage in the act another day (9 times out of the 23 offers in the data). Sometimes a specific day is given, and sometimes the phrase OTHER TIME or the sign IN-THE-FUTURE is used. Second, the signer may offer, or suggest, that the addressee try to ask another person (four occurrences in the data). Third, the signer may provide other options for the addressee (four times in the data), such as, looking through a drawer for change for the train fare, or giving a person the number of the bus that the person can take to get to the garage.

Fourth, the signer may make an outright request of the addressee. For example, (*supervisor:*) YOU GO, YOU/nod. INFORM-ME WHAT'S-UP/ pp [*translation: Go and let me know what they cover*]; (*employee:*) DON'T-MIND/tight lips HIRE PERSON, NEW, HIRE/q [*translation: Could you hire a new person?*]. In these examples, a command and a question form are used to make a request, respectively. Such requests do not appear in the rejections in the English rejection data. This again may show a difference in relative face orientation, in which the ASL signers may be more inclined to assume cooperation and, thus, may assume they can make such a request.

As stated above, the offer/promise strategy appears in all six discourse contexts in the English data as well (from 1 to 3 instances out of the 4 rejections in each context). Example 3 shows the use of this strategy in the English data.

3. **Examples of using the offer/promise strategy in English rejections**

   E = employee, C = coworker, S = supervisor

   E: I'd like to be asked again . . . [*sunshine committee*]
   C: Maybe you could find out somebody going in that
      direction. I think [*name*] lives that way. Maybe you want
      to ask her. [*ride to the garage*]
   S: If you want to wait until the cab comes, I'll try to change
      [the 20 dollar bill] with the cabbie. [*dollar for the train*]

The offer/promise strategy is used throughout the rejection data for both language groups. This strategy mitigates threats to involvement by showing that the speaker is cooperating with the addressee even though a request has just been rejected.

Give (or Ask for) Reasons

Of all the involvement strategies, give reasons appears in the most rejection contexts in the rejection data. In fact, this strategy is used by both groups in all of the rejections except one instance for each language group. This one exception in the ASL data is one instance of the "sunshine committee" (–P, –R) context, in which the signer uses a direct rejection (without redress); this example is discussed below.

In the English rejection data, this strategy is used by all 4 participants in all six contexts, except in the "turning down a request to go out to lunch" (=P, –R) context, in which it is used by 3 of the 4 speakers. It is clear that giving reasons is an important part of almost any rejection in ASL and English. We will also see in the next section that giving reasons also serves a key role in indirect rejections. Some examples of the give reason strategy in ASL and English appear in Example 4.

4. **Examples of using the give reasons strategy in ASL and English rejections**

   E = employee, C = coworker, S = supervisor

   E: I have a bunch of deadlines and I really need to prioritize and give the, uh, work tasks top priority . . . [*sunshine committee*]

   E: BUT I OVERWHELM, HAVE <u>LONG-LIST-OF-THINGS, INDEX-LONG-LIST-OF-THINGS</u>/tight lips. ADD-TO-LONG-LIST/rh-q. <u>RESPONSIBLE, "WELL"</u>/pg-frown,neg . . . [*call a prospective new consumer*]

   [*translation*: But I am overwhelmed with all the work I have on my plate as it is. I just can't add another thing to all the things I'm responsible for now, really . . .]

   C: I have an appointment somewhere else at [*time*] . . . [*ride to the garage*]

   C: I HAVE-TO <u>INDEX-FAR-LEFT</u>/th DOCTOR APPOINTMENT. <u>AFTER WORK</u>/t, I <u>TAKE-OFF-LEFT</u>/puff-cheeks DOCTOR APPOINTMENT, <u>"WELL"</u>/nose wrinkle,lip curl,neg . . . [*ride to the garage*]

   [*translation*: I have to go way in the other direction for a doctor's appointment, and I've got to get going right after work (for that appointment), so . . .]

S: #STATE PERSON (INDEX-left [nondominant hand])
    COME(nondominant hand)/t, IMPORTANT/tight lips,
    CHERISH MEETING, INDEX-LEFT [nondominant hand]/tight
    lips,nod . . . [last-minute meeting]

[translation: Someone from the state is coming for an important
meeting, and I don't want to miss that meeting . . .]

S: I've got to catch a taxi. All I have is a 20 dollar bill and
    that's it . . . [dollar for the train]

Violate Relevance Maxim—Give Hint (Indirect Rejection)

There are several instances in the ASL and English rejection data in
which the speaker does not use an overt rejection when turning down
the request. This section shows that the rejection data from each language group has a similar distribution and elaborates the process by
which the addressee interprets these indirect rejections. The data indicate the distribution of *indirect rejections* is sensitive to ranking of
imposition values (easy [–R] vs. difficult [+R] rejections), and, to some
degree, power values (employee [–P] vs. coworker [=P] vs. supervisor
[+P] rejections).

In these indirect rejections, the speaker violates the Relevance maxim
and gives hints to enable the addressee to interpret the indirect rejection as a rejection, as seen in the ASL data in Examples 5, 6, and 7 below.

5. <u>Context</u>: **An employee (E) turns down a supervisor's
    request to call a potential new consumer.**
    E: (wow), (pg-frown), "WELL"(1-hand), REALLY I FULL/puff
        cheeks SCHEDULE, LIST-OF-THINGS, BEHIND/tight lips. (oo),
        "WELL"/pg-frown, MY STAFF/t, #ALL "FULL"(2-hands)/puff
        cheeks. YOU FIND OTHER PERSON FOLLOW-UP, DON'T-MIND,
        YOU/tight lips /q.

    [translation: Oh, wow. Well, you know. Actually my schedule is
    so full and there are things I'm behind on. Um, well—and my staff
    all have their hands full. Would you mind finding someone else to
    follow up on this?]

    <u>Hints</u>: give reasons, offer (by making a request)

6. <u>Context</u>: **A supervisor (S) turns down an employee's request to borrow a dollar for the train.**

   S: "WAIT"(index finger), I CHECK MY PURSE FIRST. (*mimes looking through purse*) CL-B(nondominant hand)'holding bill'/oh, INDEX-CL-B(nondominant hand)'holding bill'+/ pg. HAVE TWENTY DOLLAR. INDEX-CL-B(nondominant hand)'holding bill'+/pg-frown, MUST FLY-TO-RIGHT/tight lips. I MUST, INDEX-CL-B(nondominant hand)'holding bill'+/pg-frown, #CAB. (tight lips), I HAVE-TO CHECK DRAWER, SEE #IF HAVE COINS/q. (*mimes looking in a drawer*) (*surprise look*) #ALL PENNY, "WELL"/tight lips. I BLOW-HAND/pp('oh well' look).

   [*translation*: Hold on, I'll check in my purse first. (*mimes looking through purse*). Oh, all I have is a 20, and I have to fly out today. I need it for the cab. Let me check the drawer to see if I have any coins in there. (*mimes looking through drawer*) (*surprise look*) There are only pennies in there. Well, I don't have it [the dollar].]

   <u>Hints</u>: give reasons, offer (to look for money)

7. **Context: A supervisor (S) turns down an employee's request to borrow a dollar for the train.**

   S: I LOOK-DOWN-AT/nod. (*response to looking: pg*), ONLY HAVE TWENTY DOLLAR/pg. I EXPEND #TAXI, EXPEND/pg, FLY-TO-RIGHT, INDEX(wiggle fingers)-LIST-OF-THINGS. I DON'T-WANT MONEY SHORT/neg. SORRY/pg.

   [*translation*: I'll look. (*responds to finding the $20 bill*) I only have a 20. It's going for the taxi. I'm flying out and all of that. I don't want to be caught short on money. Sorry.]

   <u>Hints</u>: give reasons, apologize

Three primary strategies are used as hints in the indirect rejections above: give reasons, apologize, and offer/promise. However, it is only the involvement strategy, give reasons, that all of the indirect rejections have in common. This strategy is key to making an indirect rejection in both ASL and English.

To clarify how giving reasons may be interpreted as a rejection, let us take a situation in which a person is asked out to lunch. If the response is TODAY/t, I BUSY!+/pg [*translation:* I'm way too busy today], the requester takes the reason in and of itself to be a rejection. However, this is not true of an apology, for example. If the response were SORRY/tight lips,neg, the rejection itself would still seem lacking. It must include a reason or an overt rejection to be complete and to be interpreted as a rejection. Perhaps this is why when a person is seeking an apology and only gets reasons, it is not generally taken as an apology, but rather only as a rejection. Consider, for example, the responses in the two following exchanges:

Comment: "I think I deserve an apology because you promised that you would go next Monday."
Response: "Well, I have a meeting, so I can't go."

This response would not be considered much of an apology. In contrast, consider the following:

Comment: "Can you go with me next Monday?"
Response: "Well, I have a meeting, so I can't go."

In this situation, the similar response would be considered a rejection.

Turning to the English indirect rejections, we see that giving reasons is also the key to their interpretation. See Examples 8, 9, and 10 below, in which the strategies of give reasons and offer/promise appear in bold print.

8. **Context: An employee (E) turns down the supervisor's request to call a potential new consumer.**
    E: [*Name*], you know—you know what? **My caseload is really—I mean, it's way too full right now. I can just barely meet the people I'm seeing.** You know, is there any way you could give that to somebody else, or we could talk about some other way of distributing my-the people that I have because **there's no way that I can see**

that person. I-I'm really booked with the people I have right now. Maybe you could ask [name] to do, uh, that.

Hints: give reasons, offer a suggestion

9. Context: A coworker (C) turns down another coworker's request for a ride to the garage.
    C: Oh, really? Shoo[4]-normally, [name], I would, but my problem is that—that I've already—I've got to go to another meeting at [time]. I've got to head down there and it's in the opposite direction. You know, maybe you could find out somebody [who is] going in that direction. I think [name] lives that way. Maybe you want to ask her. [researcher says he will ask this person.] Good luck.

    Hints: give reasons, offer a suggestion

10. Context: A supervisor (S) turns down the employee's request to borrow a dollar for the train.
    S: Oh, my God. All I have is a 20 dollar bill and I need it to, um, take the taxi. I don't have any other change on me.

    Hints: give reasons

In each of these cases, as in the ASL examples above, the speaker turns down the request by giving a reason, and the hearer interprets the utterance as a rejection, but the speaker never makes the rejection outright. The distribution of these indirect rejections in the ASL and English data is shown in Tables 4.7 and 4.8.

Tables 4.7 and 4.8 show that indirect rejections are associated primarily with difficult (+R) rejections for both language groups. There is also some interaction with the power variable as well; this association with employee (+P) rejections and supervisor (–P) rejections is especially apparent in the ASL data. However, clearly *both* ASL signers and English speakers use indirect rejections and clearly the give

---

4. The participant begins to say *shoot*, but does not complete the word.

Table 4.7 The Distribution of Indirect Rejections in the ASL Rejection Data

	Employee's rejection (–Power)	Coworker's rejection (=Power)	Supervisor's rejection (+Power)	Total:
Easy rejections (–Ranking)	1/7	1/7	0/7	2/21
Difficult rejections (+Ranking)	3/7	0/7	4/7	7/21
Total:	4/14	1/14	4/14	

Note. $N = 7$ native ASL signers, 42 DCT ratings (6 ratings per participant). Total occurrences of indirect rejections reported over total number of elicitations (7 participants per discourse context).

reasons strategy is key to the interpretation of these utterances as rejections. This finding is significant in that it provides strong evidence for the use of an indirect speech act in ASL and challenges the widely held view that ASL signers do not use indirect speech acts.

Strategies That Are Not Shared

The six politeness strategies shared by each language group are the primary strategies used in making rejections. In addition, three strategies are not shared by the two groups; however, each of these strategies appears only once in the rejection data. The direct strategy—making a direct rejection—appears in ASL only; the independence

Table 4.8 The Distribution of Indirect Rejections in the English Rejection Data

	Employee's rejection (–Power)	Coworker's rejection (=Power)	Supervisor's rejection (+Power)	Total:
Easy rejections (–Ranking)	0/4	0/4	0/4	0/12
Difficult rejections (+Ranking)	2/4	1/4	2/4	5/12
Total:	2/8	1/8	2/8	

Note. $N = 4$ native English speakers, 24 DCT ratings (6 ratings per participant). Total occurrences of indirect rejections reported over total number of elicitations (4 participants per discourse context).

strategy of giving deference appears in English only; and the involvement strategy of joke appears in ASL only.

Direct Rejection (ASL Only)

There are no instances in the English rejection data of making a rejection without mitigation; however, there is one occurrence of this strategy in the ASL rejection data. The direct rejection occurs in the "turning down a supervisor's request to join the sunshine committee" (–P, –R) context. In this elicitation, the participant reports that the addressee neither has an obligation to comply nor is likely to comply with the request. See Example 11 below.

11. **Context: An employee (E) turns down a supervisor's request to join the sunshine committee.**
      E: (nose wrinkle)+. DON'T-WANT, I/neg(*sitting with hand on side of chin except when signing 'DON'T-WANT, I'*).

      [*translation*: *Nah, I don't wanna (do that).*]

This is the only rejection in all of the DCT data that does not use any mitigation at all. The fact that the signer does not feel obligated is clearly the motivation for not redressing the threat to involvement in this easy (–R) rejection.

The casualness of the signing in this case (e.g., signing with one hand and the use of *nose wrinkle*, which is only used in casual or intimate settings) indicate that the signer is very comfortable rejecting this request, and does so with a direct rejection. It is likely that this signer may also see this request as not directly relevant to her work responsibilities, so the status of herself as an employee (–P) is less important in this context.

Give Deference (English Only)

There is one independence strategy, give deference, that appears in the English rejection data but not in the ASL rejection data. It appears in only one instance in the "turning down the supervisor's request to make an initial call to a potential new consumer" (–P, +R) context. As reported in chapter 3, the give deference strategy is also used one time in a request in the ASL request data: the "requesting the day before

Thanksgiving off" (–P, +R) context. The give deference strategy in both cases is used by a subordinate when engaging in a speech act (request or rejection) with the superordinate. The give deference strategy foregrounds the status difference between the employee and the supervisor and highlights the obligation by the subordinate to comply with the supervisor's request in general. The rejection in which the give deference strategy is used appears in Example 12 below.

12. **Context: An employee (E) turns down the supervisor's request to call a potential new consumer.**

    E: Unfortunately, though I would like to honor that, um, I feel responsible to the—to the workload you've already assigned me, and I-I'm overloaded. I can't do this with the amount of time allotted. You know I already put in extra time. I can't cover this case for you. I-I really know you want me to, and **if you tell me I have to, if you order me, I understand I'll have to do it**. But it's getting to the point where, ethically, I need to consider refusing, so no, unless you order it.

Joke (ASL Only)

There is one involvement strategy that is used by an ASL signer that does not appear in the English rejection data and that is the joke strategy. See Example 13.

13. **Context: A supervisor (S) turns down an employee's request for a dollar for the train.**

    S: _"WELL," SORRY, HAVE 20 DOLLAR /bt. YOU^KNOW I FLY TODAY, I #CAB/rh-q. SORRY. "WELL"(two hands, circular movement)/bt_, HAVE-TO SAY NO/pg. **WALK HOME, YOU. (roleshift) WALK+(trudging along)/laugh jokingly.**

    [_translation_: Oh, sorry. All I have is a 20. You know, I'm flying out today and I'm taking a cab. Sorry. So, I have to say no. **You'll have to walk all the way home! (laugh jokingly)**]

In this example, the supervisor makes a joke (that, crucially, is taken as a joke) and thus, assumes a close connection between the supervisor and the employee, and the positive bond between them is maintained even though the supervisor has just engaged in a rejection. Camaraderie is maintained because the joking reinforces the fact that they are close enough for her to joke about the predicament.

Note that only the ASL signers use the involvement strategy of a joke in the data. Although there are only two such instances (in this rejection and in the request context of "asking the supervisor to give the employee one's pen" [–P, –R]), it may reflect the relative face orientation of these ASL signers, which is more characterized by assumed involvement and common identity more than by independence.

The two strategies used in ASL that are not used in English, direct rejection and joke, both assume a certain amount of closeness and involvement, which may not be assumed by the English speakers in these same contexts. On the other hand, the use of the give deference strategy by an ASL signer in a difficult (+R) request and by an English speaker in a difficult (+R) rejection seems to reflect the roles and obligations of the participants in the workplace for both language communities.

Other Rejection Strategies Used to Mitigate Rejections

Three linguistic forms used to mitigate rejections in the data are not Brown and Levinson (1987) strategies: naming and surprise expression (in English only) and NMMs (in ASL only).

Naming (English Only)

The strategy, naming, is used in rejections in the English data, but not in the ASL data (nor is the related "HANDWAVE" strategy used in any of the ASL rejections). Naming is an involvement strategy that is used to show a connection to the addressee, and is used from one to 3 times (out of 4 four elicited rejections) in all six contexts. This form is widely used in rejections in English, occurring in about half of the rejections.

Surprise Expression (English Only)

Surprise expressions, which are defined as interjections such as *oh* or *geez*, are also used in the English data, but not in the ASL data.

However, as was pointed out in chapter 3, the "HANDWAVE" sign accompanied by certain NMMs may convey a type of surprise that can be used to mitigate requests. In rejections, we see a similar phenomenon with the "WELL" sign used to hedge. As with the use of "HANDWAVE" and accompanying NNMs in requests, the "WELL" sign and associated NMMs in rejections provide a wider range of pre-emptive face-saving than do the surprise expressions in English, which are limited to a very small set.

As with the naming strategy, surprise expressions are used from one to three times in all six contexts in the English rejection data. Thus, both naming and surprise expressions appear in about half of the rejections in English.

In short, a request may begin with a surprise expression and naming to lessen the impact of the forthcoming rejection, for example, *Oh, [name],—.* The surprise expression serves to warn that an imposition is about to occur, and the naming serves to show a connection with the addressee, a way of showing involvement. These strategies often create the needed balance between independence and involvement in English rejections.

3. NMMs (ASL Only)

NMMs are used extensively in both ASL requests and rejections (see chapters 5 and 6). They serve to redress a wide range of face-threats associated with both requests and rejections. These markers are unique to ASL, and all five NMMs appear in the ASL rejection data.

These three strategies that are unique to each language—naming, surprise expressions, and nonmanual modifiers—also occur in requests. These strategies represent language-specific forms that are used to mitigate threats to face and, as we can see here, are used frequently in the rejection data.

Conclusion

Although many of the politeness strategies used by the ASL signers and English speakers in the rejection data fall within a limited set, there are notable differences in the distribution of strategies

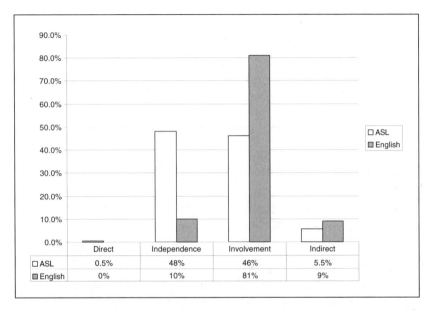

	Direct	Independence	Involvement	Indirect
□ ASL	0.5%	48%	46%	5.5%
■ English	0%	10%	81%	9%

Figure 4.1. Distribution of Politeness Strategy Types in ASL
and English Rejections

and some specific strategies used by each language group. Most of the strategies are shared by both language groups. However, the unique language forms that are used by one group but not the other (such as naming and NMMs) have a high incidence in the rejection data.

Indirect rejections, unlike indirect requests, were shown to have a similar distribution in the ASL and English data, and to primarily be used by employees and supervisors in difficult (+R) rejections. These indirect rejections provide strong evidence that ASL signers do indeed engage in indirect speech acts, contrary to current assumptions in the literature that they do not.

A major difference in the politeness strategies of these two language groups was seen in the independence strategies and involvement strategies used in making rejections. This difference can be accounted for by the fact that the relative face orientation of the ASL signers and the English speakers may well differ. ASL signers have more of an ideal social identity view of face (with more of a focus on involvement) and American English speakers have more of an ideal individual autonomy view of face (with more of a focus on independence). These English speakers may well be using more involvement strategies to mitigate rejections (which threaten involvement) because involvement is less likely to be assumed.

Figure 4.1 shows the distribution of the strategies used in making rejections by the ASL signers and the English speakers. As with requestive strategies, there is a similar overall distribution of strategies used in rejections; however, there is a notable difference in the frequency of the involvement strategies and the independence strategies in rejections. The English speakers predominantly use involvement strategies and use fewer independence strategies, and the ASL signers use about an equal number of involvement and independence strategies. This difference was attributed to differences in language forms on the one hand and differences in cultural views of face-risks in rejections on the other. However, some linguistic strategies that are unique to each language (especially NMMs which are used extensively in the ASL data) are not included in the totals shown in Figure 4.1.

5

TWO NONMANUAL MODIFIERS
THAT MITIGATE SMALLER
THREATS TO FACE

ASL signers and English speakers employ a variety of linguistic strategies when making requests and rejections. Although many of these strategies overlap, there are some unique strategies that are used by each language group. One particular kind of linguistic expression is unique to signed languages such as ASL: nonmanual modifiers (NMMs). To clarify, NMMs are specific markers that (a) occur on the mouth, such as *tight lips* which is a tightening of the lips, or (b) involve the body and head, such as a *body/head teeter* (*bt*) from side to side.[1] NMMs are different from the grammatical markers in ASL that mark specific syntactic categories (sentence types), such as the wh-question marking (a furrowed brow, head tilt forward, and direct eye gaze) used to mark a wh-word question. The grammatical markers generally make use of raised or lowered eyebrows, and body movement, such as leaning forward or back. Other types of grammatical markers are used in ASL to mark yes/no-questions, topics, and rhetorical questions. (For a discussion of these grammatical markers see Baker-Shenk & Cokely, 1980; Neidle, Kegl, MacLaughlin, Bahan, & Lee, 2000; Valli, Lucas, & Mulrooney, 2005.)

The structure of the DCT provides a tool for examining both the dimensions of ranking of imposition (easy [–R] vs. difficult [+R]) and power (employee [–P], coworker [=P], and supervisor [+P]); however, the numbers of elicited requests and rejections in this study are too small for statistical analysis. Although the differences in the power variable in particular are too small to reach any con-

---

1. This *body/head teeter* was identified as a politeness marker by Roush (1999).

clusions except in some specific contexts, the degree of ranking of imposition indicates more definite trends. The ranking of imposition is the focus of this discussion on NMMs because the data derived from the DCT for the current study show that the five NMMs can be linearly ordered, based on the relative imposition each NMM serves to mitigate (from small to extreme).

Polite Pucker—A Marker That Mitigates Small Impositions

The *polite pucker* (*pp*) marker "is made with pursed lips, sometimes with the jaw lowered" (Roush, 1999, p. 43) and appears as *mm* elsewhere in the literature, in which the focus has been on its modifying (adverbial) function, to convey the sense of *normally* or *as expected* (see, e.g., Baker-Shenk & Cokely, 1980; Bridges & Metzger, 1996). This NMM was first identified as a politeness marker by Roush. See Figure 5.1.

Previous Research on the *pp*

Roush (1999) identified the *pp* marker as one of three NMMs used by native ASL signers when making requests and rejections in a videotape segment entitled "Asking to Borrow a Truck" from the *Signing Naturally II Videotext* (Smith, Lentz, & Mikos, 1992). This

Figure 5.1. polite pucker (pp)

videotape is part of a series of educational materials designed for teaching ASL. The discourse contexts on the videotape are signed by native ASL signers to model the language for students. In this segment of the videotape, a Deaf man (Anthony) asks to borrow a truck from a series of Deaf people so that he can move a dresser he recently purchased at a furniture store. Anthony is turned down by all of them except for the last person, so requests and rejections are used throughout this segment.

The *pp* marker is used four times in the *Signing Naturally II* videotape, and it is used in each instance to express openness and willingness. For example, it is used to express willingness to comply with the request before engaging in a refusal (rejection), and it is used to express willingness to look elsewhere to borrow a truck (Roush, 1999).

> [The *pp* marker] seems to have the meaning "not bad, it's a good idea/possibility," "why don't you/I try that" or "you/I'll think about it." This seems to be used when one does not want to state a strong opinion or suggestion or wants to avoid a commitment to doing something. (Roush, p. 43)

In short, Roush suggests that the *pp* NMM is associated with acts of cooperation and solidarity.

The Use of the *pp* NMM in the DCT

The *pp* marker functions exclusively as an involvement strategy in the ASL request and rejection data. The *pp* NMM is used only when there is an assumed state of cooperation and when the threat to face is small. In addition, the *pp* marker is used mostly by the supervisor. This shows an interaction with the power dimension, in that it is consistent with the expectations that superordinates (+P) can assume more cooperation than subordinates (–P) can.

The *pp* is also the only NMM to appear more often in easy (–R) contexts than in difficult (+R) contexts, as shown in Figure 5.2. The *pp* is associated with small threats to face and appears first in the linear ordering of the NMMs, based on the relative degree of imposition that the NMMs mitigate.

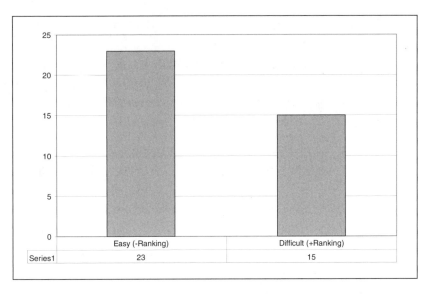

Figure 5.2 Occurrences of the Polite Pucker in Easy (–Ranking)
and Difficult (+Ranking) Contexts

The Use of the pp NMM in Requests

In the request data, the *pp* NMM is used to signal cooperation between the speaker and the addressee (i.e., to mitigate minor threats to involvement). See Examples 1 and 2, which are excerpts from longer requests that appear in the DCT. The section of the utterance that appears in bold type indicates the part that is currently under discussion.

SIGNALING COOPERATION IN REQUESTS
BY USING THE *PP*

1. **Context: An employee (E) in a grocery store asks the supervisor for the day before Thanksgiving off.**

   E: SUPPOSE YOU (roleshift) HAVE-TO/pg,cond, I **WILLING/pp**.

   [*translation:* If you say I have to (work that day), **I'll do it.**]

2. **Context**: A coworker (C) asks to borrow $50 from another coworker.

   C: don't-mind borrow money/tight lips,q. i **pay-you**/pp tomorrow.

   [*translation*: Do you mind if I borrow the money (from you)? I'll **pay you back** tomorrow.]

In both of these examples, the signer is engaging in involvement strategies. In the first instance, the signer is communicating willingness to go along with the supervisor's decision; and in the second instance, the signer is communicating cooperation by making a promise to repay the money back promptly.

The Supervisor's Use of *pp* in the Head Request in Easy (−R) Requests

See Example 3 for a typical use of the *pp* marking in the head request.

3. **Context**: A supervisor (S) asks an employee to make an initial call to a potential new consumer.

   S: you, "handwave"/oh, i (*looks right*) receive new referral client(right). ***don't-mind*/*pp*** call, ***everything-work-out*/*pp*,** #OK/q.

   [*translation*: Oh, yes. I just received a new referral. **Do you mind** making the call and **following through on that, okay?**]

The supervisor (+P) uses the *pp* marker more than either the coworker (=P) or the employee (−P); the supervisor uses *pp* in 8 of the 13 times it is used in the request data. This difference shows how the value of the power variable affects the realization of this marker. In general, the person in a higher power position uses involvement strategies more often with a subordinate than the subordinate uses with the superordinate. The increased use of the *pp* marker by the supervisor provides additional evidence for its involvement function. Although the coworker and the employee use the *pp* marker elsewhere in the making of a request (e.g., to signal willingness or cooperation, as when using the offer/promise strategy), the supervisor is the only one who uses the *pp* marker in the head request and does so only in the easy (–R) request. Its function of mitigating smaller threats to face is evident given that this marker appears in the head request in easy (–R) requests only.

THE SUPERVISOR'S USE OF *PP* IN TAG QUESTIONS IN DIFFICULT (+R) REQUESTS

There are also instances in which the supervisor uses the *pp* marker in difficult (+R) requests; however, these appear in the form of a tag question. See Examples 4 and 5.

4. <u>Context</u>: **A supervisor (S) asks an employee to complete a big project much earlier than expected.**

    S: <u>REMEMBER YOUR PROJECT *RESPONSIBLE*/tight lips ONE-MONTH/rh-q. (headshake)/pg-frown. "WELL", SORRY/pg-frown INFORM-YOU/tight lips MUST MOVE-BACK TWO-WEEKS/pg. CAN, "**WELL**"(nondominant hand, movement forward), #OK(dominant hand)/pp /q</u>

    [*translation*: You know the project you're responsible for completing in one month? Well, I'm sorry to tell you that it has to be moved back 2 weeks. **Do you think you can do that?**]

5. <u>Context</u>: **A supervisor (S) asks an employee to complete a big project much earlier than expected.**

    S: <u>"HANDWAVE"/ah, INFORM-YOU/tight lips. REMEMBER YESTERDAY *DISCUSS*/th ABOUT ONE-MONTH PROJECT, YOU/q. FIND "*HANDWAVE-NO*"/neg /tight lips, #EARLY, MOVE-BACK HAVE-TO/pg. FINISH/rh-q. NEXT-WEEK, "**WELL**"/pp, CAN, "WELL"/pg /q.</u>

    [*translation*: [Addressee's name], I need to tell you something. Remember that one-month project we talked about yesterday? Well, I just found out that it has to be done earlier. It has to be done by next week. **What do you think?** Can you finish it (by then)?]

In these two examples, we see that the *pp* marker does not occur in the head request in difficult (+R) requests, but rather, it occurs in a tag question after the supervisor in the role play has already broken the news that the employee must complete the work much earlier than originally planned. These examples provide further evidence that this NMM has an involvement function. At this point the supervisor is trying to negotiate how the project can possibly be completed in time, signaling a desire to reach out and offer support to the employee.

The *pp* marker is used to signal cooperation and solidarity in many common expressions used in everyday ASL conversations. For example, the *pp* marker co-occurs with the following: THUMB-UP/pp [*take care*], THANK-YOU/pp [*thank you*], FINE+/pp [*that's fine*], and OH-I-SEE/pp [*oh, I see*], all of which are associated with a sense of camaraderie or involvement (see Roush, 1999).

In sum, the *pp* NMM is associated with involvement strategies, such as an offer/promise. It also is used more often in the supervisor's (+P) requests and is only used in the head request of easy (–R) requests made by the supervisor (the [+P, –R] contexts). See Table 5.1 for the distribution of the *pp* marker across the discourse contexts.

The Use of the pp NMM in Rejections

The *pp* marker has a similar distribution in the rejection data and clearly serves an involvement function in rejections as well. In fact, the *pp* marker is used almost twice as often in rejections (25 times),

Table 5.1 Distribution of Polite Pucker Across Imposition Ranking and Power Dimensions for Requests

	Employee's request (–Power)	Coworker's request (=Power)	Supervisor's request (+Power)	Total:
Easy requests (–Ranking)	1/7	1/7	5/7	7/21
Difficult requests (+Ranking)	1/7	2/7	3/7	6/21
Total:	2/14	3/14	**8/14**	

Note. N = 7 native ASL signers, 42 DCT ratings (6 ratings per participant). Total occurrences of *polite pucker* reported over total number of elicitations (7 participants per discourse context).

which may threaten the addressee's involvement, as in requests (13 times), which may threaten the addressee's independence.

One might expect the *pp* to appear more than any other NMM in the rejection data because a rejection threatens involvement, but this is not the case. Although the *pp* marker signals cooperation, it is only associated with smaller threats to involvement, so in fact it has a restricted distribution in the rejection data. For example, the *pp* NMM is used much less often in difficult (+R) rejections than in easy (–R) rejections. In rejections, it only co-occurs with involvement strategies such as offer/promise, and is only used in the head rejection by the supervisor (+P).

The Supervisor's Use of *pp* in the Head Rejection in Easy (–R) Rejections

The *pp* marker is used in specific ways in the rejection data. For example, as was the case with the head request, only the supervisor uses this marker in the head rejection. That is, it is used only when actually signing the rejection (signing, "NO"), and the supervisor does so only in the easy (–R) rejection: the "turning down the request to attend a last-minute meeting" (the (+P, –R) context). The supervisor says, e.g., "NO+, I CONFLICT, PLAN/pp,neg," [*translation: No, my plans conflict*] and "*HANDWAVE-NO*"/pp, I CAN'T MAKE^#IT/neg" [*translation: No, I can't make it*]. In these examples, the *pp* marker is associated with cooperation and relatively small threats to involvement. As with requests, the employee (–P) and the coworker (=P) never use the *pp* marker in the head rejection.

Signaling Cooperation in Rejections by Using the *pp* NMM

As with requests, the *pp* marker is associated with involvement strategies in rejections and, therefore, is used to signal cooperation. These strategies include presuppose/raise/assert common ground (in five instances) and offer/promise (in nine instances). The *pp* NMM is used when the speaker points out positive feelings about either the speaker or the requested act, as when using the strategy *presuppose/raise/assert common ground*. For example, it is common for the signer to begin responses in the following ways: "WELL"(1-hand, nondominant hand)/tight lips, I DON'T-MIND/pp. PROBLEM... [*translation: Well, I wouldn't mind, but the problem is . . .*]; (oo)/slight lean back, I, INDEX-YOU, *WANT/pp* OUT LUNCH/nod, BUT . . . [*translation: Oh, I want to go out to lunch, but . . .*]. In each of these examples, the signer responds in some way to the request itself, e.g., by signing "WELL" and using the NMM, *tight lips* (see discussion below), then engages in other face-work. The *pp* marker, however, is only used to signal cooperation and willingness in these cases.

THE USE OF *PP* TO OFFER/PROMISE

The most common occurrence of the *pp* marker for both requests and rejections is with the involvement strategy, offer/promise, as in OTHER TIME/t, **"WELL"/pp,nod** [translation: *Maybe another time, it might work out*]. See Examples 6 and 7.

6. <u>**Context**</u>: **A supervisor (S) turns down an employee's request for a dollar for the train.**
    S: <u>WAIT</u>(index finger). (*looks down, mimes pulling out a bill*) SHOOT![2] I TWENTY DOLLAR, INDEX-BILL. I NEED #CAB/pg. I RIDE, I GO-TO-LEFT AIRPORT(left), PLANE-TAKE-OFF FOR CONFERENCE/tight lips, INDEX-UP-LEFT CALIFORNIA, "WELL". SORRY/pg-frown. **"WELL"(one hand, circular movement)+/pp**-tight lips-pg[3](nondominant hand holding imaginary bill; thinking—looking back and forth between bill and addressee). **DON'T-MIND WITH ME CL-1(two hands)'go together to the left' #CAB, CHANGE, I GIVE-YOU, "WELL"/bt,pp,q.**

    [*translation: Hold on. (Looks down, mimes pulling out a bill.) Darn! All I have is a 20, and I need it for a cab for the ride to the*

---

2. The sign glossed as SHOOT is sometimes glossed as SHIT or CRAP elsewhere in the literature, but this sign is not generally considered an obscenity in ASL, so I have chosen to use the gloss SHOOT for this sign.

3. Note that "WELL" perseverates as the signer changes the NMMs that co-occur with it: from *pp* to *tight lips* to *pg*.

airport to go to a conference over in California, so—sorry. **Well, hmmm, geez. Would you mind coming with me to the cab, so I could get change and give it to you, how's that?]**

7. <u>Context</u>: A coworker (C) turns down another coworker's invitation to go out to lunch.

C: TOMORROW, YOU/q. SORRY/*ah, I WISH JOIN*/tight lips, CAN'T/neg. I HAVE-TO, TWELVE/t, I HAVE-TO PICK-UP DAUGHTER, INDEX-RIGHT DOCTOR APPOINTMENT. SORRY/tight lips, NO-GOOD(1-hand)/neg. *OTHER TIME* **CAN, "WELL"**/pp /browraise, **WANT YOU, WANT+**/pp,q.

[*translation*: *That's tomorrow? Oh, sorry. I wish I could do that, but I can't. I have to pick up my daughter at noon for a doctor's appointment. Sorry, that won't work.* **I could do it** *another time,* **how's that? Do you want to plan on that?**]

In each of the examples, the signer uses the *pp* marker when expressing either joint interest or joint cooperation.

WHEN THE *PP* MARKER IS NOT USED

The distribution of the *pp* marker in the rejection data is similar to its distribution in the request data in which it appears in all contexts; however, there is one notable difference. Even though the *pp* marker is relatively evenly distributed among five discourse contexts (four or five instances in each context), it is excluded from one particular context: the employee's difficult rejection. In the "turning down a supervisor's request to call a prospective new consumer" (–P, +R) context, the *pp* is not used even though this NMM is used by the employee in the easy (–R) rejection. Clearly this marker does not show the necessary deference in this context. Only *tight lips* (discussed below) and other more severe NMMs are used in this context.

THE USE OF *PP* WITH HEDGING AND APOLOGIES TO SIGNAL EFFORTS TO COOPERATE

The *pp* marker is also used with two independence strategies: three times with hedging ("WELL"/pp) and twice with apology (SORRY/ pp). This occurrence may seem to contradict the argument that the *pp* NMM only co-occurs with involvement strategies; however, the *pp* marker in these cases appears only at those moments in which the signer conveys a desire to work collaboratively with the addressee and gives the sense of *I'm stuck, but I really am cooperating with you on this*, as in Example 8.

8. <u>Context</u>: **A coworker (C) turns down another coworker's request for a ride to the garage.**
   C: **"WELL"(one-hand), SORRY/pp**. TIME CONFLICT/tight lips, I, "WELL"(two hands, circular movement)/pg-frown. OTHER TIME/nod, BUT NOW/t, (headshake)/pg-frown,neg. **COME-TO-MIND, WHY-NOT YOU CONTACT YOUR FRIEND, SPELL-OUT NAME, YOU "WELL"(signed to the right)/pp,q. #OR TAKE-SUBWAY, HAVE #BUS NUMBER SPELL-OUT GO-TO-RIGHT, "WELL"/pp,q.** (then adds:) SORRY/pg-frown.

   [*translation*: **Oh, sorry! I've got a conflict, so, hmm. If it were** *another time; I just can't do it now.* **I know, why don't you contact your friend, [name]? Or you could take the subway, or bus [number] that goes that way, how's that?** (then adds:) *Sorry.*]

In this example, the use of "WELL"(one-hand), SORRY/pp conveys involvement, in that the NMM conveys a desire to cooperate. The use of the *pp* marker with suggestions (i.e., offer/promise) also clearly indicates this function.

Compare, for example, the mitigating functions of three different accompanying NMMs when they co-occur with the sign, SORRY: SORRY/polite pucker (pp), SORRY/tight lips, and SORRY/polite grimace-frown (pg-frown) (the *tight lips* NMM is discussed below and the *pg-frown* NMM is discussed in chapter 6). As reviewed in chapter 6, when signing SORRY/pg-frown, the signer is expressing true regret about not being able to help the addressee (i.e., this NMM is used to mitigate a severe threats to face, see Figure 5.3). As discussed later in this chapter, when signing SORRY/tight lips, the signer is expressing *I just can't do that this time, but generally I would*, i.e., *tight lips* is used to mitigate moderate threats to face (see Figure 5.4). The SORRY/pp, however, conveys the sense that the signer is genuinely

TWO NONMANUAL MODIFIERS

Figure 5.3. <u>SORRY/polite grimace-frown (pg-frown)</u>: circular movement on chest

Figure 5.4. <u>SORRY/tight lips</u>: circular movement on chest

working with the addressee and the signer expects the addressee to realize that they are in this together even though this one (small) incident has not worked out (see Figure 5.5).

The *pp* marker, then, functions in a similar way in requests and rejections. Its higher incidence in rejections than in requests provides

Figure 5.5. SORRY/polite pucker (pp): circular movement on chest

additional evidence for its involvement function, and its lack of occurrence in the employee's difficult (–P, +R) rejection supports the claim that the *pp* marker is associated with small threats to face. See Table 5.2 for the distribution of the *pp* NMM across the six rejection contexts.

Table 5.2 Distribution of Polite Pucker Across Imposition Ranking and Power Dimensions for Rejections

	Employee's rejection (–Power)	Coworker's rejection (=Power)	Supervisor's rejection (+Power)	**Total:**
Easy rejections (–Ranking)	6/7	5/7	5/7	16/21
Difficult rejections (+Ranking)	0/7	5/7	4/7	9/21
Total:	6/14	10/14	9/14	

Note. N = 7 native ASL signers, 42 DCT ratings (6 ratings per participant). Total occurrences of *polite pucker* reported over total number of elicitations (7 participants per discourse context).

Figure 5.6. tight lips

Tight Lips—A Marker That Mitigates
Moderate Threats to Face

A second NMM, *tight lips*, mitigates moderate threats to face and is the most frequently occurring NMM in the ASL DCT data. The *tight lips* marker can best be described as a tightening of the lips together, as shown in Figure 5.6.[4]

The *tight lips* marker serves both an involvement function and an independence function. It is associated more with difficult (+R) contexts than is the *pp* marker and thus, is linearly ordered second to the *pp* marker based on the degree to which it mitigates face-threats. Figure 5.7 shows the percentage of occurrences of the *pp* marker and the *tight lips* marker in easy (–R) and difficult (+R) contexts, and indicates an inverse relationship between the two. Specifically, the *pp* marker is

---

4. A *tight-lips-to-the-side* NMM also appears in the data. This variation of *tight lips* includes a tensing of the lips to one side of the mouth. It occurs four times in the request data and is counted as *tight lips* in the data. It is not clear if this variation functions differently from the standard *tight lips* NMM, but this variation of the *tight lips* marker only appears in difficult (+R) contexts. This unique marker may well have a combined meaning of *tight lips* and "WELL", or *tight lips* and the *body/head teeter* NMM (see chapter 6 for a discussion of the *body/head teeter* marker).

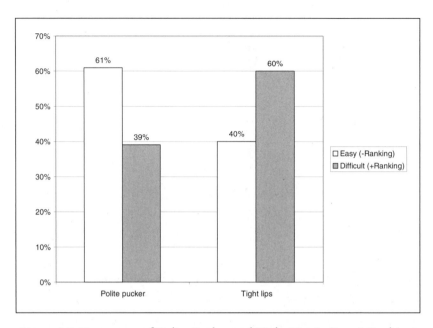

Figure 5.7 Percentage of Polite Pucker and Tight Lips in Easy (–Ranking) and Difficult (+Ranking) Contexts

associated more with easy (–R) contexts (61%) and the *tight lips* marker is associated more with difficult (+R) contexts (60%).

The Use of *tight lips* in the DCT

The *tight lips* marker is used to mitigate moderate threats to face and as such, serves as a default form (i.e., the most basic or common form) for the expression of politeness. Its wide distribution and its high co-occurrence with key lexical items such as DON'T-MIND (in requests) and "WELL" (in rejections) support this claim, in that these two lexical items are widely used in the requests and rejections, respectively.

The Use of tight lips in Requests

The *tight lips* marker is the most frequently occurring NMM in the request data, as well as the rejection data. It also has the most pervasive distribution, appearing throughout the six discourse request contexts and co-occurring with the most politeness strategies. In requests, it appears most often in the head request, in indirect apologies, in hedge/tag questions (<u>"WELL"</u>/tight lips,q), and with "HANDWAVE". The pervasiveness of the *tight lips* NMM suggests that it serves as a general default politeness marker for most requests of moderate imposition. In other words, using *tight lips* in a request is generally interpreted as conveying a desire to be polite.

TIGHT LIPS USED WITH DON'T-MIND IN THE HEAD REQUEST

The frequency with which the *tight lips* NMM co-occurs with the sign, DON'T-MIND, in the head request is particularly strong evidence for the claim that it mitigates moderate threats to face. DON'T-MIND occurs in two thirds of the requests in the ASL request data, and the *tight lips* marker is used more times than any other NMM with this sign (in 19 out of the 28 occurrences of DON'T-MIND). In these cases, *tight lips* co-occurs either with the entire head request or with just the lexical item, DON'T-MIND, as is the case in Example 9.

9. <u>**Context**</u>**: A supervisor (S) requests that an employee complete a big project much sooner than expected.**

    S: <u>YOU, COME-TO-MIND</u>/tight lips, INDEX-RIGHT, <u>I INFORM-YOU ABOUT #PROJECT, PROJECT, ONE-MONTH</u>/t, *MOVE-BACK*/tight *lips* TWO-WEEKS/neg. <u>RIGHT-WARN-ME</u>/tight lips, NEED. ***DON'T-MIND***/tight *lips* TWO-WEEKS/q. KNOW+. PATIENT+/tight lips, PLEASE.

    [<u>translation</u>: *Oh, I wanted to ask you. You know that project I told you had a month to do? It's been moved back to 2 weeks. I was just alerted that they need it (then).* **Do you mind** *finishing that in 2 weeks? I know. Please try to be patient.*]

TIGHT LIPS USED IN INDIRECT APOLOGIES

The use of the *tight lips* marker in indirect apologies provides additional evidence that the marker is associated with the mitigation of threats to independence. In addition to its use with the direct apology sign SORRY (2 times in the request data), *tight lips* is used in indirect apologies of the give overwhelming reasons sort (12 times) and the admit the impingement sort (4 times). See Example

10 in which *tight lips* mitigates both the indirect apology and the head request.

10. **Context: A supervisor (S) requests that an employee complete a big project much sooner than expected.**
    S: REMEMBER, I GRANT-YOU PROJECT, I REQUEST ONE-MONTH/
    q. (headshake), I LOOK-OVER(2-hands)/tight lips,neg.
    REALIZE I NEED TWO-WEEKS. *DON'T-MIND CL-CLAW(2-hands)'give it all to me'/tight lips*, GIVE-ME B-Y TWO-WEEKS/q.

    [*translation*: Remember that project I gave you that I asked you to have ready in a month? Well, I've looked everything over and realized I need it in 2 weeks. **Do you mind giving it all to me** within the next 2 weeks?]

The signer reports that the request in this context is difficult to ask, but that the addressee is both obligated and likely to comply with the request. In this case, the supervisor is using the standard marking—the *tight lips* marker—to mitigate both the indirect apology (having to impose a shorter deadline) and the head request.

TIGHT LIPS USED IN THE TAG QUESTION,
"WELL"/TIGHT LIPS,Q

There are eight instances in which the *tight lips* NMM co-occurs with a hedge/tag question (i.e., "WELL"/tight lips,q). The *tight lips* marker also co-occurs three times in the ASL request data with a hedge ("WELL"), which by definition occurs without question marking. See the request in Example 11.

11. **Context: An employee (E) in a grocery store asks a supervisor to have the day before Thanksgiving off.**
    E: I/pg, POSSIBLE I WEDNESDAY INDEX-RIGHT+/t, POSSIBLE,
    IF CAN/(cond), OFF I INDEX-RIGHT WEDNESDAY, "*WELL*"(1-hand)/tight lips /q. SUPPOSE YOU (roleshift) HAVE-TO/
    pg,cond, I WILLING/pp. YOU HAVE OTHER PEOPLE COVER ME,
    "*WELL*"/tight lips(1-hand, nondominant hand, move forward) /q, POSSIBLE, "*WELL*"(some circular movement)/
    (slight rocking)bt /tight lips,q.

[translation: I—is it possible for me to have this Wednesday off, **you think?** *If you say I have to work, I'll do that (of course). Perhaps someone could cover for me,* **or something?** *So is that a* **possibility at all?**]

It is common in the data for the "WELL" sign to carry the nonmanual marking even when the NMM does not co-occur with the head request or another politeness strategy.

Tight lips Used With the sign, "handwave"

The *tight lips* marker often occurs with the "HANDWAVE" sign at the beginning of a request. There are seven such instances in the request data. See, for instance, Example 12.

12. **Context: A coworker (C) asks to borrow $50 from another coworker.**

    C: *"HANDWAVE", DON'T-MIND I MOOCH[5]/tight lips* FIFTY DOLLAR/q. PAY-YOU NEXT-WEEK/nod.

    [translation: **Hey, can I bum** *50 dollars* **off you?** *I'll pay you back next week.]*

In this example, *tight lips* co-occurs with "HANDWAVE" and with much of the head request as well. When the "HANDWAVE" accompanied by *tight lips* appears at the beginning of the utterance, it serves to warn the addressee that there is a moderate threat to face forthcoming.

Tight lips Used With Give Reasons and Offer/Promise

Unlike the markers that mitigate more severe threats to face (e.g., *pg* and *pg-frown*, discussed in chapter 6), *tight lips* also co-occurs with two involvement strategies: give reasons (four instances total) and offer/promise (one instance). Although these occurrences are infrequent, the fact that these involvement strategies are mitigated by the

---

5. The gloss MOOCH is used here to represent a sign used in ASL to mean *to take an opportunity to do something*. However, the ASL sign does not inherently have the negative connotation of the English word *mooch*. In ASL, it is the accompanying NMM that communicates whether MOOCH is being used in a positive or neutral sense (e.g., MOOCH/pp or MOOCH/tight lips) or negative sense (MOOCH/th or MOOCH/shhh).

Table 5.3 Distribution of Tight Lips Across Imposition Ranking
and Power Dimensions for Requests

	Employee's rejection (–Power)	Coworker's rejection (=Power)	Supervisor's rejection (+Power)	**Total:**
Easy requests (–Ranking)	3/7	7/7	7/7	17/21
Difficult requests (+Ranking)	17/7	12/7	18/7	47/21
Total:	20/14	19/14	25/14	

Note. N = 7 native ASL signers, 42 DCT ratings (6 ratings per participant). Total occurrences of *tight lips* reported over total number of elicitations (7 participants per discourse context).

tight lips NMM provides additional evidence for its mid-range, default status in making requests, in that they show how pervasive this marker is in the request data.

The *tight lips* marker is so prevalent, in fact, that if someone wants to appear polite (in either the involvement or the independence sense), one simply needs to use this NMM. Table 5.3 shows the wide distribution of this marker, which occurs across the six discourse contexts. Note the increased use of *tight lips* in difficult (+R) requests, especially when compared to the *pp* marker above.

The Use of the *tight lips* in Rejections

The *tight lips* marker is the most widely used NMM in the rejection data as well, and *tight lips* functions in rejections as it does in requests: to mitigate moderate threats to face. In addition, *tight lips*, as with the other NMMs except for the *pp* marker, is associated with both involvement and independence strategies in rejections.

The One Instance in Which No NMM Is Used

The *tight lips* marker is used in conjunction with other NMMs 81% of the time in the elicited rejections (34 of the 42 rejections), showing the pervasiveness with which it occurs in the rejection data. In 7 of these 8 instances in which *tight lips* does not co-occur with another NMM, the signer uses only the *tight lips* marker. In the one instance of a direct rejection, however, the signer uses the *nose wrinkle* and no NMM at all; see Example 13.

13. **Context: An employee (E) turns down a supervisor's request to join the sunshine committee.**
    E: (nose wrinkle)+. DON'T-WANT, I/neg(*sitting with hand on side of chin except when signing 'DON'T-WANT, I'*).
    [*translation*: Nah, I don't wanna (do that).]

As discussed in chapter 4, the signer in this example is using a casual register. The *nose wrinkle* is associated with communication between intimates, and when the *nose wrinkle* is used with the negation marker (a shaking of the head), it is comparable to saying, "Nah," in English. Because the participant reports that this rejection is an easy one and that the employee is neither obligated nor likely to comply with the request, a simple rejection without accompanying NMMs is sufficient. Apparently, the signer feels there is no need to use a NMM, not even *tight lips*.

The Use of *tight lips* With a Direct Apology (sorry)

The frequent use of the *tight lips* marker with direct apologies (i.e., the sign SORRY) provides additional evidence for the claim that *tight lips* is associated with rather generic, middle-of-the-road rejections. The use of this NMM with SORRY implies an appropriate, but average, sense of regret, and this is the reason this marker appears so frequently with strategies such as direct apologies. Of the 20 times SORRY is used in the rejection data, 70% (fourteen) involve the use of *tight lips*.

The Use of *tight lips* With Offer/Promise, and Hedge/Tag Questions

In some rejections, the signer makes a suggestion in the form of a request (uses the offer/promise strategy) after the rejection itself is made. Take, for instance, the following example: DON'T-MIND/*tight lips* HIRE PERSON, NEW, HIRE/q [*translation*: Could you hire a new person?]. The *tight lips* NMM is used in two of the three outright requests that the employee makes of the supervisor during rejections.

There are two instances in which no NMM is used in the head rejection, but rather, a hedge/tag question is used accompanied by the *tight lips* marker. For example, CAN YOU GIVE-RIGHT OTHER PERSON DO, *"WELL"*/tight lips /q [*translation*: So, can you give this to someone else to do?], and YOU FIND OTHER PERSON FOLLOW-UP, *DON'T-MIND,* YOU/tight lips /q [*translation*: Could you find someone else to follow up on that?]. The use of *tight lips* in these examples demonstrates again the moderate level of face-threat associated with this NMM.

It seems consistent with the professional roles of these participants to have the employee make such requests of the supervisor. There is also one instance in which a direct request is made by a supervisor, who has the authority to make an outright request during a rejection: YOU GO, YOU/nod. INFORM-ME WHAT'S-UP/pp [*translation*: Go ahead and go, and let me know what's going on]. The *pp* NMM is used in this case, signifying that the supervisor is assuming cooperation on the employee's part. It is unlikely that the *pp* marker would be used by an employee in a direct request to a supervisor, as it would seem too presumptuous.

The Use of *tight lips* With a Variety of Politeness Strategies

The *tight lips* NMM is associated with a variety of politeness strategies in rejections and is used in all six of the discourse contexts (from 7 to 18 instances in each context). The *tight lips* marker is most associated with hedges (e.g., *"WELL"*/tight lips), giving reasons, a direct apology (SORRY), and the head rejection. It also may co-occur with *"WELL"* (often at the beginning of the utterance), and with THANK-YOU (in the two instances in which it occurs). This distribution shows the pervasiveness of the *tight lips* marker in the rejection data, and its function to mitigate moderate threats to both involvement and independence. See Table 5.4 for the distribution of the *tight lips* marker in the ASL rejections. Note that this marker often occurs multiple times in a single rejection.

In sum, the *tight lips* marker has the highest frequency of all the NMMs in the DCT data and also has the widest distribution, in that it appears in each discourse context across the requests and rejec-

Table 5.4 Distribution of Tight Lips Across Imposition Ranking
and Power Dimensions for Rejections

	Employee's rejection (–Power)	Coworker's rejection (=Power)	Supervisor's rejection (+Power)	Total:
Easy rejections (–Ranking)	7/7	11/7	18/7	36/21
Difficult rejections (+Ranking)	17/7	12/7	13/7	42/21
Total:	24/14	23/14	31/14	

Note. N = 7 native ASL signers, 42 DCT ratings (6 ratings per participant). Total occurrences of *tight lips* reported over total number of elicitations (7 participants per discourse context).

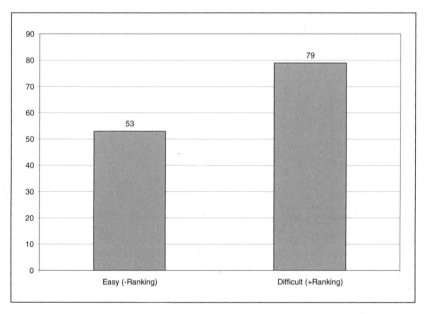

Figure 5.8 Total Occurrences of Tight Lips in Easy (–Ranking)
and Difficult (+Ranking) Contexts

tions. This distribution shows its default status in mitigating moderate threats to involvement and independence. Unlike the *pp* NMM, the *tight lips* marker occurs almost 50% more often in difficult (+R) contexts as in easy (–R) contexts. Although the *tight lips* marker has this increased frequency in difficult (+R) contexts, its frequency of occurrence in difficult (+R) contexts is still less than that of the remaining three NMMs (*polite grimace, polite grimace-frown,* and *body/head teeter*), and thus the *tight lips* marker can be linearly ordered next to the *pp* marker in terms of the degree of imposition which it mitigates. See Figure 5.8 on previous page.

6

THREE NONMANUAL MODIFIERS THAT MITIGATE MORE SEVERE THREATS TO FACE

Two nonmanual modifiers (NMMs)—the *polite pucker* (*pp*) and *tight lips*—that are associated with small to moderate threats to face are the most commonly used NMMs in the data collected in the discourse completion test (DCT). Three additional NMMs are used to mitigate more severe threats to face, and these markers can be ordered linearly as follows, based on the relative ranking of imposition that each NMM serves to mitigate: *polite grimace* (significant threats to face), *polite grimace-frown* (severe threats to face), and *body/head teeter* (extreme threats to face).

Polite Grimace—A Marker That Mitigates Significant Threats to Face

The *polite grimace* (*pg*) marker mitigates significant threats to both involvement and independence. In the DCT data, it occurs most often in difficult (+R) contexts, which supports this claim and indicates that this NMM should be linearly ordered after the *tight lips* marker.

Previous Research on the *pg*

Roush (1999) first identified the politeness function of the *pg*, and describes it as "a tight symmetrical smile (with or without teeth showing)" (p. 34). See Figure 6.1 for an example of the *pg* marker. For this study the *pg* marking is defined as showing teeth, distinguishing it from the *tight lips* NMM.

Figure 6.1. polite grimace

Roush (1999) states that the use of the *pg* marker "seems to be an important modifier in mitigating the negative impact of an utterance in ASL" (p. 35), in that the marker "seems to add the meaning of 'sorry, can't do it,' 'I don't think it can be done' or 'I don't agree'" (p. 35).

Roush discusses four instances of the *pg* marker in his data. In one example, the *pg* NMM serves as a "prefacing cue before requesting the truck" (p.34), in that the signer (Anthony) uses this marker when he explains he cannot transport the dresser in his small car. The *pg* marker is also used in a direct apology (sorry/pg,neg) and in two instances, to indicate reluctance in complying with the request. In one case, Pat shows this reluctance by giving reasons why Anthony may not be able to use the truck, and in the other case, Anthony states that he will check elsewhere and will only come back to request the truck if he is not able to borrow one from someone else.

The Use of the *pg* in the DCT

The Use of the pg in Requests

For requests, the *pg* marker is associated with more significant threats to face because it appears primarily in difficult (+R) contexts. Also, there is an interaction between the *pg* NMM and the participant's ranking of likelihood of compliance with the request.

THE USE OF THE *PG* MARKER WITH INDIRECT APOLOGIES IN
DIFFICULT (+R) REQUESTS

In the DCT request data, more than one third of the instances of
the *pg* marker occur with the independence strategy of indirect apology (in 12 of the 30 instances of the *pg* marker). In fact, it is the *pg*
NMM that co-occurs the most often with this strategy. See, for instance, Example 1 in which the indirect apology is of the give overwhelming reasons type.

1. <u>Context</u>: **A coworker (C) asks to borrow $50 from another
   coworker.**

   C: <u>"HANDWAVE"</u>, I WONDER CURIOUS/tight lips, THINK POSSIBLE
   BORROW 50 DOLLAR/q. *NEXT-WEEK / CS* FRIDAY PAY CHECK/t,
   WILL PAY #BACK, <u>"WELL"</u>/pp. CAN BORROW 50 DOLLAR,
   <u>"WELL"</u>(1-hand)/q; **I NEED MONEY FOR CAR REPAIR/pg.**
   NEED CAR WEEK-END/intense eyes. *DON'T-MIND*/tight lips
   BORROW 50 DOLLARS, <u>"WELL"</u>/tight lips /q.

   [*translation*: [Addressee's name], I was wondering if you think it'd
   be possible to borrow $50. I'll pay you back next Friday, okay? So
   can I borrow the $50? *I have to pay to have my car fixed* and I
   need the car this weekend. So, do you mind lending it to me?]

The *pg* NMM in this example is associated with a relatively high
degree of imposition to independence; note the other instances of
face-work in this example as well (e.g., hedging and offer/promise).

   Another example of an indirect apology involves admitting the
impingement. This *pg* marking is associated with this strategy in two
instances in the request data. In both instances, it is used in the "requesting the day before Thanksgiving off" (–P, +R) context and the
signer makes use of the KNOW-THAT sign. See Example 2.

2. <u>Context</u>: **An employee (E) in a grocery store asks a
   supervisor for the day before Thanksgiving off.**

   E: <u>"HANDWAVE"</u>/tight lips, ***"WELL", I KNOW-THAT***
   ***WEDNESDAY*/t, 'WOW'/pg** TEND-TO PEOPLE FLOCK-TO <u>BUY+</u>
   /tight lips FOR TOMORROW THANKSGIVING, BUT "WELL"
   (wiggle fingers) REALLY MY FAMILY LIVE <u>VERY-FAR</u>/puff

cheeks [*state*]. I SEE "WELL"/tight lips, ONCE, TWICE YEAR/
pg. 'WELL,' CAN I OFF THAT WEDNESDAY, "WELL"/bt/pg/q.

[*translation*: [*Supervisor's name*], **well, I know Wednesday, geez**, is
a busy day with all the shoppers getting ready for Thanksgiving.
But, well, my family lives really far from here, in [*state*], and I just
get to see them once or twice a year. So, well, um, can I have that
Wednesday off, you think that's possible at all?]

THE USE OF THE *PG* MARKER IN DIFFICULT (+R) AND EASY (−R) REQUESTS

There is a strong tendency to use the *pg* marker in difficult (+R)
requests. In fact, of the 30 instances of this marker in the request
data, only 6 appear in easy (−R) requests. In Example 3 below, one
participant uses this NMM in the "asking the supervisor to pass
one's pen" (−P, −R) context.

3. **Context: An employee (E) asks the supervisor to pass one's pen.**

   E: "HANDWAVE"/oh. COME-TO-MIND, NOTICE-INDEX/tight lips
   #PEN. REALIZE INDEX MY+, INDEX(nondominant hand).
   DON'T-MIND/pg GIVE-ME #PEN/q. INDEX(nondominant
   hand) MY FAVORITE. PLEASE[1] DON'T-MIND GIVE-ME/q.

   [*translation*: Oh, I just realized my pen is right there. **Would you
   mind** handing it to me? It's my favorite one. Please, would you
   mind?]

Before signing this example, the participant states that this is what
would be signed if this pen were the person's favorite pen, which
changes the context by matter of degree. It seems reasonable that a
combination of making the request from a superior and the fact that
the pen has extra value to the addressee would result in the use of
the *pg* marking in a situation in which the participant reports that
normally such a request would be easy to make.

---

1. The sign, PLEASE, in this utterance does not include a circular movement
(i.e., it is made with the flat hand briefly resting on the chest).

This participant relates further that when asking to borrow a pen from a coworker (=P, –R context), one needs to know whether it is a special pen or not. The participant was asked to sign the request both ways. Example 4 shows the participant's use of the *tight lips* marker when the pen was not a special pen, and Example 5 shows the use of the *pg* marker when it was a special pen. These examples provide clear evidence that the *pg* marker is associated with the mitigation of significant threats to face, i.e., greater threats to face than those mitigated by the *tight lips* marker.

4. **Context: A coworker (C) asks to borrow a pen from another coworker to write an address.**

   C: DON'T-MIND+, "HANDWAVE", DON'T-MIND+, #PEN, DON'T-MIND++/tight lips,q.

   [*translation*: Do you mind—Hey, do you mind (handing me) your pen?]

5. **Context: A coworker (C) asks to borrow a special pen from another coworker to write an address.**

   C: "HANDWAVE". ***DON'T-MIND/pg*** I BORROW YOUR #PEN/q.
   I KNOW-THAT YOUR FAVORITE. ***DON'T-MIND/pg*** I WRITE/q.
   I STAY! HERE!/'open-sh',lean forward.

   [*translation*: Hey, do you mind if I borrow your pen? I know it's your favorite. **Do you mind** if I use it to write with? I'll stay right here!]

THE USE OF THE *PG* MARKER IN THE HEAD REQUEST IN DIFFICULT (+R) REQUESTS

The NMM *pg* occurs 6 times within the head request in difficult (+R) contexts (out of the 21 difficult requests). In these instances, the likelihood that the addressee will comply is rated by the participant as low to moderate. The requester, then, is fairly certain that the addressee will turn down the request. See Example 6.

6. **Context: An employee (E) in a grocery store asks a supervisor to have the day before Thanksgiving off.**

   E: "HANDWAVE"/ah, I COME-TO-MIND. KNOW-THAT DAY/t,
   DON'T-MIND/tight lips I OFF ONE-HALF DAY/q. **SHOP**

THANKSGIVING/pg, <u>"WELL"</u>/pg-frown. I KNOW-THAT HARD
INDEX-PLURAL <u>REMIND-YOU++(2-hands, alt.)</u>/th, BUT <u>I
WONDER CAN LEAVE, OFF THAT DAY/(worried look),pg,q.</u>
[_translation_: Oh, I wanted to ask you something. I know that day
(is a bad one to take off), but would you mind if I take off half a
day that day (Wednesday)? **I need to do shopping for
Thanksgiving**, really. I know that makes it hard around here
and will make more work for other people to cover, but **I was
wondering if I could take (some time) off that day?**]

In this example, the signer perceives the request as a big imposition
as evidenced by the extensive face-work used. This face-work not
only includes the use of the _pg_ marker, but also a number of other
politeness strategies. The likelihood that the request will be turned
down seems to be the motivation for the extensive face-work.

THE USE OF THE _PG_ MARKER WITH THE GIVE DEFERENCE
STRATEGY

The independence strategy, give deference, is used only one time in
the request data, in a difficult (+R) context, and the _pg_ marker co-
occurs with it in this context. See Example 7.

7. <u>Context</u>: **An employee (E) in a grocery store ask a
   supervisor to have the day before Thanksgiving off.**
   E: <u>I/pg</u>, POSSIBLE I WEDNESDAY INDEX-RIGHT+/t, POSSIBLE, _IF
   CAN/cond_, OFF I INDEX-RIGHT WEDNESDAY, <u>"WELL"(1-hand)/
   tight lips/q</u>. SUPPOSE YOU (roleshift) HAVE-TO/<u>pg,cond</u>, I
   WILLING/pp. YOU HAVE OTHER PEOPLE COVER ME, <u>"WELL"/
   tight lips(1-hand, nondominant hand, move forward) /q</u>,
   <u>POSSIBLE, "well"(some circular movement)/(slight rocking)bt
   /tight lips,q</u>.

   [_translation_: I—is it possible for me to have this Wednesday off, you
   think? **If you say I have to**, I'll do that (of course). Perhaps someone
   could cover for me, or something? So is that a possibility at all?]

The use of the _pg_ marker with the give deference strategy provides
further evidence for its independence function, and its function to

mitigate significant threats to face. That is, the *pg* NMM conveys the appropriate amount of deference in a difficult (+R) request of one's supervisor.

THE USE OF THE *PG* MARKER WITH "HANDWAVE"

In some instances the *pg* NMM co-occurs with "HANDWAVE" at the beginning of the utterance. For example, ""**HANDWAVE**", I KNOW-THAT/**pg** BAD TIME ASK-YOU, 'rub hands'/pg" [*translation: [Oh], [name], I know that it's a bad time to be asking, 'but, well . . .'*], and ""**HANDWAVE"/pg**, REALLY SORRY/tight lips INFORM-YOU/pg . . ." [*translation: [Oh], [name], I'm really sorry to tell you this . . .*]. These instances serve to signal the severity of the imposition right at the beginning of the request.

The *pg* marker is associated with independence strategies such as indirect apology and give deference and is associated with significant threats to face as determined by the rating of the likelihood of compliance with the request as low to moderate. See Table 6.1 for the distribution of the *pg* marker in the request data, and especially note the total used in making difficult (+R) requests (this total appear in bold) that shows its higher frequency in contexts that require greater mitigation of face-threats.

Table 6.1 Distribution of Polite Grimace Across Imposition Ranking and Power Dimensions for Requests

	Employee's request (–Power)	Coworker's request (=Power)	Supervisor's request (+Power)	**Total:**
Easy requests (–Ranking)	1/7	5/7	0/7	6/21
Difficult requests (+Ranking)	14/7	1/7	9/7	**24/21**
Total:	15/14	6/14	9/14	

Note. N = 7 native ASL signers, 42 DCT ratings (6 ratings per participant). Total occurrences of *polite grimace* reported over total number of elicitations (7 participants per discourse context).

The Use of the pg Marker in Rejections

As with requests, the *pg* marker is associated with significant threats to face in rejections. Also, just as with requests, the rejection data suggest an interaction between the *pg* marker and likelihood of compliance with a request on the one hand, and the *pg* marker and difficult (+R) rejections on the other.

THE USE OF THE *PG* MARKER IN THE HEAD REJECTION

The *pg* marker frequently occurs in the head rejection to mitigate the threat to involvement that results from the rejection. For example, REALLY I HONEST CAN'T ACCEPT/*pg*; I, "WELL"/tight lips/neg [*translation*: Really, I can't honestly do this, I'm really stuck] and I FEEL HAVE-TO SAY NO/pg,neg [*translation*: I feel I have to say, "No"]. In fact, approximately 40% of the instances of the *pg* marker are associated with the mitigation of threats to involvement (17 of the 31 instances of the *pg* marker in the elicited rejections).

THE USE OF THE *PG* MARKER WITH THE STRATEGY, GIVE REASONS, IN DIFFICULT (+R) REJECTIONS

The involvement strategy, give reasons, reflects one's efforts to be cooperative by providing reasons for the exception to being able to cooperate in this case. For example, SHOOT! I TWENTY DOLLAR, INDEX-BILL. I NEED #CAB/pg [*Darn! I only have this 20 dollar bill. I have to use it for the cab*]. When the *pg* marker is used with the give reasons strategy, it clearly communicates that the signer is very reluctant to turn down the request, and it serves to mitigate the significant threat to involvement.

THE USE OF THE *PG* MARKER WITH OPENING MATERIAL

There are a few instances in which the signer opens the response with the *pg* marker to signal the upcoming rejection and to begin the face-work. For example, "HANDWAVE", "WELL"(one hand), I, "WELL"(one hand)/pg,neg, . . . [[Addressee's name], well, I, uh, well . . .]; (pg)² I/pg,slight neg, . . . [Uh, I . . .]. In these instances, the speaker

---

2. This initial *pg* marking occurs before the signer produces the first sign in the utterance.

is indicating reluctance about not being able to comply with the request and is attempting to maintain the working relationship with the addressee. By signaling the rejection early, the addressee is expected to understand the signer's face-saving intent.

THE USE OF THE *PG* MARKER WITH HEDGES IN REJECTIONS

The *pg* NMM also appears with the independence strategy of hedging ("WELL") seven times in the rejection data. These hedges (<u>"WELL"/ pg</u>) are associated with the head rejection in three instances, with the give reasons strategy in three instances, and with the opening in one instance.

When the *pg* marker accompanies the "WELL" sign, it is almost always mitigated further by the use of the *body/head teeter* (*bt*) marker (discussed later in this chapter) or the incorporation of a circular movement in the sign "WELL". In every instance in which the *pg* marker occurs with "WELL" (with the exception of one) in the rejection data, it (a) co-occurs with the *bt* marker (four times) or (b) the "WELL" sign is of the 'circular movement' variety (two times). That is, the *pg* marker in these cases is usually mitigated further by the *bt* marker or the circular movement of the "WELL" sign. See Figures 6.2 and 6.3. Both strategies—"WELL"(circular movement) and the *bt* marker—are used together with the *pg* NMM in this example:

Figure 6.2. <u>'WELL'/polite grimace, body,head teeter</u>—body teeters from side to side

Figure 6.3. 'WELL'(circular movement)/polite grimace: hands move in alternating forward circles

"WELL"(two hands, circular movement)/bt, HAVE-TO SAY NO/pg [*translation: So I'm really stuck; I have to say no"*]. The one instance in which the "WELL" sign occurs with the *pg* marker but without *bt* or circular movement is when giving a reason: NOT ENOUGH STAFF HERE, *"WELL"/pg/neg* [*translation: We don't have enough staff; we really don't*].

THE USE OF THE *PG* MARKER WITH DIRECT APOLOGIES IN REJECTIONS

The *pg* NMM also co-occurs with the independence strategy, direct apology (SORRY), in three instances. See Example 8. Note that the *pg* marker in this example appears without accompanying any signs after the participant roleplays looking for a dollar bill, with the give reasons strategy, and then with the sign SORRY.

8. **Context: A supervisor (S) turns down an employee's request to borrow a dollar for the train.**

    S: I LOOK-FOR/nod. **(response to looking: pg)**, ONLY HAVE TWENTY **DOLLAR/pg**. I EXPEND #TAXI, EXPEND/pg,

FLY-TO-RIGHT, INDEX(wiggle fingers)-LIST-OF-THINGS. I DON'T-WANT MONEY SHORT/neg. **SORRY**/pg.

[*translation:* I'll look. (*response to looking: oh!*) I only have a 20 dollar **bill** and **I need that for the taxi** to get me to the airport and all of that. I don't want to be caught short. **I'm really sorry.**]

The *pg* marker, like the *tight lips* marker, serves to mitigate threats to both involvement and independence in the data, whereas the *pp* marker has only an involvement function. The use of the *pg* marker in both the head rejection and head request supports this claim. This marker is used to reflect one's willingness but inability to cooperate in the case of the head rejection, which shows its involvement function, and conversely, one's desire not to impose in the case of the head request, providing evidence for its independence function. Its use with the involvement strategy, give reasons, as well as with the independence strategy, direct apology, also shows that the *pg* marker serves both an involvement and independence function in the DCT data.

THE *PG* MARKER IN REJECTIONS WHERE THE ADDRESSEE IS LIKELY TO COMPLY

The *pg* marker co-occurs most often in rejection contexts in which the request is rated an easy (–R) request and, crucially, the likelihood of compliance is ranked by the participant as high or moderate. The fact that an easy (–R) request usually makes for a difficult (+R) rejection, and the fact that of the 31 instances of *pg* in the rejection data, 20 occur in the rejection of difficult (+R) requests, provide additional evidence that the *pg* marker is associated with significant threats to face. See Example 9 from the "turning down the supervisor's request to call a prospective consumer" (–P, +R) context. All of the participants stated that in this context the request was an easy one and that the likelihood of compliance was high. All of the participants mitigate the rejection in this case by using more severe NMMs and by engaging in extensive face-work.

9. **Context: An employee (E) turns down a supervisor's request to make an initial call to a potential consumer.**
    S: (mouthing: *wow*), (***pg-frown***), "WELL"(1-hand), REALLY I FULL/puff cheeks SCHEDULE, LIST-OF-THINGS, BEHIND/tight

Table 6.2 Distribution of Polite Grimace Across Imposition Ranking
and Power Dimensions for Rejections

	Employee's rejection (–Power)	Coworker's rejection (=Power)	Supervisor's rejection (+Power)	**Total:**
Easy rejections (–Ranking)	6/7	2/7	3/7	11/21
Difficult rejections (+Ranking)	6/7	1/7	**13/7**	**20/21**
Total:	12/14	3/14	16/14	

Note. $N = 7$ native ASL signers, 42 DCT ratings (6 ratings per participant). Total occurrences of *polite grimace* reported over total number of elicitations (7 participants per discourse context).

<u>lips</u>. (*oo*), **"WELL"/pg-frown**, MY STAFF/t, #ALL "FULL"(2-hands)[3]/puff cheeks. YOU FIND OTHER PERSON FOLLOW-UP, ***DON'T-MIND, YOU**/tight lips /q.*

*[translation: **Oh**, wow. Well, you know. Actually my schedule is so full and **there are things I'm behind on**. Um, well—and my staff all have their hands full. **Would you mind** finding someone else to follow-up on this?]*

The face-work in this example includes the use of give reasons and offer/promise (which in this case is a request to find someone else to make the call); the use of *pg-frown* and *tight lips* NMMs, as well as the mouthing of *wow*; and the use of an indirect rejection (in that the signer does not actually make the rejection outright).

Table 6.2 shows the distribution of the *pg* marker in the rejection data. Note especially that the frequency of the *pg* marker is nearly doubled in difficult (+R) contexts. Also note that the *pg* marker is most used by the employee and the supervisor (especially the supervisor in difficult [+P, +R] requests), but is used least in the coworker (=P) contexts. Thus, this form is also more associated with the roles of the employee (–P) and the supervisor (+P).

---

3. This sign, "FULL", is not like the sign, FULL, used in FULL SCHEDULE in this utterance, but rather is the natural gesture meaning *I am full* (signed with the open hand under the chin).

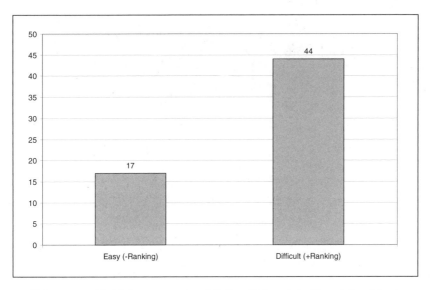

Figure 6.4. Total Occurrences of Polite Grimace in Easy (–Ranking) and Difficult (+Ranking) Contexts

Summary of the Use of the pg *Marking in Requests and Rejections*

The *pg* marking serves to mitigate significant threats to both involvement and independence. The higher frequency of occurrence in difficult (+R) contexts supports this claim. This higher rate of frequency in difficult (+R) contexts also supports the claim that the *pg* marker should be ranked next to the *tight lips* marker in the linear ordering of the NMMs by degree of imposition. See Figure 6.4 for the distribution of the *pg* marker in easy (–R) and difficult (+R) contexts.

Polite Grimace-Frown—A Marker That Mitigates Severe Threats to Face

There is a NMM that emerged in this study that is similar to the *pg* marker discussed above, but serves to mitigate severe threats to face. This NMM is termed the *polite grimace-frown (pg-frown)* because, like the *pg* NMM, the *pg-frown* is characterized by a tight, symmetrical smile with teeth showing (a grimace), but, in addition, it has an

Figure 6.5. polite grimace-frown (pg-frown)

accompanying frown: a downward turn of the sides of the mouth. This NMM includes a noticeable tightening of the neck muscles that occurs when producing the *pg-frown* marker. See Figure 6.5.

The Use of the *pg-frown* in the DCT

The *pg-frown* marker, like the *pg* NMM, is also associated with both involvement and independence strategies in the DCT data; however, its distribution differs from that of the *pg* marker. Specifically, the *pg-frown* marker appears almost exclusively in difficult (+R) contexts except for one instance in requests and four instances in rejections, which are discussed below. The *pg-frown* NMM is associated with greater threats to face than the *pg* marker is, and thus should be linearly ordered after the *pg* marker. In addition, its distribution is associated with the participant's ranking of the addressee's sense of obligation to engage in the requested act, as opposed to the expected likelihood of compliance.

The Use of the pg-frown in Requests

The *pg-frown* marking is used to address severe threats to the addressee's face in the request data, in that with only one exception the *pg-frown* marker occurs in difficult (+R) requests. It co-occurs with such strategies as direct apologies, indirect apologies, the "HANDWAVE" sign, and tag questions. It is also associated with a lower degree of obligation on the addressee's part to comply with the request.

THE USE OF THE *PG-FROWN* IN DIRECT AND INDIRECT APOLOGIES

The *pg-frown* NMM occurs with the independence strategy, direct apology, as when "WELL", SORRY/pg-frown is used in the "complete a big project much earlier than expected" (+P, +R) context. It is also used when acknowledging the circumstances that make the addressee less obligated to comply with the request (e.g., I KNOW-THAT YOU REQUIRE/pg-frown ALL GO-TO [WORK] . . . [*translation: I know that we're all required to work . . .*]) in the "requesting the day before Thanksgiving off" (–P, +R) context, which is an indirect apology of the admit the impingement sort.

THE USE OF THE *PG-FROWN* MARKER IN TAG QUESTIONS AND WITH "HANDWAVE" IN REQUESTS

The *pg-frown* marker is commonly associated with a tag question that repeats the request at the end of the utterance even though the *pg-frown* does not occur in the head request. For example, CAN, QUESTION-MARK(wiggle)/pg-frown,q [*translation: Do you think I can, at all?*], which follows the request to borrow $50. Additionally, the *pg-frown* may also occur initially in the utterance with "HANDWAVE", as in, I, "HANDWAVE"/pg-frown, I WONDER I CAN . . . [*translation: I—[Name], I'm wondering if I could . . .*]. When occurring with "HANDWAVE", the *pg-frown* marker forewarns the addressee of the degree (severe) and type (independence) of face-threat of the forthcoming discourse.

THE *PG-FROWN* MARKER IN AN EASY (–R) REQUEST

In only one instance is the *pg-frown* marker used in an easy (–R) request and that is in the "asking the supervisor to pass one's pen" (–P, –R) context. See Example 10.

10. <u>Context</u>: **An employee (E) asks a supervisor to pass one's pen.**

    E: DON'T-MIND—SEEM MY PEN, <u>CL-1'roll over by you'/th</u>,
    **DON'T-MIND GIVE-ME, DON'T-MIND PLEASE, DON'T-
    MIND/pg-frown,q**. *(researcher hands her an imaginary
    pen)* THANK-YOU/pp, THANK-YOU.

    *[<u>translation</u>: Would you mi—. It seems my pen has rolled over by
    you. **Would you mind giving it to me please, if you don't mind?**]
    (Researcher hands her an imaginary pen) [Thank you, thanks.]*

The use of the *pg-frown* marker conveys a relatively high level of deference in a context that at first blush seems to not require much face-work. This result may seem particularly surprising given that all of the participants rate this request as easy to ask, and also state that the addressee is both likely and obligated to comply with the request.

The head request in this (–P, –R) context, in fact, generates the greatest range of NMMs of all the head requests.[4] The range seems to stem from participants' response to the fact that they are in an employee role talking to a supervisor. They may well have certain perceptions of how to behave with supervisors, even those with whom they share a common language and cultural background and with whom they get along.

In Example 10 above, there are two types of evidence other than the *pg-frown* marker that indicate the high degree of deference the employee is giving the supervisor. The first is the reason given for the request. The fact that the signer states the pen rolled over near the supervisor seems much more intrusive, and thus a greater face-threat, than merely discovering that the pen is resting on the table near the supervisor. The nonmanual adverbial modifier, *th*, has the meaning of *carelessly* or *haphazardly*, so the use of the *th* modifier with the classifier, CL-1 (i.e., <u>CL-1 'pen roll over by you'/th</u>), implies

---

4. In the employee's easy request (–P, –R) context, participants use the following NMMs in the head request (one instance each, except where indicated): no NMM (2 instances), *pp*, *tight lips* (2 instances), *pg*, and *pg-frown*.

a greater threat to the supervisor's independence. Also, the use of PLEASE provides additional evidence that this context is perceived as a more severe threat to face. In fact, the sign PLEASE is used only five times in the request data (and not at all in the rejection data), and this is the only time it is accompanied by such a severe NMM.[5] In short, the signer seems to perceive this context as a difficult (+R) context and this is reflected by the amount of face-work that is evident in the request.

THE USE OF THE *PG-FROWN* MARKER IN REQUESTS
WITH LESS ADDRESSEE OBLIGATION

Other than the one instance in an easy (–R) request, the rest of the *pg-frown* markers occur in difficult (+R) requests. In most of these contexts the addressee's obligation to comply is rated by the participant as low to moderate. See Examples 11 and 12. Note the amount of face-work in which the signer engages in these examples.

11. <u>Context</u>: **An employee (E) at a grocery store asks the supervisor to have the day before Thanksgiving off.**

E: *I+*, *"WELL"*, *WANT DISCUSS*, *SEE I CAN/pg* #OFF(2-hands), THURSDAY, (headshake), BEFORE, WEDNESDAY/q. WHY/rh-q. [*NUMBER*] FROM [*STATE*] CALL-ME, COME-FROM-FAR-LEFT TUESDAY NIGHT. I, <u>WEDNESDAY, DO-ALL-THAT-LEFT</u>/t, SAME-TIME SHOP-RIGHT+. THURSDAY/t, THANKSGIVING/tight lips,nod. #SO **MOVE-THINGS-AROUND(2-hands)/pg**. STUCK(2-hands)/tight lips. (lean right) I **KNOW-THAT YOU REQUIRE/pg-frown** ALL GO, BUT CAN, *"WELL"*/bt/q. #OR FIND TRADE-WITH-LEFT BRING-IN-FROM-LEFT HELP, QM(wg), *"WELL"(1-hand)/tight lips* /q.

---

5. Only the employee and the supervisor use PLEASE with each other (two times and three times, respectively). PLEASE is never used with coworkers in the data. In the other four instances in which the sign is used, in three instances no NMM accompanies the sign and in one instance the *tight lips* NMM accompanies the sign.

[*translation*: **I**—*well, wanted to discuss something with you, to see if—* **could** *I have, not Thursday, but Wednesday off? I'm asking because I got a call and [number of] people are coming in all the way from [state] on Tuesday night. So I have a lot to do with them on Wednesday and I still need to shop (for groceries) for Thanksgiving on Thursday. So **I've looked at moving things around**, and I'm really stuck. **I know that you require** everyone to work (that day), but do you think it's possible at all that I can have that day off? Or find someone else to trade with me, that could help. So what do you think, huh?*]

12. <u>**Context:**</u> **A supervisor (S) requests that an employee complete a big project much earlier than expected.**

   S: YOU+, REMEMBER YESTERDAY I *INFORM-YOU/tight lips* INDEX-RIGHT(UP) RIGHT-INFORM-ME THAT INDEX-SECOND-ON-LIST PROJECT DUE, I GIVE-YOU/q. INDEX-RIGHT(UP) ONE-MONTH/t, FINE. NOW/t, CHANGE, TWO-WEEKS. (*lean right*) **"WELL", I KNOW-THAT MOVE-BACK TWO WEEKS/pg-frown. CAN WORK-OUT YOUR SCHEDULE, YOU/pg-frown,q.**

   [*translation*: *Oh, yes. Remember yesterday I told you that I was informed that other project I gave you is due in a month, and we were fine with that. Now, it's changed. It's due in 2 weeks. **So, I know, that means 2 less weeks. Can you work that out given your schedule, do you think it's possible?***]

THE USE OF THE *PG-FROWN* MARKER IN CONTEXTS WITH HIGH ADDRESSEE OBLIGATION?

In two instances the signer has rated the addressee's obligation to comply as high and yet uses the *pg-frown* marker. See Example 13.

13. <u>**Context:**</u> **A coworker (C) asks to borrow $50 from another coworker.**

   C: *"HANDWAVE"*. *"WELL"/bt*, MONEY/pg-frown(mouth open) CL-1(2 hands)'short'/th. *DON'T-MIND I BORROW/tight lips* 50 DOLLAR, *"WELL"/bt*, q. NEXT-WEEK/t, I GIVE-YOU, PROMISE!

[translation: [Coworker's name], well, I'm really short on money. Do you mind lending me 50 dollars, if you think you can? I'll give it back to you next week. I promise!]

In Example 13, the signer is engaging in more face-work in the request than would be suggested by a context in which the addressee has a high obligation to comply with the request. Before signing this request in the DCT elicitation, the participant reports that this question would be easy to ask a person one knows well, but difficult to ask someone one does not know as well. The participant also mentions that when it comes to borrowing money, there may be an issue of trust regarding repayment. This issue of trust makes this more of a threat to face than the participant's ranking would suggest. The fact that the signer ends the request by stressing the PROMISE sign in the offer/promise—NEXT-WEEK/t, I GIVE-YOU, PROMISE! *[translation: I'll give it back to you next week. I promise!]*—strongly suggests that this request is being perceived as a severe face-threat. That is, although the participant reports that the addressee is obligated to comply with the request, this fact doesn't make the issue of asking to borrow money any easier.

The *pg-frown* is a distinct NMM associated with the mitigation of greater threats to face than the *pg* marker. It occurs, as expected, in difficult (+R) requests that involve the mitigation of more severe threats to face, with one interesting exception. This marker is also associated with a low-to-moderate degree of obligation on the addressee's part to comply with the request. See Table 6.3 for the distribution of the *pg-frown* NMM in the request data.

The Use of the pg-frown in Rejections

The *pg-frown* marker in rejections is used to mitigate greater threats to face than those mitigated by the other NMMs that appear on the mouth (the *pp*, *tight lips*, and *pg* markers), as was the case with ASL requests. Most instances of the *pg-frown* marker occur in difficult (+R) rejections, which supports this claim. The *pg-frown* marker in rejections, as in requests, also serves both involvement and independence politeness functions, but unlike in requests, the *pg-frown* NMM in

Table 6.3 Distribution of Polite Grimace-Frown Across Imposition Ranking
and Power Dimensions for Requests

	Employee's request (–Power)	Coworker's request (=Power)	Supervisor's request (+Power)	**Total:**
Easy requests (–Ranking)	1/7	0/7	0/7	1/21
Difficult requests (+Ranking)	3/7	4/7	5/7	12/21
Total:	4/14	4/14	5/14	

Note. N = 7 native ASL signers, 42 DCT ratings (6 ratings per participant). Total occurrences of *polite grimace-frown* reported over total number of elicitations (7 participants per discourse context).

rejections occurs most often when there is a higher degree of obligation on the addressee's part to comply with the request. That is, there
is a greater threat to face when the participant turns down a request
for which there is a high degree of obligation to comply.

The Use of the *PG-FROWN* Marker in Difficult (+R) Rejections

The *pg-frown* marker appears almost exclusively in difficult (+R)
rejections, which shows the more severe face-work that is accomplished by this NMM. In fact, 24 out of the 28 instances of the *pg-
frown* occur in difficult (+R) rejections, that is in the rejection of
requests that have been rated as easy (–R) by the participant.

The Use of the *PG-FROWN* Marker in Contexts With More Addressee Obligation

Although the *pg-frown* NMM in rejections is associated with easy (–
R) requests, there are two exceptions in the rejection data. In both
cases, the participants have rated the request as difficult to make and
more likely easier to turn down, and yet the addressee is obligated to
comply with the request. In these two difficult (+R) rejections—"turning down a coworker's request for a ride to the garage" (=P, +R) and
"turning down an employee's request for a dollar for the train" (+P,
+R)—the *pg-frown* marker is used in the mitigation of the reasons, as

in the following: I HAVE-TO GO-RIGHT PICK-UP/pg-frown KID [*translation: I have to go in the other direction to pick up my kid*] and I MUST, INDEX CL-B(nondominant hand)'holding bill'+/pg-frown, #CAB [*translation: I have to use this (20 dollar bill) for the cab*]. As with requests, these examples demonstrate the effect that the addressee's sense of obligation in rejections has on the use of the *pg-frown* marker, in that the *pg-frown* marker is only used in contexts in which either the request is rated easy to ask or the addressee's obligation to comply is rated as high.

THE USE OF THE *PG-FROWN* MARKER IN EASY (–R) REJECTIONS BY THE SUBORDINATE

The *pg-frown* marker is associated with difficult (+R) contexts, which accounts for all but four instances in the rejection data. These four instances all appear in one particular easy (–R) rejection: the "turning down the supervisor's request to serve on the sunshine committee" (–P, –R) context. In fact, only the employee (–P) uses the *pg-frown* marker in easy (–R) rejections, which reflects the more severe facework done in general by the subordinate, who uses the *pg-frown* marker more than twice as often as the supervisor does in rejections (10 times and 4 times, respectively).

THE USE OF THE *PG-FROWN* MARKER IN THE "RIDE TO THE GARAGE" (=P, +R) REJECTION

One specific discourse context accounts for half of the *pg-frown* marker occurrences in the rejection data. This is the "turning down a coworker's request for a ride to the garage" (=P, +R) context. The frequency of the *pg-frown* marker in this context can be attributed to a greater personal face-threat in this difficult (+R) rejection, in that the interlocutors are not performing a more established role, as is the case for the employee and the supervisor. That is, a coworker feels more of a personal obligation to comply with a fellow worker who needs help in a difficult situation.

THE USE OF THE *PG-FROWN* MARKER IN HEDGES

The high use of the *pg-frown* marker in hedges ("WELL"), in particular, highlights the function of this marker in mitigating severe face-threats. Unlike the *pg* marker's high frequency of co-occurrence with "WELL", which often includes the *bt* or the "WELL"(circular movement) sign, the *pg-frown* marker only occurs one time with the *bt* marker and one time with the "WELL"(circular movement) sign. That is, in these same contexts, when using *pg,* participants use additional mitigators (*bt* or the incorporation of circular movement with the "WELL" sign) to achieve what is conveyed by the *pg-frown* marker alone. This fact provides strong evidence for the ordering of the *pg-frown* marker above the *pg* marker in the degree of imposition mitigated by these two markers.

The two contexts in which these two hedging instances occur in particular—the "turning down the supervisor's request to serve on the sunshine committee" (–P, –R) and "turning down a coworker's request for a ride to the garage" (=P, +R) contexts—seem to involve a personal request, increasing the personal face-threat in the rejection. The two instances of *bt* and "WELL"(circular movement) with the *pg-frown* marker are: (a) BUT I LIST-OF-THINGS, BEHIND. "WELL"/ bt,pg-frown, I FEEL INDEX-LIST-OF-THINGS DUTY/pg-to-the-side[6] [*translation:* But I have a list of things I'm behind on. I'm not sure what to do; I'm obligated to do these other things], and (b) TIME CONFLICT/tight lips, I, "WELL"(two hands, circular movement)/pg-frown [*translation:* I've got a conflict, so, um (I'm not sure what to do)].

The *PG-FROWN* Marker in Both Involvement and Independence Strategies

In the rejection data, the *pg-frown* marker appears with both involvement and independence strategies, as well as the head rejection and openings (with the hedge, "WELL", or without an accompanying sign). For example, it occurs with the give reasons strategy (e.g.,

---

6. This example involves a variation of *pg* marker that can best be described as *pg-to-the-side* (i.e., the *pg* marker is produced with the lips tensing to one side of the mouth) which appears only one time in the DCT data (and is counted as *pg* in the data). As is the case of *tight-lips-to-the-side* reported in chapter 5, it is not clear if this variation of the *pg* marker functions any differently from the standard *pg* NMM. However, *pg-to-the-side* may well serve to intensify the function of the *pg* marker by combining a sense of "WELL" or the *bt* to this NMM.

"WELL"/pg-frown, MY STAFF/t, #ALL "FULL"(2-hands)/puff cheeks [*translation:* Well, you know, my staff is already overloaded]), direct apology (I SORRY/pg-frown [*translation:* I'm so sorry]), and in the head rejection (e.g., HAVE-TO THANK˄EXCUSE/pg-frown; CAN'T, I/neg, "WELL"(1-hand)pg-frown [*translation:* I have to decline. I just can't do that with all that's going on]), and in opening of the response (e.g., "HANDWAVE", "WELL"(one hand), I, "WELL"(one hand)/pg-frown,neg . . . [*translation:* [Addressee's name], well, I (feel stuck) . . .]). This distribution across involvement and independence strategies shows that the marker serves both involvement and independence functions.

In sum, the *pg-frown* marker is associated with difficult (+R) rejections, but does also appear in one easy (–R) rejection: the "turning down the supervisor's request to serve on the sunshine committee" (–P, –R) context. That is, in easy (–R) rejections, the *pg-frown* NMM is used only by subordinates. The high frequency of occurrence of the *pg-frown* marker in difficult (+R) contexts supports the claim that this marker is associated with severe threats to face. See Table 6.4. Note that the distribution of *pg-frown* in rejections differs from the distribution of the *pg* marker, which appears at least once in each context in the DCT data. In addition, the *pg-frown* marker serves both involvement and involvement functions, and is rarely further mitigated by the *bt* marker or the "WELL" (circular movement) sign.

Table 6.4 Distribution of Polite Grimace-Frown Across Imposition Ranking and Power Dimensions for Rejections

	Employee's rejection (–Power)	Coworker's rejection (=Power)	Supervisor's rejection (+Power)	Total:
Easy rejections (–Ranking)	4/7	0/7	0/7	4/21
Difficult rejections (+Ranking)	6/7	14/7	4/7	24/21
Total:	10/14	14/14	4/14	

Note. N = 7 native ASL signers, 42 DCT ratings (6 ratings per participant). Total occurrences of *polite grimace-frown* reported over total number of elicitations (7 participants per discourse context).

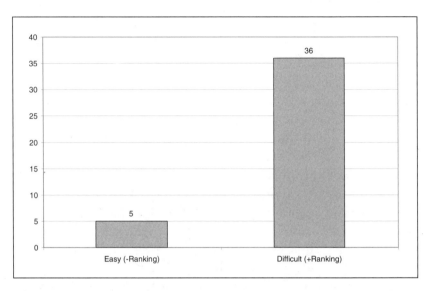

Figure 6.6. Total Occurrences of Polite Grimace-Frown in Easy (–Ranking) and Difficult (+Ranking) Contexts

Summary of the Use of the pg-frown *in Requests and Rejections*

Figure 6.6 shows the *pg-frown* marker is strongly associated with difficult (+R) requests and rejections. This fact supports the two claims made about this NMM: (a) the *pg-frown* marker mitigates severe threats to both involvement and independence and (b) the *pg-frown* marker should be placed after the *pg* marker in its ordering relative to the degree of imposition that the marker mitigates. In sum, as revealed by the current data, the linear ordering of the four NMMs that appear on the mouth, in lock-step order from lowest imposition to highest imposition, is as follows: *pp < tight lips < pg < pg-frown.*

Body/Head Teeter—A Marker That Mitigates Extreme Threats to Face

The *body/head teeter* (*bt*) marker is used to mitigate extreme threats to involvement and independence in one of two ways. First, when the marker co-occurs with other NMMs, it serves to intensify those

NMMs. Second, when *bt* appears without an accompanying NMM, it functions to question the possibility of compliance with a request or to question the possibility of an option working out.

Previous Research on the *bt*

The *bt* is the only NMM of the five discussed here that involves the body and head rather than the mouth and face. Roush (1999), who first identified the politeness function of this NMM, describes it as a "side to side head movement or shifting of weight between one foot and the other" (p. 43). See Figure 6.7. Roush further reports that it "seems to have a similar meaning to *pg* (and sometimes produced simultaneously)—[i.e.,] 'I don't think this is going to work'" (p. 43).

Roush (1999) gives two instances in which the *bt* marker is used in the "Asking to Borrow a Truck" segment of the *Signing Naturally II Videotext* (Smith, Lentz, & Mikos 1992), and both of these co-occur with the *pg* marker. In one instance, the signer (Anthony) uses the *bt* marker as "a prefacing cue before requesting the truck" (p.36). In the other instance, the signer engaging in a rejection (Pat) uses

Figure 6.7. body/head teeter (*bt*): body teeters from side to side

the *bt* marker to indicate resistance when she begins her response with both the *pg* and *bt* markers (without any accompanying signing) before providing a reason for why she cannot lend him the truck. Roush uses these examples to propose that the *bt* marker is similar to the *pg* marker in its function.

The Use of the *bt* in the DCT

The Use of the bt *in Requests*

The *bt* marker is used the least of all of the NMMs in the DCT request data, occurring only 10 times in the 42 requests (7 participants each signing 6 requests). It most often accompanies three other NMMs: *tight lips* (five times), *pg* (one time), and *pg-frown* (two times). It is the only NMM to occur exclusively in difficult (+R) contexts in the request data, and for this reason, it is ranked last in terms of the level of imposition it serves to mitigate. When co-occurring with other NMMs in requests, the *bt* marker serves to intensify the NMMs. However, when the marker is used alone without other NMMs (in two instances) in requests, it mitigates the face-threat by questioning the possibility of compliance.

THE *BT* MARKER SERVES AS AN INTENSIFIER OF OTHER NMMS IN DIFFICULT (+R) REQUESTS

The *bt* NMM occurs only in the three difficult (+R) contexts in the request data: "requesting the day before Thanksgiving off" (−P, +R), "requesting to borrow $50" (=P, +R), and "complete a big project much earlier than expected" (+P, +R). The fact that the *bt* marker only occurs in difficult (+R) requests provides strong evidence for its serving an intensifier function. See Examples 14, 15, and 16. Example16 differs from the other two examples in that it was not part of the DCT, but rather resulted when a participant was asked to produce two utterances, one which was directed to someone she knew well, and a second one, shown in Example 16, which was directed to someone whom she did not know well.

14. <u>Context</u>: **An employee (E) in a grocery store asks a supervisor to have the day before Thanksgiving off.**

E: I/pg, POSSIBLE I WEDNESDAY INDEX-RIGHT+/t, POSSIBLE, *IF CAN*/*cond*, OFF I INDEX-RIGHT WEDNESDAY, "*WELL*"(*1-hand*)/*tight lips*/q. SUPPOSE YOU HAVE-TO/pg,cond, I WILLING/pp. YOU HAVE OTHER PEOPLE COVER ME, "*WELL*"/*tight lips*(*1-hand, nondominant hand, move forward*)/q, POSSIBLE, **"*WELL*"(*some circular movement*)/(*slight rocking*)bt** /tight lips,q.

[*translation: I—is it is possible that I could have Wednesday off, you think? If I have to work, I certainly will. But maybe other people could cover for me, do you think? **Do you think there is the remotest possibility?**]*

15. **Context: An employee (E) in a grocery store asks a supervisor to have the day before Thanksgiving off.**

    E: "HANDWAVE"/oh. DON'T-MIND, I/tight lips "WELL"/ah KNOW-THAT, NEAR+ THANKSGIVING TOMORROW, #SO I *NOT-YET*/th BUY FOOD/neg. I WONDER #OK, **"*WELL*"/*tight lips,bt**, I #OFF WORK TOMORROW, *BUY*+ *FOOD*/pg, '*WELL*(*one hand*)'/*tight lips,bt* /q.

    [*translation: Say, do you mind if I—well, I know that it's close to Thanksgiving, but I haven't been able to buy groceries yet. I wonder if it is okay if, **well**, I take tomorrow off to do my grocery shopping, **do you think that's a possibility?**]*

16. **Context: A coworker (C) asks to borrow $50 from another coworker whom he or she does not know well.**

    C: **(pg-frown, bt)**[7] I *NOT KNOW YOU GOOD*/*neg*, BUT, **"*WELL*"(two hands,circular movement), HOPE YOU TRUST ME**/bt, pg-frown, #SO, "WELL"/tight lips, *CAN BORROW FIFTY DOLLAR*/tight lips FOR SOMETHING INDEX-RIGHT, **"*WELL*"/*pg, bt*** /q. #IF NOT/neg,cond, [I UNDERSTAND+/pp. #IF NO-TO ME/neg,cond, UNDERSTAND+/pp.] (Note: For the segment enclosed in square brackets ([ ]), the participant signs YOU with the nondominant hand.)

---

7. These NMMs are used before the first sign is produced.

[translation: Well, um, I know I don't know you very well really, I don't know if it's possible, but, you know, I'm hoping you can just trust me with this. So, well, could I borrow 50 dollars, is that at all possible? If not, I'll certainly understand. If you have to tell me no, I'll understand.]

These examples show that the *bt* marker serves to intensify the other NMMs in requests. Compare, for example, "WELL"/tight lips,q with its mitigation of a moderate threat to face (meaning *Is that possible?*) with "WELL"/bt,tight lips,q which, in a request, conveys something along the lines of *Is that a possibility at all?* Likewise, compare "WELL"/pg,q, which could be interpreted to mean *Do you think it could work out?* with "WELL"/bt,pg,q which conveys *Do you think there is any chance at all that it could work out?*

THE *BT* MARKER MAY OCCUR IN DIFFICULT (+R) REQUESTS WITHOUT OTHER NMMS

The *bt* marker occurs alone without any accompanying NMM in two instances. In both of these instances, the marker occurs in a tag question (with "WELL"), e.g., BUT CAN, "WELL"/bt /q [*translation: But, well, do you think it's possible that I can do that?*] in the "requesting the day before Thanksgiving off" (–P, +R) context. In both of these instances, the *bt* marker alone questions the possibility of compliance with a request. That is, it conveys the meaning *Is this a possibility (at all)?*, which is the distinctive function of the *bt* marker.

THE *BT* MARKER MAY BE INCORPORATED INTO "WELL" AS A CIRCULAR MOVEMENT

The *bt* marker commonly co-occurs with the sign "WELL". In addition to the sign, "WELL"/bt, there is a unique variation of this sign discussed above: "WELL"(circular movement), which involves an alternating circular movement forward of the open hands used in producing the "WELL" sign. See Figure 6.3 for a sample of "WELL" (circular movement)/pg. In this sign, the movement of the body (the body teetering) becomes incorporated into the movement of the "WELL" sign and the resulting sign appears to have the same semantic

value as "WELL"/bt. That is, "WELL"/bt and "WELL" (circular movement) are comparable in meaning and function: to question the
possibility of compliance. This sign (in either its one-hand or two-
hand version) may appear at the beginning of the utterance, within
an utterance, or as a tag. See Example 17, which like Example 16
above, is a request to a coworker whom the signer does not know
well.

17. **Context: A coworker (C) asks to borrow $50 from
another coworker whom she does not know well.**
C: **"WELL"(one hand; circular movement), FEEL A-
LITTLE/pg-frown** AWKWARD, I/tight lips, "WELL"/pg-
frown. REALLY I TIGHT-BUDGET/pg. **DON'T-MIND I
BORROW FIFTY DOLLAR, "WELL"(two-hands; circular
movement)/pg-frown,q.** #IF/cond, CHECK NEXT WEEK/
t, I WILL PAY-YOU NEXT-WEEK, WILL, I/nod.

[*translation*: **Well, um.** This feels a little *awkward, really. My
budget's really tight.* **Would you mind letting me borrow 50
dollars? Is there any way you could do that?** *If you can, I'll pay
you back on payday next week, really I will.*]

Note the incorporation of the circular movement into the sign
"WELL"(circular movement)/pg-frown in Example 17. This example
shows how the function of the *bt* marker is incorporated into the
"WELL"(circular movement) sign by this change in production.

Another variation of "WELL" appears in the data: "WELL" (movement forward), which is produced with both hands (but may also
be signed with a single hand) moving forward toward the addressee
and has the added meaning of a suggestion. In fact, it looks like a
reduced form of the ASL sign, SUGGEST. It appears to only serve as a
tag question. The meaning of this sign matches Roush's (1999) fifth
definition for the "WELL" sign: "'What do you think?', 'How does
that sit with you?'" (p. 35). However, none of six meanings offered
by Roush match the meaning of "WELL"(circular movement), other
than in rejections where the meaning of "WELL"(circular movement)
is similar to Roush's description, "'What can I say,' "well"" (p. 42).

Table 6.5 Distribution of Body/Head Teeter Across Imposition Ranking
and Power Dimensions for Requests

	Employee's request (–Power)	Coworker's request (=Power)	Supervisor's request (+Power)	**Total:**
Easy requests (–Ranking)	0/7	0/7	0/7	0/21
Difficult requests (+Ranking)	5/7	3/7	2/7	**10/21**
Total:	5/14	3/14	2/14	

Note. N = 7 native ASL signers, 42 DCT ratings (6 ratings per participant). Total occurrences of *body/head teeter* reported over total number of elicitations (7 participants per discourse context).

In sum, when the *bt* marker occurs without accompanying NMMs, it functions to question the possibility of compliance with the request. When the marker co-occurs with other NMMs (that appear on the mouth), it serves to intensify those NMMs by questioning the possibility of compliance. Its occurrence exclusively in difficult (+R) requests supports the claim that it serves an intensifier function and mitigates extreme threats to involvement and independence. The *bt* marker may also be incorporated into the "WELL" sign by the use of circular movement to convey the same meaning (to question the possibility of compliance). See Table 6.5 for the distribution of the *bt* marker in requests.

The Use of the bt in Rejections

The *bt* NMM is clearly associated with extreme face-work involved in trying to work things out in a difficult situation. In rejections, it also functions to question the possibility of a particular act or option and intensifies the functions of other NMMs that are being used to redress threats to both involvement and independence (i.e., *pp*, *tight lips*, *pg*, and *pg-frown*).

The BT Marker Serves an Intensifier Function With Other NMMs, Including PP

The *bt* marker is most often associated with difficult rejections and so most often appears with *pg* (eight instances). In addition, it co-occurs with *pg-frown* (one instance) and *tight lips* (one instance), but also appears alone (in two instances with hedge) and with *pp* (in one instance). The use of the *bt* marker to intensify the *tight lips* and *pg* markings has been discussed with requests. The co-occurrence of the *bt* NMM with the *pp* marker in rejections provides additional evidence for its intensifier function: to question the possibility of an act or of an option.

The co-occurrence of *bt* and *pp* is used by the supervisor in the "turning down an employee's request for a dollar for the train" (+P, +R) context. In this instance, the participant first provides reasons and engages in the rejection (using the *pg*, *tight lips*, and *pg-frown* markers) and then offers the following: DON'T-MIND WITH ME CL-1(two hands)'go together to the left' #CAB, CHANGE, I GIVE-YOU, "WELL"/bt,pp,q [*translation*: *Would you mind coming with me to the cab and I could get change and give it to you, how's that?*]. This example plainly shows that the *bt* marker questions the possibility of an act or option. The specific degree to which face is mitigated and the specific type of face mitigated (involvement, in this case) are determined by the accompanying NMM. In the case of the co-occurrence with the *pp* marker, the degree of possibility is assumed to be relatively high, as would be expected with a small threat to face (which the *pp* marker serves to mitigate). However, when *bt* co-occurs with *pg*, the degree of possibility is assumed to be low, and when it co-occurs with *tight lips*, the degree of possibility is assumed to be moderate.

When the *bt* marker appears with the "WELL" sign in rejections, it is used to convey that the signer is thinking of possible options. For example, the signer uses "WELL"/bt as an opener in one context (to show consideration of options) and "WELL"/bt to hedge on an offer/promise in another (with the same intent). These examples further show this unique function.

The fact that *bt* appears with a full range of NMMs (including the *pp* marker) provides counterevidence for Roush's (1999) claim that the *bt* marker as "a similar meaning to *pg*. . . [which is] 'I don't think this is going to work'" (p.35). The marker may, in fact, have this meaning when it accompanies a marker such as *pg*; however, when it co-occurs with the *pp* marker, we find that it intensifies the involvement function of that marker by conveying, *Don't you think this is going to work?*

THE *BT* MARKER MAY OCCUR WITHOUT OTHER NMMs

In the "turning down a coworker's request for a ride to the garage" (=P, +R) context, one participant turns down the request by using *tight lips* with a hedge, giving reasons, and then offering the following: YOU REQUEST OTHER, "WELL"(1-hand)/bt,q [*translation: Maybe you could ask someone else, is that a possibility?*]. This example shows that the *bt* marker in isolation conveys cooperation and option building, and that the *bt* marker in itself conveys a sense of possibility or options.

It is this possibility function that serves to intensify the meaning of other NMMs when it co-occurs with them. See Example 18, in which the *bt* NMM co-occurs with the *pg* marker.

18. **Context: An employee (E) turns down a supervisor's request to make an initial call to a potential consumer.**
    E: **(bt,pg(open mouth, roll eyes)), #WELL/bt,pg(open mouth, roll eyes)**, MY SCHEDULE FULL+. AND MANY CLIENT+/t, REALLY I OVERWHELMED, "WELL"/tight lips. *DON'T-MIND*/tight lips HIRE PERSON, NEW, HIRE/q. REALLY, "WELL", SORRY/pg-frown, "WELL"/tight lips.

    [*translation:* **Oh, geez, well (I don't know that it's possible).** *My schedule is all filled up, and I'm overwhelmed with all the clients I have. So, could you hire a new person? Really [I mean it]. So, sorry.*]

In this example, the *bt* marker conveys the fact that the signer wants to provide options (i.e., to cooperate), but sees none, and this colors the intensity of the *pg* marker by indicating an even stronger desire to cooperate and save face.

THE *BT* MARKER OCCURS IN ONE EASY (−R) REJECTION

There is one easy (−R) rejection in which the *bt* marker occurs: the "turning down the supervisor's request to serve on the sunshine committee" (−P, −R) context. In this instance, it co-occurs with the *pg-frown* marker, which seems inconsistent given the severity of face-threat that this combination of markers mitigates. This instance is shown in Example 19.

19. <u>Context</u>: **An employee (E) turns down a supervisor's request to serve on the sunshine committee.**

    E: (*oh-wow*), INDEX <u>FINE(wiggle)</u>/oo, BUT I LIST-OF-THINGS, BEHIND. <u>"WELL"</u>/bt,pg-frown, I FEEL INDEX-LIST-OF-THINGS <u>DUTY</u>/pg-to-the-side. FOR NOW/t, I <u>NO</u>/neg, FOR NOW.

    [*translation*: Oh, wow. *That would be nice, but I'm behind on so many things. **I don't see how it would work at all.** I've got to give priority to all these obligations, so for now, I have to say no. At least for now.*]

Although this context was rated as an easy rejection by this signer, it is clear—based on what we know about how the *bt* and *pg-frown* markers work in ASL—that the signer is treating this as an extreme threat to face. The NMMs and politeness strategies used contradict this person's rating.

Take, for example, the response of another ASL signer to this same (–P, –R) context, which was discussed in chapter 5: "<u>(nose wrinkle)</u>+. DON'T-WANT, I/neg(*sitting with hand on side of chin except when signing 'DON'T-WANT, I')*" [*translation*: Nah, I don't wanna (do that)]. The contrast is quite clear. It should also be pointed out that the signer in Example 19 above is emphasizing the other work she has to do: I FEEL INDEX-LIST-OF-THINGS <u>DUTY</u>/pg-to-the-side. This signer may well be responding this way for one of two reasons: (a) she is perceiving that the rejection of the supervisor's request as a greater face-threat than she reports, or (b) her reason for rejecting the request is so extreme that this is reflected in her use of NMMs. The extreme reason (which is a sticky subject in its own right) would most likely increase the face-threat, in that the signer feels she cannot take on one more task. Regardless of what the motivation is, it is clear that the combination of the *bt* and *pg-frown* markers signals that this response, indeed, involves extreme face-work.

In sum, the *bt* marker serves the function of questioning the possibility of an act or an option in face-work, and as such, serves to

Table 6.6 Distribution of Body/Head Teeter Across Imposition Ranking and Power Dimensions for Rejections

	Employee's rejection (−Power)	Coworker's rejection (=Power)	Supervisor's rejection (+Power)	**Total:**
Easy rejections (−Ranking)	1/7	0/7	0/7	1/21
Difficult rejections (+Ranking)	3/7	1/7	8/7	**12/21**
Total:	4/14	1/14	8/14	

Note. N = 7 native ASL signers, 42 DCT ratings (6 ratings per participant). Total occurrences of *body/head teeter* reported over total number of elicitations (7 participants per discourse context).

intensify the face-work of the NMM with which it occurs. The high distribution in difficult (+R) rejections, as shown in Table 6.6, provides additional evidence for this intensifier function and its use in mitigating extreme threats to both involvement and independence.

Summary of the Use of the bt *in Requests and Rejections*

For both requests and rejections, the *bt* marker mitigates extreme face-threats in one of two related ways: (a) by questioning the possibility of compliance or the possibility of an act or option, which is especially evident when the *bt* marker occurs without accompanying NMMs; or (b) by intensifying the involvement and independence function of the NMM with which it occurs. Because of its intensifying function, this marker has the highest distribution in difficult (+R) contexts in the data and based on this data is linearly ordered at the extreme end of the NMMs in terms of the degree of imposition that these NMMs mitigate. See Figure 6.8 for the distribution of the *bt* marker in the DCT data.

Ranking of the Use of These Five NMMs in Both Requests and Rejections

Five NMMs are associated with the mitigation of face-threats in requests and rejections: *pp, tight lips, pg, pg-frown,* and *bt.* Three of

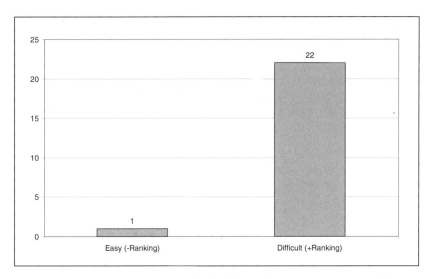

Figure 6.8. Total Occurrences of Body/Head Teeter in Easy (–Ranking) and Difficult (+Ranking) Contexts

these (*pp, pg,* and *bt*) have been previously identified by Roush (1999) and the other two were identified in this DCT (*tight lips* and *pg-frown*). Only the *pp* marker exclusively mitigates threats to involvement, whereas the other NMMs mitigate threats to both involvement and independence.

All five NMMs are sensitive to ranking of imposition (R) values. See Figure 6.9. The *pp* marker is the only NMM associated more with easy (–R) contexts than with difficult (+R) contexts, and when it does appear in difficult (+R) contexts, it is only used in the mitigation of smaller threats to involvement. The high incidence of the *tight lips* marker in both requests and rejections shows that it is a default marker for the mitigation of moderate threats to face. Although the *tight lips* marker appears more in difficult (+R) contexts than in easy (–R) contexts, it does not appear in difficult (+R) contexts to the extent that the *pg, pg-frown*, and *bt* markers do. These three markers in particular show a sharp increase of use in difficult (+R) contexts, which reflects their greater degree of face-work.

Given the discussion above concerning the form, function, and distribution of the five NMMs in the DCT data, I propose a linear

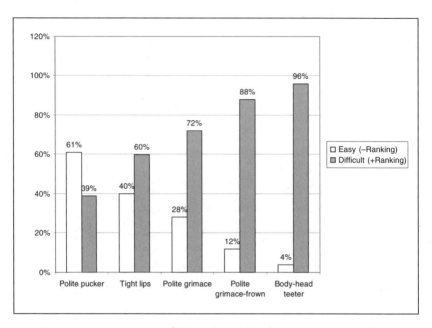

Figure 6.9. Percentage of Nonmanual Markers in Easy (–Ranking) and Difficult (+Ranking) Contexts

ordering of these markers by the degree to which they mitigate threats to face (from small imposition to extreme imposition). The *pp* marker is used only for small threats to involvement and shows a high degree of cooperation, so this marker provides the least mitigation for face-threats, and should be ordered first. The other markers are associated with the mitigation of threats to both involvement and independence. The *tight lips* marker is the most prevalent and mitigates moderate threats to face and should be ordered second. The *pg* marker is used to mitigate significant threats to face, followed by the *pg-frown* marker, which is used to mitigate severe face-threats; these markers should appear third and fourth in the linear ordering of the NMMs. Finally, the *bt* marker, which mitigates extreme threats to face, should be ranked fifth (and last). See Table 6.7, which shows the percentage of each NMM used in easy (–R) contexts.

Table 6.7 The Linear Ordering of Nonmanual Modifiers by the Degree
to Which They Mitigate Face-Threats

pp	tight lips	pg	pg-frown	bt
small imposition; cooperation is assumed; involvement function only	moderate imposition; both involvement and independence function	significant imposition; both involvement and independence function	severe imposition; both involvement and independence function	extreme imposition; both involvement and independence function
		% of use in easy (−R) contexts		
61%	40%	28%	12%	4%

Figure 6.10. don't mind/pp: beginning and end of sign

Figure 6.11. don't mind/tight lips: beginning and end of sign

Figure 6.12. don't mind/pg: beginning and end of sign

THREE NONMANUAL MODIFIERS

Figure 6.13. DON'T MIND/pg-frown: beginning and end of sign

This ranking of the NMMs is readily apparent when comparing DON'T-MIND/pp, DON'T-MIND/tight lips, DON'T-MIND/pg, and DON'T-MIND/pg-frown. See Figures 6.10, 6.11, 6.12, and 6.13, respectively. The *bt* does not seem to occur alone with DON'T-MIND, so it is not included here. The *bt* marker, of course, would further intensify these markers.

The review of strategies used by these two language groups and of the NMMs in the ASL requests and rejections, lays the foundation for an examination of the age of acquisition of ASL and its effect on the use of politeness strategies.

7

LANGUAGE FLUENCY
AND POLITENESS

Deaf persons are not always born to Deaf culture and ASL. In fact, only a small minority of deaf people are born to deaf parents. Although researchers commonly report that 5% to 10% of deaf people are born to deaf parents (e.g., Lane, Hoffmeister, & Bahan, 1996; Moores & Meadow-Orlans, 1990; Neidle, Kegl, MacLaughlin, Bahan, & Lee, 2000), in at least one study's findings this figure is less than 5% (Mitchell & Karchmer, 2004). It is apparent that the American Deaf community is not only composed of native ASL signers. Therefore, native ASL is not the only way of signing found in the Deaf community.

Introduction

The signing in the Deaf Community varies from native ASL in two primary ways. First, many deaf people are bilingual in ASL and (written or spoken) English to varying degrees, and thus may be more language-dominant in either ASL or English, or may at times mix the two languages or code-switch (i.e., switch to different language usage) to more English-like signing (contact signing) (see, e.g., Baker-Shenk & Cokely, 1980; Kannapell, 1993; Lane et al., 1996; Lucas & Valli, 1992; Neidle et al., 2000). Second, some deaf people vary in their relative fluency in ASL. There are ASL signers who are native to ASL, those who learn ASL early (e.g., when entering a school for deaf students for the first time), and those who learn ASL later in life (e.g., when in high school or as an adult).

To determine the effect that the age of acquisition of ASL has on politeness strategies, 3 signers completed the ASL DCT: a native

ASL signer, a near-native ASL signer, and a late learner of ASL. All 3 are deaf female professionals who work as directors of programs in social service agencies, and have been deaf since birth. At the time of the study, these women ranged in age from their mid-30s to mid-40s and lived in New England. All 3 were of European descent. These 3 deaf persons were selected because they represent the range of signers (in terms of age of ASL acquisition) found within the Deaf community.

The results from the ASL DCT administered to these 3 different participants are compared with the larger native ASL group that participated in the study discussed earlier in this book. The results of these DCTs reveal that the treatment of requests and rejections varies across these language users. The comparison between the native ASL signer and the near native ASL signer reflects some individual variation. However, the results of the DCT administered to the late learner of ASL reveal an interesting mixture of ASL and English politeness strategies, which are particularly idiosyncratic. The results have implications in terms of how these signers are viewed by others, the degree to which their social meaning may be misinterpreted by others, and the value of early acquisition of ASL.

The Near-Native User of ASL

The near-native user of ASL began learning ASL around the age of 5 when she entered a residential school for deaf students. The politeness strategies used by this signer in the ASL DCT are quite similar to the native ASL signers' use of those strategies. In terms of politeness strategies, she uses conventionalized indirectness, a direct request (command), and indirect rejections in the same contexts as do the native ASL signers. Likewise, the distribution of the other strategies such as hedge, direct apologies, indirect apologies, and give reasons parallel those of the native ASL signers.

She differs, however, in her use of one specific NMM: the *polite pucker* (*pp*). She appears to overuse the *pp* marker in requests and makes no use of this marker in rejections. Although she uses the more severe NMMs as the native ASL signers do in requests, she differs in that she uses the *pp* marker in all requests except for the "complete a big project much earlier than expected" (+P, +R) context. And although she uses only the more severe NMMs in rejections, she does not use the *pp* marker in rejections at all, unlike the native ASL signers who use the *pp* NMM with involvement strategies such as offer/promise and presuppose/raise/assert common ground. Another difference of note is that she mouths English glosses for signs more often than the native ASL signers, especially in making requests. Otherwise, her strategies parallel those of the native ASL signers.

Although this signer's use of politeness strategies is quite similar to the group of 7 native ASL signers, the differences highlight two important aspects of learning a language early in life rather than from birth. First, there may be some overgeneralization of specific strategies, such as the use of the *pp* NMM by this signer, and the lack of the *pp* marker in rejections. Second, the increased use of mouthing may reduce the amount of NMMs used, in that this signer seems to mouth English glosses at times rather than using some NMMs.

Given that the vast majority of deaf children are born to hearing parents, the majority of ASL signers are early learners of ASL (but not native signers of ASL), so this signer's use of politeness strategies, although unique to her as an individual, may reflect some tendencies of early learners of ASL. They may use some strategies more often or less often than native ASL signers.

The Native ASL Signer

The native ASL signer has both Deaf parents and Deaf siblings, and attended a residential school for deaf students.[1] In short, this signer was exposed to ASL since birth. Her requestive strategies conform to the overall requestive strategies of the native ASL signers. Her choice of strategies appears to differ slightly in two contexts; however, her use of strategies in these two contexts elaborates how certain politeness strategies are used by native ASL signers.

In short, this native ASL signer is a good example of a typical native ASL signer. She uses the strategy, conventionalized indirect-

---

1. This native ASL signer is one of the 7 native ASL signers who participated in the final ASL DCT.

ness, in all contexts except the "request to complete a big project much earlier than expected" (+P, +R) context in which she uses a variety of politeness strategies as expected: a tag question; give reasons or indirect apologies in all contexts. She also uses NMMs as appropriate (more on this below); questions and hedges in the expected contexts; and offer/promise and minimize the imposition in the "borrow $50 from a coworker" (=P, +R) context.

Her use of NMMs shows a sensitivity to the ranking of imposition (R), in that more severe NMMs appear in difficult (+R) requests and rejections. Her use of NMMs also shows a sensitivity to variations in power (P). Her use of NMMs in the head request in easy (–R) contexts varies from the *pp* marker in the supervisor's (+P) request, to the *tight lips* marker in the coworker's (=P) requests, and the *pg-frown* marker in the employee's (–P) request. The one instance of the *pg-frown* marker, used to mitigate severe threats to face, in the "asking a supervisor to pass one's pen" (–P, –R) context seems inconsistent with the expectations for this context. However, this signer actually signs two versions of this request. Looking at the two versions clarifies why the *pg-frown* marker is being used in this easy (–R) request. See Examples 1 and 2.

1. **Context: An employee (E) asks to borrow a pen from a supervisor.**

   E: DON'T-MIND GIVE-ME PEN, BORROW, DON'T-MIND GIVE-ME/pp,q.

   [*translation:* Do you mind handing me your pen (to borrow)?]

2. **Context: An employee (E) asks a supervisor to hand the employee his/her pen.**

   E: DON'T-MIND—SEEM MY PEN, CL-1'roll over by you'/th,
   DON'T-MIND GIVE-ME, DON'T-MIND PLEASE, DON'T-MIND/pg-frown,q.

   [*translation:* Do you mind—it seems that my pen has rolled over by you. Do you mind giving it to me please, if you don't mind?]

The first utterance, Example 1, was signed in error, in that the elicited situation was to request that the supervisor pass one's *own* pen (not ask to borrow a pen). The participant was asked to sign the request again using the correct context; this second elicitation is shown in Example 2 above. The context the signer assumes for each of these utterances differs greatly. In the first instance, she assumes the request is a common one of requesting to borrow a pen and uses conventionalized indirectness (DON'T-MIND . . ./pp,q) and the involvement marker, *pp*, (assuming cooperation) when making the request of the supervisor.

However, in the second instance (Example 2), she again uses conventionalized indirectness, but uses an indirect apology (of the give overwhelming reasons type) and the severe politeness marker, *pg-frown*. This second example signals a greater imposition to the supervisor's independence.

These examples show that this signer's use of the *pp* marker and the *pg-frown* marker conforms to the linear ranking proposed in chapters 5 and 6. Namely, the *pp* marker is used to mitigate small threats to involvement, in that asking to borrow a pen from someone is perceived as a cooperative act and a small imposition with the expectation that the addressee will comply; and the *pg* marker is used to mitigate severe threats to face, as in the case of when the pen has accidentally rolled into the supervisor's personal space. These two examples highlight how native ASL signers determine which NMM to use and when to engage in more face-work.

Of the strategies associated with rejections in the native ASL data, this participant conforms to all of them except one. The one in which she differs is the hedge strategy ("WELL"), which in the native ASL DCT data is used in most difficult (+R) rejections. This ASL signer uses this strategy only in the "turning down a supervisor's request to call to a potential new consumer" (–P, +R) context. That is, she uses hedging in the context in which the rejection is made to one's supervisor (superordinate) only. However, in the other difficult (+R) rejections, this signer does not use "WELL", but rather uses a direct apology (SORRY) accompanied by the *tight lips* NMM in one instance and the *pg* NMM in the other. It may well be that because apologizing indicates the signer's acceptance of the responsibility for the imposition, it may be more definitive in mitigating a rejection than the use of hedging ("WELL"); therefore, "WELL" may not be needed in such cases. In short, these strategies (using a direct apology and an accompanying NMM) may be used for the same desired effect.

In both cases in which this native ASL signer seems to differ from the ASL baseline, further analysis shows that she in fact conforms to the ASL signers' use of politeness strategies overall. In the first case, she visualizes a context that is a greater imposition than the elicited context would suggest and uses strategies that match her expectations; and in the second case, this signer uses either a direct apology (SORRY) or hedging ("WELL") in difficult (+R) rejections, which seems to be an appropriate use of these strategies in ASL.

The Late Learner of ASL

The late learner of ASL began to learn the language when she entered high school, and she differs in the politeness strategies she uses for both requests and rejections. When making rejections in particular, she uses a set pattern that differs from both the native ASL signers and the native English speakers.

Some of the politeness strategies used by this signer in making requests and rejections are in keeping with the native ASL signers. For example, she uses the following, as do the native ASL signers: offer/promise, minimize the imposition, give reasons, indirect apology, question, and hedge.

This signer differs in her requestive strategies in two important respects. First, she makes the request in the "complete a project much earlier than expected" (+P, +R) context by making an indirect request. Given that none of the native ASL signers use indirect requests in this context and 3 of the 4 English speakers do use indirect requests in this context, in this instance her strategy clearly matches the English speakers' strategy. In this respect, the late learner of ASL differs greatly from the native ASL signers.

Second, this signer typically mouths English words (glosses) that are associated with the signs she is producing, so the NMMs that she uses are used sparingly. Although the distribution of the NMMs used by this signer (*pp, tight lips, pg,* and *bt*) show that she is using NMMs as would be predicted by the ASL baseline, there is one notable exception. This exception appears in the "asking the supervisor to pass one's pen" (–P, –R) context, in which the signer mouths English glosses throughout the request and uses no NMMs at all.

The scope of this signer's NMMs in requests differs from that of the native ASL signers. When this signer uses these markers, they are almost always associated with specific lexical items (signs). For the native ASL signers, NMMs may co-occur with an entire sentence, a tag, or a single lexical item (sign) only. That is, the scope of the NMM for the native ASL signers seems to be dependent on the pragmatic function of the particular utterance.

Actually, many native ASL signers at times partly mouth English glosses associated with particular signs. This practice seems to be dependent on an individual's signing environment. For example, if the person knows or uses speech and speechreading to a great extent, or if other members of the person's signing environment (family, friends, etc.) sign in this way, the signer is more likely to mouth the English glosses. In fact, the amount of mouthing when signing ASL also may represent a regional variation, in that ASL signers in some parts of the country do more mouthing of English glosses than in other parts of the country. However, in the ASL DCT data, this English-like mouthing is generally replaced with the appropriate politeness NMMs at those points in which the NMMs are used to mitigate threats to involvement or independence.

In requests, the NMMs of the late learner of ASL in this study co-occur with lexical items, rather than with larger linguistic units (phrases or clauses) as can be the case with the native ASL signers. Examples 3 and 4 show the scope of this signer's NMMs in two elicited requests.

3. **Context: An employee (E) in a grocery store requests to have the day before Thanksgiving off.**
   [English mouthing is indicated by bold type.]

   E: "HANDWAVE"/closed mouth, **KNOW-THAT TOMORROW, WEDNESDAY,** *YOU BUSY+/closed mouth,intense eyes.* **THURSDAY THANKSGIVING**/brow raise, UP-TO-NOW/tight lips, **KNOW**-THAT. **PEOPLE** HORDE/tongue-side-to-side,

LANGUAGE FLUENCY AND POLITENESS

KNOW-THAT+/brow furrow. **BUT POSSIBLE I #OFF**/brow furrow, lean forward, I, "WELL"/bt,pg,lean forward,slight q marking.

[translation: [Supervisor's name], I know tomorrow's Wednesday and you [sic] will be so busy with Thanksgiving, like we always have been. I know we'll be swamped with shoppers, I know. But is it possible for me to have that day off? Do you think it's at all possible?]

4. **Context: A supervisor (S) requests an employee to make an initial call to a potential new consumer.**
   [English mouthing is indicated by bold type.]

   S: **PERSON** CALL-ME/pp, **SEEM POSSIBLE NEW CLIENT. WANT** GRANT-YOU/pp **CALL-ON-TTY, FOLLOW-UP, SEE WHAT'S-UP,** "WELL"(hands move forward)/pp,lean forward, #OK/pp.

   [translation: A person (someone) called me. It seems we possibly have a new client. I want you to call to follow up and see what's going on, okay?]

In these examples, some nonmanual adverbial modifiers are used lexically by this signer, as expected in ASL (e.g., BUSY+/closed mouth,intense eyes and HORDE/tongue-side-to-side). Note, however, that the politeness NMMs also appear lexically, as in "WELL"/bt,pg in Example 3 and GRANT-YOU/pp in Example 4. Adjectival and adverbial markers in ASL (e.g., pursed lips [meaning very thin or very small], cs (a tensing of the cheek muscles to one side and a tilting of the head toward the shoulder on that side [meaning just or recently]) are usually associated with lexical items; however, the NMMs used to mitigate threats to involvement and independence vary in their scope in the DCT of the native ASL signers.

In a follow-up interview, this participant reports that she first learned to sign in her late teens and learned ASL by interacting with other deaf people, which indicates she learned ASL as a second language. Second language learners of ASL have been found to acquire facial expressions associated with affective and linguistic functions in the following sequence: they first acquire affective markers which indicate such feelings as joy or sadness; second, they acquire adverbial markers (e.g., *cs*, *pursed lips*, and *pah*); and third, they acquire grammatical markers (e.g., wh-question marking, yes/no-question marking, and topicalization; Reilly & McIntire 1988). Only affective markers and adverbial markers are mostly associated with lexical items in ASL. This late learner of ASL seems to have acquired these politeness NMMs at the lexical level.

This signer's level of second language fluency in ASL is also revealed by the nonmanual behaviors she uses with various syntactic structures. For example, the marking associated with this signer's yes/no questions is inconsistent (and, of course, yes/no-questions appear frequently in the request data). At times, she uses all of the behaviors associated with a yes/no question: a lean forward, a brow raise, and direct eye gaze. However, in most instances one of the following is used: (a) a lean forward only (with no accompanying brow raise), (b) a lean forward and a furrowed brow (instead of a brow raise), or (c) a slight yes/no-question marking. That is, the syntactic marking is made either in part, as with the case of using only a lean forward, or with a marking that is not part of the yes/no marking in ASL (i.e., the furrowed brow). In contrast, the furrowed brow (as an affective marker) in the native ASL request data co-occurs only with phrases such as I WONDER or YOU THINK, but not with the embedded yes/no-question, which is marked by the yes/no-question marking.

The brow furrow this signer uses in making yes/no-questions is quite different from the yes/no-question marking used by the native ASL signers. First, unlike the yes/no-question marking in ASL, this furrowed brow looks like an affective facial expression that is used to convey wondering. Second, the brow furrow is similar to the lowered brows associated with wh-questions in ASL, and is not used to mark a yes/no-question in ASL. Such idiosyncratic linguistic behavior (as Reilly & McIntire [1988] report) is to be expected with second language users of ASL.

It has been shown that when deaf children are exposed to inconsistent, inadequate, or inaccessible language input, they develop their own idiosyncratic grammar (see, e.g., Mounty, 1989). This may be the case for deaf children who do not have access to a full language due to inaccessibility to the spoken word or due to communication exclusively with nonnative ASL signers, who may provide the child with inconsistent signed language input. Thus, these children acquire an idiosyncratic grammar based on limited input. This process is called *nativization*. As deaf children's language becomes more standardized (denativized) by more complete and consistent language input, the children show improvement in language development and show greater variability in style shifts (making changes in communication styles) with different signers (Mounty).

The late learner of ASL may well be in the process of developing standardized grammatical and pragmatic competence (regarding social meaning) in ASL. However, she may also have fossilized in this regard. That is to say, her ASL acquisition may have frozen in her idiosyncratic use of these features of the language.

The rejection strategies of the late learner of ASL exhibit some similarities with the strategies used by the native ASL signers, but also exhibit some strategies that differ greatly. She particularly differs in her use of a unique sequence of strategies in rejections.

This signer's strategies in rejections are similar to the native ASL signers in that she uses the give reasons strategy in all six requests, as is done by many of the native ASL participants; however, she differs in that she uses hedging ("WELL") in every rejection. The native ASL signers use "WELL" more often in difficult (+R) rejections, but do not use it in every rejection.

In addition, this signer uses an indirect rejection in the "turning down an employee's request for a dollar for the train" (+P, +R) context, in that she gives reasons and apologizes directly, but does not overtly engage in the rejection, which is in keeping with the baseline of the native ASL signers. The signer uses the direct apology (SORRY) strategy in only this one instance. These strategies fall within the baseline of the native ASL signers in this context.

However, this use of the direct apology strategy actually represents the only instance in which the signer varies from a set pattern in her rejections. The pattern is composed of the following: (a) engage in the rejection, (b) give reasons, and (c) hedge (by using "WELL", usually accompanied by NMMs). See Examples 5 and 6. This pattern is not shared by the native ASL signers, in that these signers generally use a mixture of strategies, including such involvement strategies as presuppose/raise/assert common ground and offer/promise.

This signer's use of NMMs in rejections differs slightly from what was reported for requests above. Although she uses *tight lips*, *pg*, and *pg-frown* in rejections, she does not use the *pp* marker in rejections at all. Native ASL signers may use the *pp* marker in rejections in the right contexts (e.g., when engaging in an offer/promise). There is no such use in this signer's rejections, nor does this signer use the *bt* marker in rejections.

The distribution of this signer's use of the *tight lips* and *pg* markers seems to differ in rejections when compared to requests, in that these markers may spread over entire clauses, which was not the case with the NMMs used by this signer in making requests. However, even in rejections, the tendency is for these markers to be associated with lexical items (signs) as shown below in Examples 5 and 6.

5. **Context: A coworker (C) turns down another coworker's request for a ride to the garage.**
   [English mouthing is indicated by bold type.]

   C: "HANDWAVE", I CAN'T/neg /pg. **WHY**/slight lean back. (*lean left*) I INDEX-LEFT **KID HOME,** I GO-TO-LEFT, PICK-UP KID. (*lean right*) #IF INDEX-RIGHT(circle around)/th, (*lean left, open eyes*) **ARRIVE LATE,** I STUCK, "WELL"/pg.

   [translation: Well, I can't, because I have to pick up my kid and I go way in the other direction to get home. I'd be late (picking up my kid), so I'm stuck (with that situation), geez.]

6. **Context: A supervisor (S) turns down an employee's request to attend a last-minute meeting.**
   [English mouthing is indicated by bold type.]

   S: NO/tight lips, **CAN'T**/neg. **STATE COME.** I **HAVE-TO**/brow raise MEET-RIGHT INTERACT-WITH-RIGHT/tight lips, "WELL"/ tight lips,nod.

[*translation*: No, I can't. (Someone from) the state is coming and I have to meet with them, so.]

In Example 5, the *pg* marking spreads over the entire head rejection. This spread does not occur with the NMMs in Example 6, and yet, the *tight lips* marking has a wider scope than was typical in the signer's requests. In this example, the *tight lips* marker co-occurs with two verbs and the "WELL" sign.

In sum, the late learner of ASL differs in many respects from the native ASL signers. Although this signer shares some requestive strategies with the ASL signers, she differs in her use of an indirect request in the "requesting the employee complete a big project much earlier than expected" (+P, +R) context and the NMMs this signer employs in requests are associated with specific lexical items rather than with a range of linguistic structures. The signer's rejections, however, differ from her requests in that there is some spreading of the scope of NMMs over several signs rather than just one lexical item. Unlike the native ASL signers, this signer's rejections follow a set pattern, which lacks the diversity of strategies commonly found among the native ASL signers (e.g., she does not use the presuppose/raise/assert common ground and offer/promise strategies). This signer also overuses the "WELL" sign in rejections and does not use the *pp* marking in rejections at all.

Summary and Implications

The comparison of the individual DCT results of the native ASL signer, the near native ASL signer, and the late learner of ASL to the baseline created by the DCT results of the native ASL signers overall has revealed some differences among these signers. For a comparison of the requestive strategies of these signers with the native ASL signers overall, see Table 7.1, and for a comparison of the rejection strategies of these signers with the native ASL signers, see Table 7.2. For the native ASL signer and the near native ASL signer, the differences in how requests and rejections are mitigated are small. However, there were major differences noted in the politeness

Table 7.1 DCT Requestive Strategies of the 3 Deaf Professionals Compared
to the DCT Baseline of the 7 Native ASL Signers

	Native ASL signer	Near-native signer	I. Late learner of ASL
conventionalized indirectness			(one indirect request)
question, hedge			
off-record apology/ give reason			
offer, promise			
minimize the imposition			
NMMs		(overuse of *pp*)	(used lexically)

Note. DCT = Discourse completion test, NMMs = Nonmanual modifiers. The **shaded cells** indicate similar tendencies between these individual signers and the group of native ASL signers. Differences appear in **unshaded cells** and a brief description of the difference appears in parentheses in these cases.

Table 7.2 DCT Rejection Strategies of the 3 Deaf Professionals Compared to
the DCT Baseline of the 7 Native ASL Signers

	Native ASL signer	Near-native signer	II. Late learner of ASL[1]
question, hedge			
apology			
give reason			
offer/promise			(not used)
common ground			(not used)
NMMs		(no use of *pp*)	(used phrasally; no use of *pp*)

1. The late learner of ASL uses the following pattern in her rejections: (a) make the rejection, (b) give reasons, and (c) hedge (use 'WELL').

Note. DCT = Discourse completion test, NMMs = Nonmanual modifiers. The **shaded cells** indicate similar tendencies between these individual signers and the group of native ASL signers. Differences appear in **unshaded cells** and a brief description of the difference appears in parentheses in these cases.

strategies employed by the late learner of ASL. These differences seem to be due to this signer's second-language fluency in ASL.

Because members of the Deaf community learn ASL at a variety of ages, this study has important implications for deaf children learning ASL. The results of this pilot study suggest that the earlier that deaf children learn ASL, the more competent they are likely to become at mitigating threats to involvement and independence. Given that politeness strategies communicate about one's relationship (at the metamessage level), it seems that having less pragmatic competence in a language could lead to greater misunderstanding of one's social meaning and could result in being deemed less socially competent. Given that politeness strategies can make or break a relationship, the importance of such pragmatic competence in face-to-face interaction cannot be underestimated, and the earlier a child learns such pragmatic features of a language, the more socially competent the child can become.

8

WHY IT MATTERS HOW
YOU SAY IT

All language users communicate at least four levels of meaning in any given utterance: content, function, textual meaning, and social meaning. In this study I investigated a particular area of social meaning in ASL and English: the linguistic expression of politeness. The data from the ASL and English versions of the discourse completion test (DCT) reveal general trends regarding specific linguistic strategies used by ASL signers and English speakers when making requests and rejections. Although the ASL signers may use more direct and involvement-oriented strategies at times when English speakers may use more indirect and independence-oriented strategies, both language groups use many similar strategies. In addition, each language group uses some language-specific strategies.

One of the goals of this study was to determine whether or not ASL signers use a variety of strategies in the mitigation of speech acts because it was not clear in the literature that ASL signers use any strategy other than directness (except for some examples from Roush, 1999, and Valli, Lucas, & Mulrooney, 2005). Indirect speech acts in ASL were especially in question. The DCT results show that ASL signers do use a variety of strategies in making requests and rejections. Although the English speakers make indirect requests in only the "requesting the employee complete a big project much earlier than expected" (+P, +R) context, none of the ASL signers make such indirect requests. The only instance of an indirect request in the ASL DCT data is a joke. On the other hand, both ASL signers and English speakers make indirect rejections, especially in difficult (+R) rejections. The use of indirect rejections by ASL signers and the joke (as an indirect request) by one ASL signer provides empirical evidence that ASL signers indeed use, at least, these two types of indirect speech acts.

This investigation is important because how an interlocutor says something can result in possible misinterpretation, negative perceptions, and perpetuation of stereotypes. Cross-cultural communication can be improved with the understanding that more than one kind of politeness is at work in face-to-face interaction. Therefore, the results of the current study have implications for interactional sociolinguistics and cross-cultural studies, as well as for ASL instruction and ASL/English interpretation.

Misinterpreting Another's Way of Speaking— Moving Away From Stereotyping

Learning a particular way of speaking is part of one's acquisition of a language and becoming a full member of a language community. That is to say, people learn to express themselves in socially appropriate ways. When encountering the utterances of those who use the same way of speaking, addressees generally know how to interpret the various levels of meaning, including the social meaning, of those utterances, and the discourse usually flows naturally. However, speakers also encounter language communities that have quite different ways of speaking.

When interlocutors' politeness strategies differ, there may be one of three results. First, the addressee may misinterpret the speaker by interpreting the speaker's meaning (social or otherwise) based on the addressee's way of speaking. Second, the addressee may judge the speaker harshly and may reject the speaker as being either too forward or too evasive. Third, the addressee may recognize the speaker as an outsider who has a different way of speaking, and either attempt to understand communicative differences or discount the speaker as a deviant who does not know how to interact well with others.

These first impressions are made quickly and often without much thought. One's way of speaking marks someone as either an insider or an outsider, showing that differences in politeness strategies are interpreted as having a social meaning.

An increased awareness of how people express themselves in different contexts is an important first step in reducing the misinterpretation of social meaning and the subsequent judging, misinterpreting, or discounting of speakers that can occur in cross-cultural communication. For example, it is helpful for ASL signers to recognize that English-speaking supervisors may use indirect requests when making a difficult (+R) request. This is an example where an ASL signer may misinterpret the supervisor's request and may judge the supervisor to be unnecessarily vague or uncooperative.

Likewise, the judging of ASL signers as too direct, which appears to be a folk stereotype, may be used as a way to discount this linguistic minority. The evidence from the ASL DCT provides evidence that ASL signers, in fact, are not always direct. Although at times they were more likely to engage in direct requests and direct rejections apparently due to different cultural expectations, they in fact engage in a variety of strategies to mitigate threats to face, and many of these strategies are similar to those of English speakers. In addition, the use of indirect rejections by the ASL signers in the DCT data provides strong counterevidence to the prevailing view that ASL signers do not use indirect strategies. This is not to say that ASL signers and English speakers do not differ in their ways of speaking; there are actually many differences. The function of nonmanual modifiers (NMMs) to mitigate threats to face, in particular, seems to have been overlooked. Nonetheless, this multidimensional investigation of differences helps move the focus away from a dichotomy based on one dimension. By using multiple dimensions, researchers can more accurately characterize the complexity of language use among the members of each language community.

It's *How* You Say It

Cross-linguistic differences can be better understood by looking at three possible levels of analysis: cultural, discourse style, and interaction. Some trends may be made about cultural dimensions that affect the linguistic tendencies of a linguistic community, and trends may also be made about discourse styles. However, it is the interactional level of analysis that provides evidence regarding how linguistic devices are used in their complexity by language users in changing day-to-day interactions, and it is this level that has been the focus of this book.

There is no question that people alter the way they express themselves depending on the context they are in. The data presented here show that at the level of face-to-face interaction, both ASL signers and English speakers use politeness strategies that reveal that they consider both involvement and independence in making requests and rejections. For example, when supervisors make requests or rejections of subordinates, they use certain strategies depending on the perceived supervisor-employee (+P) relationship and the relative weight of the threat to involvement or independence. When supervisors are with their colleagues (other supervisors), they may use different strategies, and when addressing their own superiors, they make different linguistic choices. At the interactional level of analysis, we see the dynamic use of language to maintain face, and the interlocutors' relationship, within the social context of the interaction.

A language community's expectations and perceptions regarding the mitigation of threats to involvement and independence reflect a way of interacting that is unique to that community. Indeed, to express oneself contrary to the community's expectations is to mark oneself as an outsider.

Using an interactional approach and a politeness framework, the current study reveals that there are strong tendencies regarding the mitigation of requests and rejections based on the relative weight of the imposition. These correspond to the variables of ranking of imposition and to some degree, power relations. However, the variable of social distance was controlled in this study, as this factor has been the most disputed in the literature, especially the dimensions of familiarity and affect, and the dimension of liking in particular (Kasper, 1990; Meyer, 1994).

More face-work is generally expected for those speech acts that are ranked as being more difficult (+R) and in which the speaker is in a lower power position (–P). This is indeed the case in the DCT data. In contrast, the supervisor (+P) uses fewer politeness strategies, and overall, fewer strategies are used to mitigate easy (–R) requests and rejections. Consider the two employee (–P) requests, which are signed by the same ASL signer, in Examples 1 and 2:

1. **Context: An employee (E) asks a supervisor to pass one's pen.**

   E: <u>INDEX/*tight lips*, MY #PEN/(*wondering*)</u>, <u>DON'T-MIND GIVE-ME, DON'T-MIND GIVE-ME/*tight lips,q.*</u>

   [*translation*: *I think that's my pen. Do you mind—Do you mind handing it to me?*]

2. **Context: An employee (E) in a grocery store asks the supervisor for the day before Thanksgiving off.**

   E: I/pg, <u>POSSIBLE I WEDNESDAY INDEX-RIGHT+/t</u>, <u>POSSIBLE, *IF CAN/cond*, OFF I INDEX-RIGHT WEDNESDAY, *"WELL"(1-hand)/ tight lips* /q</u>. <u>SUPPOSE YOU HAVE-TO/pg,cond, I WILLING/</u> pp. <u>YOU HAVE OTHER PEOPLE COVER ME, *"WELL"/tight lips(1-hand, nondominant hand, move forward)* /q</u>, <u>POSSIBLE, *"WELL"(some circular movement)/(slight rocking)bt* /tight lips,q</u>.

   [*translation*: *I—is it possible for me to have this Wednesday off, you think? If you say I have to work, I'll do that (of course). Perhaps someone could cover for me, or something? So is that a possibility at all?*]

These two examples are markedly different, and demonstrate some uses of the politeness strategies reported in this study. Example 1 shows use of the sign DON'T-MIND, the *tight lips* marker, and a question form. Example 2 shows use of the sign POSSIBLE (hedging); four different NMMs: *pg, bt,* and *tight lips* during the head request, and *pp* during the offer/promise strategy; the give deference strategy (<u>SUPPOSE YOU HAVE-TO/pg,cond, I WILLING/pp</u>); an offer/promise (<u>YOU HAVE OTHER PEOPLE COVER ME, *"WELL"/tight lips(1-hand, nondominant hand, move forward)* /q</u>); as well as the use of the question form in the head request.

In most cases, one would not expect the politeness strategies used in Example 2, a difficult (+R) request, to be used in an easy (–R) request, such as Example 1. The implication would be that there was a great threat to face, which seems unlikely in such a request. In a typical context in which an employee is asking a supervisor to pass the employee's pen, the extensive face-work would seem extreme and would imply that something more is at stake.

Conversely, if one uses the politeness strategies used in an easy (–R) request, such as Example 1, in a context in which there is a perceived greater threat to face, the addressee may be offended or may wonder why the signer is making light of the request. In other words, the lack of face-work on the signer's part would imply that the content and function were taking precedent over the social meaning and the mitigation of the larger threat to independence. Example 3 shows what this type of incongruous request might look like, i.e., if an employee were to do little face-work when making a difficult (+R) request.

3. <u>Context</u>: **An employee (E) in a grocery store asks the supervisor for the day before Thanksgiving off.**

   E: wednesday, day before thanksgiving/t, don't-mind, off, I/pp,q.

   [*translation: Do you mind if I have the day before Thanksgiving off?*]

All of the native ASL signers engage in more face-work (e.g., use more severe NMMs) in this difficult (+R) rejection made by the employee than appears in this example. Clearly the appropriate and expected face-work is not being conveyed in this example. The supervisor would wonder why the employee is presuming to make light of such a big imposition, especially given that the *pp* marker (which is used only for small threats to involvement) is being used to make a difficult (+R) request.

When it comes to social meaning and the linguistic expression of politeness, what matters is not only what language users say, but how they say it. Human beings are not only conveying content, function, and textual meaning in interaction, they are also maintaining an image of themselves and their relationship with others; they are conveying social meaning. The linguistic decisions they make, which are generally made unconsciously, provide the glue that helps maintain our social interactions.

Two Kinds of Face Politeness Systems, Not One

When most people in the United States think of politeness, they tend to think of the traditional view of politeness as it is expressed in books on etiquette. This social norm view of politeness reflects a prescriptive view of polite behavior and, therefore, may assume that a polite way of speaking is more akin to independence, in that the speaker does not want to impede the addressee's wants, actions, and values. When it comes to linguistic politeness, however, speakers often mitigate threats to both involvement and independence. Involvement, when the speaker affirms the addressee's wants, actions, and values as desirable, reaffirms the relationship between the interlocutors and a sense of solidarity and connectedness. Whereas linguistic communities may be more independence-oriented or involvement-oriented; in actuality, both kinds of face-needs are mitigated in face-to-face interaction.

The general lack of awareness of the involvement politeness system (at least in the majority culture of the United States) is unfortunate. As has been suggested in this book, some language communities, such as the American Deaf community, assume involvement as the predominant face politeness system, where acceptance in common membership takes precedence over independence. The implication of this cultural tendency is that there may be less concern with threats to independence.

This difference in expectations regarding independence and involvement is reflected in some comments made by English speakers. For example, some English speakers have said that ASL signers do not say "please" and "thank you" enough. This criticism seems to be based on differing cultural expectations regarding the linguistic expression of politeness. Given that independence (characterized by the desire to not impose or assume the addressee will agree) is the predominant face politeness system in the majority culture, these English speakers may well be assuming an independence face politeness system and judging those who do not conform to their expectations.

ASL signers, in fact, do use the signs, PLEASE and THANK-YOU, among themselves at times to mitigate threats to independence. Both of these signs appear in the ASL data in this study. However, it is likely that ASL signers are using PLEASE and THANK-YOU the Deaf way and not in the specific contexts that some English speakers would expect to hear the words, *please* and *thank you*, in everyday usage. It would also follow that PLEASE and THANK-YOU would be used less often in a linguistic community that operates primarily under the involvement face politeness system because the degree to which these signs are used may well be lessened by the general assumption of cooperation and common membership.

Some English speakers also have said that ASL signers don't say, "you're welcome," enough as well. In actuality, expressions such as THANK-YOU or FINE+ [*That's fine*], often marked by the *pp* marker or the *tight lips* NMM—rather than YOU WELCOME — are used in ASL as a response to the act of thanking. A nodding of the head, often marked with either the *pp* or *tight lips* NMM, is also a common marker used in the language for this purpose.

The difference in face politeness systems may also account for why some ASL signers say that English speakers (hearing people) BE-VAGUE (*are vague* or *are indirect*). There may well be many contexts in which English speakers say things in a more roundabout way by using more face-work than many ASL signers (Deaf people) would expect at that moment in the interaction. The use of indirect requests by English speakers certainly attests to such a difference in difficult (+R) requests by the supervisor (+P). In addition, ASL signers—using the involvement face politeness system—may use more of a deductive rhetorical strategy (topic-first), even more than English speakers.

Scollon and Scollon (2001) have suggested that Americans tend to use a deductive (topic-first) rhetorical strategy; however, when American ASL signers are compared to American English speakers,

ASL signers may have more of a preference for this rhetorical strategy than do American English speakers. The use of the deductive rhetorical strategy is a matter of degree, and the attribution to any particular group may depend in part on what groups are being compared. The stereotyping regarding their different ways of speaking as direct or indirect also seems to be based on this dichotomy, which—like most stereotypes—has some basis in fact.

Holding a more independence oriented view of linguistic politeness may actually blind some people to the strategies used by a member of a community that is more involvement oriented. The recognition of two types of face politeness systems and the strategies used to mitigate them is an important contribution of the face-saving view to politeness. It provides a framework for better understanding the range of strategies that are employed by particular language users at the level of face-to-face interaction.

Future Research

The findings presented here clarify how these two groups of language users manage requests and rejections. Although this study has helped to clarify many of these issues, future research is needed in at least three related areas.

First, more research is needed regarding the politeness strategies used by a variety of signed language users. These include signers of other signed languages, second language users of ASL (especially considering the findings of the pilot study reported in chapter 7), and ASL signers of various dialects, including blue-collar (grass-roots) ASL signers and ASL signers who differ in their ethnicity, race, gender, and regional backgrounds. More research is also needed regarding various dialects of English, second language users of English, and other spoken languages.

Second, use of politeness strategies in settings other than the workplace should be researched. Research into casual conversations, medical appointments, the classroom setting, or other settings should help reveal how requests and rejections are handled differently as determined in part by the speech event, sociolinguistic differences, and variables that determine the weight of the imposition: power, social distance, and ranking.

Third, researchers need to investigate how ASL signers mitigate other speech acts, such as complaints, compliments, and so on. There is a particular need for empirical investigation into the mitigation of other speech acts by second language users of ASL and signers of various ASL dialects.

Implications

The findings reported here have implications for interactional sociolinguistics and cross-cultural studies, as well for ASL instruction and ASL/English interpretation. First, regarding sociolinguistic and cross-cultural studies, it is important when developing a DCT for a comparative language study to verify similar expectations for the contexts by the two language groups, as was done in this study. In addition, when administering a DCT, the ranking of the discourse contexts by the participants before the elicitation of linguistic data is important for accurate analysis and interpretation of the data.

Second, the findings of the DCT in this study show that these language users employ many well-documented politeness strategies (e.g., politeness strategies proposed by Brown & Levinson, 1987) to mitigate requests and rejections, and, in addition, use some distinct language forms (e.g., NMMs, "HANDWAVE," naming, and surprise expressions). This study provides new findings that can contribute to the understanding of cross-linguistical politeness strategies. In particular, the recognition of NMMs (Roush, 1999) reveals the unique nature of ASL in using nonmanual features to mitigate speech acts, which may be unique to signed languages. It is important for studies that involve a signed language to attend to such nonmanual features.

The implications for ASL instruction and ASL/English interpretation are threefold. First, the area of politeness is not generally taught in ASL or interpreter education programs. If such differences are currently addressed in the curriculum, they are usually attributed to cross-cultural differences in general. The findings of the current study, the face-saving view of politeness, and the approach used in the cross-linguistic study presented here (especially determining the weight of the imposition by considering power, social distance, and ranking of imposition) can provide educators with an approach to educate students and interpreters about this specific area of language usage.

Second, ASL instructors should be concerned about the competence of their students in terms of expressing social meaning as well as content, function, and textual meaning. The findings presented here show that there are certain aspects of social meaning that are integral to ASL instruction and to the goal of fostering pragmatic competence in second language users of ASL. For interpreters, an awareness of these four levels of meaning is also key to effective interpretation, as all four levels of meaning are conveyed in every interpreted interaction.

Third, ASL/English interpreters may focus on interpreting a speaker's meaning as text (as though it were a monologue) and may, therefore, overlook important features of face-to-face interaction in their interpretations (see Hoza, 1999; Metzger, 1999; Roy, 2000a, 2000b; Wadensjö, 1998). ASL/English interpreters need to understand the politeness strategies used by ASL signers and English speakers because they make decisions regarding how to convey speakers' politeness strategies (their social meaning) in interpreted interaction. How these strategies are rendered by the interpreter could have a profound effect on the interaction and how the primary speakers perceive each other as participants.

Having proficiency in a language, whether the language is a first or second language, involves competence in one's ability to alter language usage to accommodate different social contexts. People convey their intent, their social images, and their view of the relationship by the language choices they make. These levels of language usage guide how an addressee construes a speaker's social meaning, and yet language users usually interpret these powerful messages unconsciously. Given that these linguistic decisions are based on social factors that lie beneath the surface of every interaction, every face-to-face encounter involves some consideration of politeness concerns.

WHY IT MATTERS HOW YOU SAY IT

A major barrier to successful cross-cultural communication is to take for granted a stereotype about another person's way of speaking based on one or two dimensions of that group's language usage. Although ASL signers and English speakers may lean toward certain strategies, the empirical findings presented here challenge a limited view of these two language groups. ASL signers and English speakers, like all language users, employ a rich variety of strategies in interaction at any given moment. In short,

DEAF/t, BE-DIRECT, BE-VAGUE, *BOTH!* HEARING/t, BE-VAGUE, BE-DIRECT, *BOTH!*
[*translation:* Deaf people are <u>both</u> direct and indirect, and hearing (non-Deaf) people are <u>both</u> indirect and direct].

An awareness of this fact is one step away from stereotyping and a step toward understanding ways of speaking that may differ from one's own.

APPENDIX I
TRANSCRIPTION CONVENTIONS

Example

Explanation

SEE

a capitalized English word represents a single sign in ASL

DON'T-KNOW

hyphenated words represent a single ASL sign

THEY(RIGHT), INFORM-RIGHT

signs that appear with a direction indicate the location in space used by the signer, e.g., THEY(RIGHT) is signed on the right and INFORM-RIGHT is signed toward the right

#BUT

lexicalized fingerspelling

INDEX

a specific "pointing" sign used in ASL as a pronoun, determiner, or adverb of location (no distinction is made in this book among these three functions)

"WELL", "HANDWAVE"

natural gesture used in ASL

"WELL"(one-hand)

the one-handed version of the sign is used, rather than the standard two-handed version

"HOLD-ON"(two-hands)

the two-handed version of the sign is used, rather than the standard one-handed version

APPENDIX I

USE^AGENT	two glosses joined by a caret (^) represents a compound sign
<u>C</u>ONSUMER	When the first letter of a gloss is underlined, this indicates that the sign is initialized (e.g., compare <u>C</u>ONSUMER and USE^AGENT)
[state], [name]	glosses or words appearing in square brackets indicate that the specific information has been replaced by a generic term (to either protect the identity of the subjects in the study or to indicate the rough equivalent in a translation)
(reaches for an imaginary pen)	comments appearing in italics in parentheses indicate an action or some other description of the context
PROMISE!	the use of an exclamation point after a sign indicates that the sign is being stressed by the signer
"WELL", SORRY	**bold** type indicates that this part of the utterance is being highlighted in the example (for discussion purposes only)
FINE+	the symbol, +, indicates that the sign is repeated
CL-1 'pen rolls over by you'	CL is used to represent a particular classifier, whose handshape is identified (in this case, a "1" handshape) and whose meaning appears in single quotes

Nonmanual grammatical marker	**Explanation**
wh-q	wh-word question
q	yes/no-question

TRANSCRIPTION CONVENTIONS

rh-q	rhetorical question
cond	conditional clause
t	topicalization
neg	negation
nod	nodding (used in assertions)

Nonmanual modifier (NMM)	Explanation
th, cs, sh	adverbial modifiers in ASL
pp, tight lips, pg, pg-frown, bt	specific nonmanual modifiers that are associated with the mitigation of threats to involvement and independence in ASL

Scope of marking

Example	Explanation
<u>DON'T-MIND I BORROW</u>/<u>*tight lips*</u> <u>50 DOLLAR, "WELL"</u>/*bt* /q.	The <u>underlined</u> portion of the utterance indicates the scope (or spread) of the nonmanual grammatical marker or NMM. In the example above, the "q" marking accompanies the entire utterance.

The portions that are both <u>*italicized and underlined*</u> indicate that BOTH the primary and a secondary marking co-occur with these signs. In the example above, *tight lips* NMM and the 'q' marking are both associated with DON'T-MIND I BORROW, and the *bt* NMM and the 'q' marking are both associated with "WELL".

APPENDIX II
DISCOURSE COMPLETION TEST

The discourse contexts used in the discourse completion test (DCT) completed by the English speakers are given below in their entirety. The same contexts appeared on videotape in ASL for the ASL signers. In all cases, the participants were told they were talking to someone whom they know well, like, and get along with. In addition, ASL signers were told that the signer and the addressee in these contexts were both fluent ASL signers and members of Deaf culture (i.e., STRONG #ASL and STRONG DEAF).

Part I. Requests

AN EMPLOYEE MAKES AN EASY REQUEST OF THE SUPERVISOR

As an employee, you are having a meeting with your supervisor when you notice your pen is sitting very near your supervisor; you ask the supervisor to pass it to you.

AN EMPLOYEE MAKES A DIFFICULT REQUEST OF THE SUPERVISOR

As an employee in a grocery store, you ask your supervisor for the day before Thanksgiving off, the busiest grocery shopping day of the year (you do this during a supervision meeting).

A COWORKER MAKES A DIFFICULT REQUEST OF ANOTHER COWORKER

As an employee, you ask a coworker to let you borrow $50 until payday—which is Friday of next week (you two are sitting together, alone, during a break).

A COWORKER MAKES AN EASY REQUEST OF ANOTHER COWORKER

As an employee, you just remember that you need to write down an address, so you ask a coworker to let you borrow a pen (you two are sitting together, alone, during a break).

DISCOURSE COMPLETION TEST

A SUPERVISOR MAKES AN EASY REQUEST OF AN EMPLOYEE

<u>As a supervisor</u>, you ask an employee to make an initial call to a potential new consumer who was just referred to your agency.

A SUPERVISOR MAKES A DIFFICULT REQUEST OF AN EMPLOYEE

<u>As a supervisor</u>, you recently gave an employee a big project and said s/he had one month to finish it. Now, you meet with the employee and ask him/her to complete it in 2 weeks instead of a month.

Part II. Rejections

AN EMPLOYEE ENGAGES IN AN EASY REJECTION OF A SUPERVISOR'S REQUEST

<u>As an employee</u>, your supervisor has just asked you if you are interested in serving on the sunshine committee, which is not part of your regular work responsibilities. You turn down the request because you are overloaded with work that has deadlines that are coming up soon.

AN EMPLOYEE ENGAGES IN A DIFFICULT REJECTION OF A SUPERVISOR'S REQUEST

<u>As an employee</u>, your supervisor has just asked you to make an initial call to a potential new consumer who was referred to your agency. You feel your caseload is already too full because there isn't enough staff, and you turn down the request.

A COWORKER ENGAGES IN A DIFFICULT REJECTION OF ANOTHER COWORKER'S REQUEST

<u>As an employee</u>, a coworker has just asked you for a ride to a garage to pick up his/her car this afternoon (after work); the garage is 5 miles away. You tell the coworker you can't give him/her a ride (you two are sitting together, alone, during a break).

A COWORKER ENGAGES IN AN EASY REJECTION OF ANOTHER COWORKER'S REQUEST

<u>As an employee</u>, a coworker has just asked you out to lunch tomorrow, but you turn him/her down (you two are sitting together, alone, during a break).

A SUPERVISOR ENGAGES IN AN EASY REJECTION OF AN EMPLOYEE'S REQUEST

<u>As a supervisor</u>, an employee asks if you will attend a last-minute meeting tomorrow at 2:00 about some minor changes in the payroll schedule.

You look at your appointment book and see that an important person from the state will be at your agency all afternoon, so you turn down this request because you need to meet with this person (all afternoon).

A SUPERVISOR ENGAGES IN A DIFFICULT REJECTION OF AN EMPLOYEE'S REQUEST

<u>As a supervisor</u>, you have just completed a meeting with an employee. It's the end of the day, and the employee and you are alone in the office. The employee tells you s/he doesn't have any money for the train and wants to borrow $1. All you have is a $20 bill and you need it to take a taxi to the airport, so you tell the employee you can't.

APPENDIX III
BROWN AND LEVINSON'S (1987) POLITENESS STRATEGIES
Arranged by the Categories Used in This Book[1]

DIRECT (*WITHOUT REDRESSIVE ACTION, BALDLY*) **STRATEGIES**[2]
(no specific strategies other than to make the speech act directly)

INVOLVEMENT (*POSITIVE POLITENESS*) **STRATEGIES**
(summarized from Brown & Levinson 1987, p. 102):

CLAIM "COMMON GROUND"
(1) Notice, attend to Hearer (the Hearer's interests, wants, needs, goods)
(2) Exaggerate (interest, approval, sympathy with Hearer)
(3) Intensify interest to Hearer
(4) Use in-group identity markers
(5) Seek agreement
(6) Avoid disagreement
(7) Presuppose/raise/assert common ground
(8) Joke

CONVEY THAT SPEAKER & HEARER ARE COOPERATORS
(9) Assert or presuppose Speaker's knowledge of and concern for Hearer's wants
(10) Offer/promise
(11) Be optimistic

---

1. Brown and Levinson also have the category, don't do the FTA (face-threatening act); however, because not doing the FTA is not linguistically expressed, it is not included in this study. This study focused only on linguistic expressions.

2. This book uses the terms *direct strategies, involvement strategies, independence strategies,* and *indirect strategies* rather than Brown and Levinson's (1987) terms for these categories of strategies.

(12) Include both Speaker and Hearer in the activity
(13) Give (or ask for) reasons
(14) Assume or assert reciprocity

FULFILL HEARER'S WANT (FOR SOME X)

(15) Give gifts to Hearer (goods, sympathy, understanding, cooperation)

INDEPENDENCE (*NEGATIVE POLITENESS*) STRATEGIES

(summarized from Brown & Levinson 1987, p. 131)

BE DIRECT/BE INDIRECT

(1) Be conventionally indirect
(2) Question, hedge

DON'T COERCE HEARER

(3) Be pessimistic
(4) Minimize the imposition
(5) Give deference

COMMUNICATE SPEAKER'S WANT TO NOT IMPINGE ON HEARER

(6) Apologize
(7) Impersonalize Speaker and Hearer
(8) State the FTA as a general rule
(9) Nominalize

REDRESS OTHER WANTS OF HEARER *(Also (5) above)*

(10) Go on record as incurring a debt, or as not indebting Hearer

INDIRECT (*OFF-RECORD*) STRATEGIES

(summarized from Brown & Levinson 1987, p. 214)

VIOLATE RELEVANCE MAXIM

(1) Give hints
(2) Give association clues
(3) Presuppose

VIOLATE QUANTITY MAXIM

(4) Understate
(5) Overstate
(6) Use tautologies

VIOLATE QUALITY MAXIM

(7) Use contradictions
(8) Be ironic
(9) Use metaphors
(10) Use rhetorical questions

VIOLATE MANNER MAXIM (*be vague or ambiguous*)

(11) Be ambiguous
(12) Be vague
(13) Overgeneralize
(14) Displace Hearer
(15) Be incomplete, use ellipsis

REFERENCES

American Heritage Dictionary (4th ed.). (2001). New York: Dell.

Araújo Carreira, M. A. (2005). Politeness in Portugal: How to address others. In L. Hickey & M. Stewart (Eds.), *Politeness in Europe* (pp. 306–316). Clevedon, UK: Multilingual Matters.

Baker, C. (1977). Regulators and turn-taking in American Sign Language discourse. In Lynn Friedman (Ed.), *On the other hand: New perspectives on American Sign Language*. New York: Academic Press.

Baker-Shenk, C., & Cokely, D. (1980). *American Sign Language: A teacher's resource text on grammar and culture*. Silver Spring, MD: TJ.

Barke, A., & Uehara, S. (2005). Japanese pronouns of address: their behavior and maintenance over time. In R. Lakoff & S. Ide (Eds.), *Broadening the horizon of linguistic politeness* (pp. 301–313). Amsterdam: John Benjamins.

Battison, R. (1978). *Lexical borrowing in American Sign Language*. Silver Spring, MD: Linstok Press.

Blum-Kulka, S. (1987). Indirectness and politeness: Same or different. *Journal of Pragmatics, 11*, 147–160.

Blum-Kulka, S. (1997). *Dinner talk: Cultural patterns of sociability and socialization in family discourse*. Mahwah, NJ: Erlbaum.

Blum-Kulka, S., & House, J. (1989). Cross-cultural and situational variation in requesting behavior. In Shoshana Blum-Kulka, Julianne House, and Gabriele Kasper. *Cross-cultural pragmatics: Requests and apologies* (pp. 123–154). Norwood, NJ: Ablex Publishing Corporation.

Blum-Kulka, S., House, J., & Kasper, G. (1989). *Cross-cultural pragmatics: Requests and apologies*. Norwood, NJ: Ablex.

Bridges, B., & Metzger, M. (1996). *Deaf tend your: Non-manual signals in American Sign Language*. Silver Spring, MD: Calliope.

Brown, P., & Levinson, S. (1987). *Politeness: Some universals in language usage*. Cambridge, MA: Cambridge University Press.

Fraser, B. (1990). Perspectives on politeness. *Journal of Pragmatics 14*, 219–236.

Fraser, B. (1999). *The form and function of politeness in conversation*. Unpublished manuscript.

Fraser, B. (2005). Whither politeness. In R. Lakoff & S. Ide (Eds.), *Broadening*

REFERENCES

the horizon of linguistic politeness (pp. 65–83). Amsterdam: John Benjamins.

Fraser, B., & Nolen, W. (1981). The association of deference with linguistic form. *International Journal of Sociology of Language, 27,* 93–111.

Fredsted, E. (2005). Politeness in Denmark: Getting to the point. In L. Hickey & M. Stewart (Eds.), *Politeness in Europe* (pp. 159–173). Clevedon, UK: Multilingual Matters.

Fretheim, T. (2005). Politeness in Norway: How can you be polite and sincere? In L. Hickey & M. Stewart (Eds.), *Politeness in Europe* (pp. 145–158). Clevedon, UK: Multilingual Matters.

Goffman, E. (1967). On face work. In E. Goffman. *Interaction ritual* (pp. 5–46). New York, NY: Anchor Books.

Grice, P. (1975). Logic and conversation. In P. Cole & J. Morgan (Eds.), *Syntax and semantics: Vol. 3. Speech acts* (pp. 41–58). New York: Academic Press.

Gu, Y. (1990). Politeness phenomena in modern Chinese. *Journal of Pragmatics 14,* 237–257.

Hall, E. T. (1976). *Beyond culture.* Garden City, NY: Anchor Press/Doubleday.

Hall, S. (1989). Train-Gone-Sorry: The etiquette of social conversations in American Sign Language. In S. Wilcox (Ed.), *American deaf culture: An anthology* (pp. 89–102). Burtonsville, MD: Linstok Press.

Haumann, S., Koch, U., & Sornig, K. (2005). Politeness in Austria: Politeness and impoliteness. In L. Hickey & M. Stewart, (Eds.), *Politeness in Europe* (pp. 82–99). Clevedon, UK: Multilingual Matters.

Hickey, L. (1991). Surprise, surprise, but do so politely. *Journal of Pragmatics, 15,* 367–372.

Hickey, L. (2005). Politeness in Spain: Thanks but no "thanks." In L. Hickey & M. Stewart (Eds.), *Politeness in Europe* (pp. 317–330). Clevedon, UK: Multilingual Matters.

Hickey, L., & Stewart, M. (Eds.). (2005). *Politeness in Europe.* Clevedon, UK: Multilingual Matters.

Hill, B., Ide, S., Ikuta, S., Kawasake, A., & Ogino, T. (1986). Universals of linguistic politeness: Quantitative evidence from Japanese and American English. *Journal of Pragmatics, 10,* 347–371.

House, J. (2005). Politeness in Germany: Politeness in *Germany?* In L. Hickey & M. Stewart (Eds.), *Politeness in Europe* (pp. 13–25). Clevedon, UK: Multilingual Matters.

Hoza, J. (1999). Saving face: The interpreter and politeness. *Journal of Interpretation, 39–68.*

Hoza, J. (2004). Using discourse completion tests in cross-linguistic studies. In E. Maroney (Ed.), *Proceedings of the 15th Convention of the Conference of Interpreter Trainers. CIT: Still Shining After 25 Years* (pp. 93–104).

REFERENCES

Huszcza, F. (2005). Politeness in Poland: From "titlemania" to grammaticalised honorifics. In L. Hickey & M. Stewart (Eds.), *Politeness in Europe* (pp. 218–233). Clevedon, UK: Multilingual Matters.

Ide, S. (1989). Formal forms of discernment: Two neglected aspects of linguistic politeness. *Multilingua, 59,* 223–248.

Ide, S. (2005). How and why honorifics can signify dignity and elegance: The indexicality and reflexivity of linguistic rituals. In R. Lakoff & S. Ide (Eds.), *Broadening the horizon of linguistic politeness* (pp. 45–64). Amsterdam: John Benjamins.

Ide, S., Hill, B., Carnes, Y., Ogino, T., & Kawasaki, A. (1992). The concept of politeness: An empirical study of American English and Japanese. In R. J. Watts, S. Ide, & K. Ehlich (Eds.), *Politeness in language* (pp. 281–297). Berlin: Mouton de Gruyter.

Janney, R. W., & Arndt, H. (1992). Intracultural tact versus intercultural tact. In R. J. Watts, S. Ide, & K. Ehlich (Eds.), *Politeness in language* (pp. 21–41). Berlin: Mouton de Gruyter.

Kannapell, B. (1993). *Language choice—identity choice.* Burtonsville, MD: Linstok Press.

Kasper, G. (1990). Linguistic politeness: Current research issues. *Journal of Pragmatics 14,* 193–218.

Katriel, T. (1986). *Talking straight: Dugri speech in Israeli Sabra culture.* Cambridge, England: Cambridge University Press.

Keevallik, L. (2005). Politeness in Estonia: A matter of fact style. In L. Hickey & M. Stewart (Eds.), *Politeness in Europe* (pp. 203–217). Clevedon, UK: Multilingual Matters.

Kerbrat-Orecchioni, C. (2005). Politeness in France: How to buy bread politely. In L. Hickey & M. Stewart (Eds.), *Politeness in Europe* (pp. 29–44). Clevedon, UK: Multilingual Matters.

Lakoff, R. (1973). The logic of politeness, or, minding your p's and q's. *Chicago Linguistic Society, 9,* 292–305.

Lakoff, R., & Ide, S. (Eds.). (2005). *Broadening the horizon of linguistic politeness.* Amsterdam: John Benjamins.

Lane, H., Hoffmeister, R., & Bahan, B. (1996). *A journey into the Deaf-world.* San Diego, CA: DawnSignPress.

Le Pair, R. (2005). Politeness in The Netherlands: Indirect requests. In L. Hickey & M. Stewart (Eds.), *Politeness in Europe* (pp. 66–81). Clevedon, UK: Multilingual Matters.

Leech, G. (1983). *Principles of pragmatics.* London: Longman.

Lucas, C., & Valli, C. (1992). *Language contact in the American Deaf community.* San Diego, CA: Academic Press.

Manno, G. (2005). Politeness in Switzerland: Between respect and acceptance. In L. Hickey & M. Stewart (Eds.), *Politeness in Europe* (pp. 100–115). Clevedon, UK: Multilingual Matters.

REFERENCES

Mao, L. (1994). Beyond politeness theory: "Face" revisited and renewed. *Journal of Pragmatics 21*, 451–486.

Martin, J. (1982). *Miss Manners' guide to excruciatingly correct behavior: The ultimate handbook for modern etiquette.* New York: Gallahad Books.

Mendoza, M. (2005). Polite diminutives in Spanish: A matter of size? In R. Lakoff & S. Ide (Eds.), *Broadening the horizon of linguistic politeness* (pp. 163–173). Amsterdam: John Benjamins.

Metzger, M. (1999). *Sign language interpreting: Deconstructing the myth of neutrality.* Washington DC: Gallaudet University Press.

Mey, J. (Ed.). (2003).About face [Focus-on issue]. *Journal of Pragmatics, 35.*

Meyer, J. (1994). Effect of situational features on the likelihood of addressing face needs in requests. *Southern Communication Journal, 59,* 240–254.

Mindess, A. (2006). *Reading between the signs: Intercultural communication for sign language interpreters.* (2nd ed.). Boston, MA: Intercultural Press.

Mindess, A., & Holcomb, T. (2001). *See what I mean: Differences between D/deaf and hearing culture.* Salem, OR: Sign Enhancers.

Mitchell, R., & Karchmer, M. (2004). Chasing the mythical 10%: Parental hearing status of deaf and hard of hearing students in the United States. *Sign Language Studies, 4 (2),* 138–163.

Moores, D., & Meadow-Orlans, K. (1990). *Educational and developmental aspects of deafness.* Washington, DC: Gallaudet University Press.

Mounty, J. (1989). Beyond grammar: Developing stylistic variation when the input is diverse. *Sign Language Studies, 62,* 43–62.

Neidle, C., Kegl, J., MacLaughlin, D., Bahan, B., & Lee, R. G. (2000). *The syntax of American Sign Language: Functional categories and hierarchical structure.* Cambridge, MA: MIT Press.

Nekvapil, J., & Neustrupny, J. V. (2005). Politeness in the Czech Republic: Distance, levels of expression, management and intercultural contact. In L. Hickey & M. Stewart (Eds.), *Politeness in Europe* (pp. 247–262). Clevedon, UK: Multilingual Matters.

Padden, C., & Humphrey, T. (1988). *Deaf in America: Voices from a culture.* Cambridge, MA: Harvard University Press.

Padden, C., & Humphrey, T. (2005). *Inside Deaf culture.* Cambridge, MA: Harvard University Press.

Preston, P. (1994). *Mother father deaf: Living between sound and silence.* Cambridge, MA: Harvard University Press.

Reilly, J., & McIntire, M. (1988). Nonmanual behaviors in L1 and L2 learners of American Sign Language. *Sign Language Studies, 61,* 351–375.

Rinnert, C., & Kobayashi, H. (1999). Requestive hints in Japanese and English. *Journal of Pragmatics, 31,* 1173–1201.

REFERENCES

Roush, D. (1999). *Indirectness strategies in American Sign Language: Requests and refusals.* Unpublished master's thesis, Gallaudet University, Washington, DC.

Roy, C. (2000a). *Innovative practices for teaching sign language interpreters.* Washington, DC: Gallaudet University Press.

Roy, C. (Ed.). (2000b). *Interpreting as a discourse process.* Oxford, England: Oxford University Press.

Scollon, R., & Scollon, S. W. (2001). *Intercultural communication: A discourse approach* (2nd ed.). Malden, MA: Blackwell.

Sifianou, M., & Antonopoulou, E. (2005). Politeness in Greece: The politeness of involvement. In L. Hickey & M. Stewart (Eds.), *Politeness in Europe* (pp. 263–276). Clevedon, UK: Multilingual Matters.

Smith, C., Lentz, E. M., & Mikos, K. (1992). *Signing naturally: Student workbook level 2, Student videotext.* San Diego, CA: DawnSignPress.

Stewart, M. (2005). Politeness in Britain: "It's only a suggestion . . ." In L. Hickey & M. Stewart (Eds.), *Politeness in Europe* (pp. 116–129). Clevedon, UK: Multilingual Matters.

Supalla, S. (1992). *The book of name signs: Naming in American Sign Language.* San Diego, CA: DawnSign Press.

Takahashi, T., & Beebe, L. (1993). Cross-linguistic influence in the speech act of correction. In Gabriele Kasper & Shoshano Blum-Kulka (Eds.). *Interlanguage pragmatics* (pp. 138–157). New York, NY: Oxford University.

Tan, A. (2004). Yes & no. In W. Lesser (Ed.), *The genius of language* (pp. 25–25). New York: Anchor Books.

Tannen, D. (1986). *That's not what I meant! How conversational style makes or breaks relationships.* New York: Ballantine Books.

Tannen, D. (1990). *You just don't understand: Women and men in conversation.* New York: Ballantine Books.

Terkourafi, M. (2005). Politeness in Cyprus: A coffee or a small coffee? In L. Hickey & M. Stewart (Eds.), *Politeness in Europe* (pp. 277–291). Clevedon, UK: Multilingual Matters.

Turnbull, W., & Saxton, K. (1997). Modal expressions as facework in refusals to comply with requests: I think I should say "no" right now. *Journal of Pragmatics, 27,* 145–181.

Valli, C., Lucas, C., & Mulrooney, K. (2005). *Linguistics of American Sign Language: An introduction.* (4th ed.). Washington, DC: Clerc Books, Gallaudet University Press.

Wadensjö, C. (1998). *Interpreting as interaction.* New York: Addison Wesley Longman.

Watts, R. J. (1989). Relevance and relational work: Linguistic politeness as politic behavior. *Multilingua, 8,* 131–166.

REFERENCES

Watts, R. J. (1992). Linguistic politeness and politic verbal behavior: Reconsidering claims of universality. In R. J. Watts, S. Ide, & K. Ehlich (Eds.), *Politeness in language* (pp. 43–69). Berlin: Mouton de Gruyter.

Weizman, E. (1989). Requestive hints. In S. Blum-Kulka, J. House, & G. Kasper (Eds.), *Cross-cultural pragmatics: Requests and apologies* (pp. 71–95). New York: Oxford University Press.

Wilcox, S. (Ed.). (1989). *American Deaf culture: An anthology.* Burtonsville, MD: Linstok Press.

Woodward, J. (1982). *How you gonna get to heaven if you can't talk with Jesus: On depathologizing deafness.* Silver Spring, MD: TJ Publishers.

Yli-Vakkuri, V. (2005). Politeness in Finland: Evasion at all costs. In L. Hickey & M. Stewart (Eds.), *Politeness in Europe* (pp. 189–202). Clevedon, UK: Multilingual Matters.

Zimmer, J. (1992). Appropriateness and naturalness in ASL/English interpreting. In J. Plant-Moeller (Ed.). *Proceedings of the Twelfth National Convention of the Registry of Interpreters for the Deaf: Expanding Horizons.* Silver Spring, MD: RID Publications, 81–92.

INDEX

Page numbers in italics denote figures or tables.

apologies: NMMs use with, 135–37, *137*; *polite grimace*, 151–52, *158*, 158–61, *160–61*; *polite grimace-frown*, *163*; in rejections, 108–9, *109*; in requests, 86–89, *87*, *89*; *tight lips*, 141–42, 145

Asian languages, 39–40. *See also specific languages*

ASL: conventionalized indirectness, 68–74, *69*, *71*, *73*; direct rejections, 120; direct requests, 64–68; DON'T MIND sign, 70–72, *71*, 141, *186*, *187*; "HANDWAVE" sign, *13*, 100–1, *101*, 143, 155, *163*; independence strategies (rejections), *107*, 107–9, *109*; independence strategies (requests), 74–89, *78–79*, *87*, 98; indirect rejections, 115–19, *119*, 202–4; indirect requests, 93–96, 98–99, 202–4; instruction, 211–13; involvement strategies (rejections), 110–15, *111–12*, 121–22; involvement strategies (requests), 89–93, *91*, 98–99; joking in, 94–96, 98–99, 121–22; PLEASE sign, 99–100, 165, 165n5, 208–9; THANK-YOU sign, 208–9; WELL sign, *11*, *79*, 78–80, 176–77, *179*. *See also* ASL-English distinctions; NMMs

ASL-English distinctions: deductive (topic first) rhetorical strategies, 209–10; independence vs. involvement orientation, 208–9; in rejections, 111–12, *113*, 122, 123–24, *124*; in requests, 73–74, *73*, 95–96, 102–5, *104*

ASL instruction, 211–13

Austrian, 49

Bahan, B., 37, 62
Baker-Shenk, C., 61
Beebe, L., 54–55
Blum-Kulka, S., 25–26, 39, 44–45, 52–53, 55–56
Brown, P., 21–22, 44

Chinese, 5–6, 25–26, 27, 48
CI (conventionalized indirectness): about, 43–45; in ASL, 68–74, *69*, *71*, *73*; in English, 68–74, *69*, *73*
CODA (children of deaf adults), 61–62
Cokely, D., 61
commands, 64–68. *See also* direct requests
common ground strategy, 97–99, 110–12, *111–12*
conversational contract view, 20–21
conversational maxims: indirect requests and, 41–43; joking and, 95; quality maxim, 98–99; relevance maxim, 93–96, 115–19, *119*
conversational maxim view, 17–20
cultural level of analysis, 20, 25–26, *31*

DCT (Discourse Completion Test), 56–62, 218–220
deductive (topic first) rhetorical strategies, 209–10
deference strategy, 98, 120–21, 154–55
diminutive forms, 53
directness, 1–4, 202–4, 209–10

direct rejections, 35–40, 52–53, 120
direct requests, 35–40, 52–53, 64–68
discourse style level of analysis, 27–29,
  30–31, *31*
DON'T MIND sign, 70–72, *71*, 141, *186*, 187

East-West distinctions, 39, 48
English: conventionalized indirectness,
  68–74, *69*, *73*; direct requests, 64–68;
  independence strategies (rejections),
  107–9, *108–9*, 120–21; independence
  strategies (requests), 74–89, *75*, *83*, *89*,
  96–98; indirect rejections, 115–19, *119*;
  indirect requests, 93–96; involvement
  strategies (rejections), 110–15, *112*;
  involvement strategies (requests), 89–
  93, *92*, 96–98; Israeli compared to, 25–
  26, 37; Japanese compared to, 37, 46–
  48; naming, 100–1, 122; please, use of,
  99–100; preparatory statements, 102;
  surprise markers, 55, 102–3, *103*, 122–
  23. *See also* ASL-English distinctions
Estonia, 39

face-saving view, 21–24. *See also* relative
  face orientation
face-threatening acts (FTAs), 22–23, 96–
  97
FFAs (face-flattering acts), 22–23
fluency: about, 188–89; comparison, 199–
  201, *200*; late learner, 193–99, *200*, 201;
  native signer, 150–53, *200*; near-native
  user, 189–90, *200*
form vs. function, 7–11
Fraser, B., 20
French, 39, 44, 48–49, 52–54
FTAs (face-threatening acts), 22–23, 96–97

gender differences, 28–29, *29*
German, 38, 52
Goffman, E., 21
Greek, 39, 54
Grice, P., 18, 41

"HANDWAVE" sign, *13*, 100–1, *101*, 143, 155,
  163

HC (high-context) communication, 47
hedges: about, *53*; in ASL rejections, *107*,
  107–8; in ASL requests, 78–81, *79*;
  polite grimace, *157–58*, 157–58; *polite
  grimace-frown*, 169–70; *polite pucker*,
  135–36; *tight lips*, 142–43, 145–46
hesitations, 81. *See also* hedges
Hickey, L., 55
Hoffmeister, R., 37
Holcomb, T., 2
House, J., 38, 39
Hoza, J., 59
humor. *See* joking

imperative forms, 64–68. *See also* direct
  requests
imposition, ranking of. *See* ranking of
  imposition
independence strategies: about, 22–23,
  27, *28*; in American English
  community, 208–9; NMMs and, 183,
  185; paralinguistic and nonverbal cues,
  50–51; in rejections, *107–9*, 107–9, 120–
  21; in requests, 74–89, *75*, *78–79*, *83*, *87*,
  89, 96–99; social meaning and, 34; in
  Western languages, 40
indirectness, 1–4, 202–4, 209–10. *See also*
  CI (conventionalized indirectness)
indirect rejections, 40–43, 115–19, *119*,
  202–4
indirect requests, 40–43, 93–96, 98–99,
  202–4
interactional level of analysis, 29–31, *31*
interpreters, implications for, 211–13
involvement strategies: about, 22–23, 27,
  28; in American Deaf community, 208–
  9; in Asian languages, 40; NMMs and,
  183, *185*; paralinguistic and nonverbal
  cues, 50–51; *polite pucker*, 128–38, *129*,
  132, *137–38*; in rejections, 110–15, *111–
  12*, 121–22; in requests, 89–93, *91*, *92*,
  96–98; social meaning and, 34
irony. *See* joking
Israeli, 25–26, 37, 55–56

Japanese, 37, 45–48

INDEX

Jewish American culture, 55–56
joking, 94–96, 98–99, 121–22

Katriel, T., 25–26
Kegl, J., 62
Kerbrat-Orecchioni, C., 54
Kobayashi, H., 42

Lakoff, R., 18–19
Lane, H., 37
LC (low-context) communication, 47
Lee, R., 62
Leech, G., 19
Le Pair, R., 39
Levinson, S., 21–22, 44
Lucas, C., 3

MacLaughlin, D., 62
Mao, L., 25, 48, 73
McIntire, M., 196
Mindess, A., 2–3, 37
minimize the imposition strategy, 85–86
misinterpretations, 203–4
mitigated directness, 52–53
modals, 53, 84
Mounty, J., 196–97
mouthing, 193–94
Mulrooney, K., 3

naming, 100–1, 122
nativization, 197
negative politeness. *See* independence
    strategies
Neidle, C., 62
NMMs (nonmanual modifiers): about, 65–
    66, 67, 101, 126; apologies with, 135–37,
    137; location in requests, 81; pessimism
    strategy and, 85; *polite grimace*, 67, 149–
    61, 150, 155, 157–58, 160–61; *polite
    grimace-frown*, 161–72, 162, 168, 171–72;
    polite pucker, 127, 127–38, 129, 132, 137–
    38, 139–40, 140; ranking of use, 182–84,
    183–87, 187; *teeter, body/head*, 67, 157,
    172–82, 173, 178, 182–83; *tight lips*, 67,
    139–40, 139–48, 144, 147
nonverbal cues, 49–51, 81

nose wrinkle, 145

offer/promise strategy, 91, 92, 91–93, 112–
    13, 134–35, 143–44, 145–46

paralinguistic cues, 49–51, 81
pessimism strategy, 82–85, 83
PLEASE/*please*, 99–100, 165, 165n5, 208–9
Polish, 49
polite grimace-frown (pg-frown), 161–72,
    162, 168, 171–72
polite grimace (pg), 67, 149–61, 150, 155,
    157–58, 160–61
politeness: about, 11–12; conversational
    contract view, 20–21; conversational
    maxim view, 17–20; face-saving view,
    21–24; levels of analysis, 24–31; levels
    of meaning, 12–15; social norm view,
    15–17
polite pucker (pp), 127, 127–38, 129, 132,
    137–38, 139–40, 140
positive politeness. *See* involvement
    strategies
positive remarks, 54–55
power variables: about, 57, 205–7;
    independence strategies (rejections),
    107, 107–8, 109, 109; independence
    strategies (requests), 83, 83–84, 87, 88–
    89, 89; indirect rejections, 118–19, 119;
    involvement strategies (rejections),
    110–12, 111; involvement strategies
    (requests), 92, 92; *polite grimace*, 160,
    160; *polite grimace-frown*, 163–65, 168,
    169, 171; *polite pucker*, 130–32, 132, 133,
    135, 138; surprise markers, 102, 103;
    teeter, body/head, 178; *tight lips*, 144, 146
preparatory statements, 102
promises. *See* offer/promise strategy

quality maxim, 98–99
question strategy, 74–78, 75, 78. *See also*
    tag questions

ranking of imposition: about, 57, 205–7;
    conventionalized indirectness and, 73;
    independence strategies (rejections),

ranking of imposition (*continued*)
107, 107–8, *109*; independence
strategies (requests), *75*, *78*, 81, *83*, *87*,
89; indirect rejections, 118–19, *119*;
involvement strategies (requests), *91*,
92; NMMs (generally), 182–84, *183–87*,
187; *polite grimace*, 149, 151–55, *155*,
159–61, *160–61*; *polite grimace-frown*,
162, 163–72, *168*, *171–72*; *polite pucker*,
131–32, *132*, 133, *138*, 139–40, *140*;
surprise markers, 102, *103*; *teeter,
body/head*, 174–82, *178*, *182–83*; *tight
lips*, 139–40, *140*, 144, *144*, 146–48, *147*
reasons, give/ask for strategy, 89–93, *91*,
92, 113–15, 143–44
Reilly, J., 196
rejections: about, 32–35; ASL-English
distinctions, 111–12, 113, 122, 123–24,
124; diminutive forms, *53*; direct
rejections, 35–40, 52–53, 120;
independence strategies, 107–9, *107–9*,
120–21; indirect rejections, 40–43,
115–19, *119*, 202–4; involvement
strategies, 110–15, *111–12*, 121–22;
modals, *53*; naming, 122; NMMs
(generally), 182–84, *183–87*, 187;
nonverbal cues, 49–51; paralinguistic
cues, 49–51; *polite grimace*, 156–61,
157–58, *160*; *polite grimace-frown*, 167–
72, *171–72*; *polite pucker*, 132–34;
ritualized forms, 51–52; social
indexing, 45–49; surprise markers,
122–23; *teeter, body/head*, 178–82, *182–
83*; *tight lips*, 144–48, *147*
relative face orientation, 73–74, 113, 122,
124–25
relevance maxim, 93–96, 115–19, *119*
requests: about, 32–35; ASL-English
distinctions, 73–74, 95–96, 103–5, *104*;
conventionalized indirectness, 68–74,
69, *71*, *73*; diminutive forms, *53*; direct
requests, 35–40, 52–53, 64–68;
"HANDWAVE" sign, 100–1, *101*;
independence strategies, 74–89, *75*,

78–79, *83*, *87*, *89*, 96–99; indirect
requests, 40–43, 93–96, 98–99, 202–4;
involvement strategies, 89–93, *91*, *92*,
96–99; modals, *53*, 84; naming, 100–1;
NMMs (generally), 65, 101, 182–84,
183–87, 187; nonverbal cues, 49–51;
81; paralinguistic cues, 49–51; 81;
PLEASE/*please*, 99–100; *polite grimace*,
150–55, *155*; *polite grimace-frown*, 162–
67, *168*; *polite pucker*, 129–33, *132*;
preparatory statements, 102;
ritualized forms, 51–52; social
indexing, 45–49; surprise markers,
102–3, *103*; *teeter, body/head*, 174–78,
178, 182; *tight lips*, 140–44, *144*
Rinnert, C., 42
ritualized forms, 51–52, 99–100, 208–9
Roush, D., 3, 127–28, 149–50, 173–74,
177, 179, 183, 211

Saxton, K., 55
Scollon, R., 27–29, *28*, 208–9
Scollon, S., 27–29, *28*, 208–9
social distance, 57, 205
social indexing, 45–49
social meaning, 13–15, 33–34, 189
social norm view, 15–17
Spanish, 48, 54
stereotyping, 4–7, 203–4
surprise markers, 55, 102–3, *103*, 122–
23
Switzerland, 39

tag questions, 77–78, *78*, 131–32, 142–43,
145–46, 163
Takahashi, T., 54
Tan, A., 5–6
Tannen, D., 27–29, *29*
teeter, body/head, 67, *157*, 172–82, *173*, *178*,
182–83
textual meaning, 12–13
THANK-YOU sign, 208–9
tight lips, 67, *139–40*, 139–48, *144*, *147*
topic first rhetorical strategies, 209–10

transcription conventions, 215–17

Turnbull, W., 55

Valli, C., 3

warning markers, 55. *See also* preparatory
statements

Weizman, E., 40–41

"WELL" sign, *11, 79,* 79–80, 176–77, 179.
See also hedges

Western languages, 39–40, 48. *See also*
specific languages

Zimmer, J., 3